COMUS & LYCIDAS

JOHN MILTON

COMUS & LYCIDAS

EDITED BY

A. W. VERITY, M.A.

CAMBRIDGE
AT THE UNIVERSITY PRESS
1924

CAMBRIDGE UNIVERSITY PRESS
Cambridge, New York, Melbourne, Madrid, Cape Town,
Singapore, São Paulo, Delhi, Mexico City

Cambridge University Press
The Edinburgh Building, Cambridge CB2 8RU, UK

Published in the United States of America by Cambridge University Press, New York

www.cambridge.org
Information on this title: www.cambridge.org/9781107620018

First edition 1898
First published 1898
Reprinted 1903, 1905, 1908, 1912, 1919, 1924
First paperback edition 2013

A catalogue record for this publication is available from the British Library

ISBN 978-1-107-62001-8 Paperback

NOTE.

THIS volume is partly a recast of the earlier editions of these poems in the "Pitt Press Series," and I desire to repeat my acknowledgment of indebtedness to other Editors.

I have also the pleasure to thank the General Editor of the series for many valuable suggestions.

The Indexes were compiled for me.

A. W. V.

CONTENTS.

INTRODUCTION.

LIFE OF MILTON.

The three periods in Milton's life.

MILTON'S life falls into three clearly defined divisions. The first period ends with the poet's return from Italy in 1639; the second at the Restoration in 1660, when release from the fetters of politics enabled him to remind the world that he was a great poet, if not a great controversialist; the third is brought to a close with his death in 1674. The poems given in the present volume date from the first of these periods; but we propose to summarise briefly the main events of all three.

Born 1608; the poet's father.

John Milton was born on December 9, 1608, in London. He came, in his own words, *ex genere honesto.* A family of Miltons had been settled in Oxfordshire since the reign of Elizabeth. The poet's father had been educated at an Oxford school, possibly as a chorister in one of the College choir-schools, and imbibing Anglican sympathies had conformed to the Established Church. For this he was disinherited by his father. He settled in London, following the profession of scrivener. A scrivener combined the occupations of lawyer and law-stationer. It appears to have been a lucrative calling; certainly John Milton (the poet was named after the father) attained to easy circumstances. He married about 1600, and had six children, of whom several died young. The third child was the poet.

The elder Milton was evidently a man of considerable culture, in particular an accomplished musician, and a composer[1] whose madrigals were deemed worthy of being printed side by side with those of Byrd, Orlando Gibbons and other leading musicians of the time. To him, no doubt, the poet owed the love of music of which we see frequent indications in the poems[2]. Realising, too, that in his son lay the promise and possibility of future greatness, John Milton took the utmost pains to have the boy adequately educated; and the lines *Ad Patrem* show that the ties of affection between father and child were of more than ordinary closeness.

Early Training.

Milton was sent to St Paul's School as a day-scholar about the year 1620. He also had a tutor, Thomas Young, a Scotchman, who subsequently became Master of Jesus College, Cambridge. More important still, Milton grew up in the stimulating atmosphere of cultured home-life. This was a signal advantage. There are few who realise that the word 'culture' signifies anything very definite or desirable before they pass to the University; for Milton, however, home-life meant, from the first, not only broad interests and refinement, but active encouragement towards literature and study. In 1625 he left St Paul's. Of his extant English poems[3] only one, *On the Death of a Fair Infant*, dates from his school-days; but we are told that he had written much verse, English and Latin.

[1] See the article on him in Grove's *Dictionary of Music*.

[2] Milton was especially fond of the organ; see note on *Il Penseroso*, 161. During his residence at Horton Milton made occasional journeys to London to hear, and obtain instruction in, music.

[3] His paraphrases of *Psalms* cxiv, cxxxvi, scarcely come under this heading. Aubrey says in his quaint *Life* of Milton: "Anno Domini 1619 he was ten yeares old, as by his picture: and was then a poet."

And his early training had done that which was all-important: it had laid the foundation of the far-ranging knowledge which makes *Paradise Lost* unique for diversity of suggestion and interest.

At Cambridge.

Milton entered at Christ's College, Cambridge, commencing residence in the Easter term of 1625. Seven years were spent at the University. He took his B.A. degree in 1629, proceeded M.A. in 1632, and in the latter year left Cambridge. His experience of University life had not been wholly fortunate. He was, and felt himself to be, out of sympathy with his surroundings; and whenever in after-years he spoke of Cambridge[1] it was with something of the resentfulness of Gibbon, who complained that the fourteen months which he spent at Oxford were the least profitable part of his life. Milton, in fact, anticipates the laments that we find in the correspondence of Gray, addressed sometimes to Richard West and re-echoed from the banks of the Isis. It may, however,

[1] That Milton's feeling towards the authorities of his own college was not entirely unfriendly would appear from the following sentences written in 1642. He takes, he says, the opportunity to "acknowledge publicly, with all grateful mind, that more than ordinary respect which I found, above many of my equals, at the hands of those courteous and learned men, the Fellows of that college wherein I spent some years; who, at my parting after I had taken two degrees, as the manner is, signified many ways how much better it would content them that I would stay; as by many letters full of kindness and loving respect, both before that time and long after, I was assured of their singular good affection towards me."—*Apology for Smectymnuus*, *P. W.* III. 311. Perhaps Cambridge would have been more congenial to Milton had he been sent to Emmanuel College, long a stronghold of Puritanism. Dr John Preston, then Master of the College, was a noted leader of the Puritan party; see his *Life* by Thomas Ball, printed in 1885 by Mr E. W. Harcourt from the MS. at Newnham Court. (The abbreviation *P. W.* = Milton's Prose Works, Bohn's ed.)

be fairly assumed that, whether consciously or not, Milton owed a good deal to his University; and it must not be forgotten that the uncomplimentary and oft-quoted allusions to Cambridge date for the most part from the unhappy period when Milton the politician and polemical dogmatist had effectually divorced himself at once from Milton the scholar and Milton the poet. A poet he had proved himself before leaving the University. The short but exquisite ode *At a Solemn Music*, and the *Nativity Hymn* (1629), were already written.

The five years (1632—1637) spent at Horton.

Milton's father had settled[1] at Horton in Buckinghamshire. Thither the son retired in 1632. He had gone to Cambridge with the intention of qualifying for some profession, perhaps the Church[2]. This purpose was soon given up, and when Milton returned to his father's house he seems to have made up his mind that there was no profession which he cared to enter. He would choose the better part of studying and preparing himself, by rigorous self-discipline and application, for the far-off divine event to which his whole life moved.

It was Milton's constant resolve to achieve something

[1] As tenant of the Earl of Bridgewater, according to one account; but probably the tradition arose from Milton's subsequent connection with the Bridgewater family.

[2] Cf. Milton's own words, "The Church, to whose service by the intention of my parents and friends I was destined of a child, and in my own resolutions." What kept him from taking orders was not, at first, any difference of belief, but solely his objection to Church discipline and government. "Coming to some maturity of years, and perceiving what tyranny had invaded in the church, that he who would take orders must subscribe slave......(I) thought it better to prefer a blameless silence before the sacred office of speaking, bought and begun with servitude and forswearing."—*Reason of Church Government*, *P. W.* II. 482. Milton disliked in particular the episcopal system, and spoke of himself as "Church-outed by the prelates."

that should vindicate the ways of God to men, something great[1] that should justify his own possession of unique powers—powers of which, with no trace of egotism, he proclaims himself proudly conscious. The feeling finds repeated expression in his prose; it is the guiding-star that shines clear and steadfast even through the mists of politics. He has a mission to fulfil, a purpose to accomplish, no less than the most earnest of religious enthusiasts; and the means whereby this end is to be attained are fourfold: devotion to learning, devotion to religion, ascetic purity of life, and the pursuit of σπουδαιότης or "excellent seriousness" of thought.

The key to Milton's life.

This period of self-centred isolation lasted from 1632 to 1637. Gibbon tells us among the many wise things contained in that most wise book the *Autobiography*, that every man has two educations: that which he receives from his teachers and that which he owes to himself; the latter being often the more important. During these five years Milton completed his second education; ranging the whole world of classical antiquity and absorbing the classical genius so thoroughly that the ancients were to him what they afterwards became to Landor, what they have perhaps never become to any other English poet in the same degree, even as the very breath of his being; learning, too, all of art, especially music, that contemporary England could furnish; wresting from modern languages and literatures their last secrets; and combining these vast and diverse influences into a splendid equipment of hard-won, well-ordered culture.

[1] Cf. the second sonnet; "How soon hath Time." Ten years later (1641) Milton speaks of the "inward prompting which grows daily upon me, that by labour and intent study, which I take to be my portion in this life, joined with the strong propensity of nature, I might perhaps leave something so written to after times, as they should not willingly let it die"—*Reason of Church Government*, *P. W.* II. 477, 478.

The world has known many greater scholars in the technical, limited sense than Milton, but few men, if any, who have mastered more things worth mastering in art, letters and scholarship[1]. It says much for the poet that he was sustained through this period of study, pursued *ohne Hast, ohne Rast*, by the full consciousness that all would be crowned by a masterpiece which should add one more testimony to the belief in that God who ordains the fates of men. It says also a very great deal for the father who suffered his son to follow in this manner the path of learning[2].

Milton's lyric verse; its relation to contemporary life.

True, Milton gave more than one earnest of his future fame. The dates of the early pieces—*L'Allegro*, *Il Penseroso*, *Arcades*, *Comus* and *Lycidas*—are not all certain; but probably each was composed at Horton before 1638. We must speak of them elsewhere. Here we may note that four of them have great autobiographic value as an indirect commentary, written from Milton's coign of seclusion, upon the moral crisis through which English life and thought were passing, the clash between the careless, pleasure-seeking Cavalier world and the deepening austerity of Puritanism. In *L'Allegro* the poet holds the balance almost equal between the two opposing tendencies. In *Il Penseroso* it becomes clear to which side his sympathies are leaning. *Comus* is a covert prophecy of the downfall of the Court-party, while *Lycidas* openly "foretells the ruine" of the Established Church. The latter poem is the final utterance of Milton's lyric genius.

[1] Milton's poems with their undercurrent of perpetual allusion are the best proof of the width of his reading; but interesting supplementary evidence is afforded by the commonplace book discovered in 1874, and printed by the *Camden Society*, 1876. It contains extracts from about 80 different authors whose works Milton had studied.

[2] Cf. the poem *Ad Patrem*, 68—72, in which Milton thanks his father for not having forced him to be a merchant or lawyer.

Here he reaches, in Mr Mark Pattison's words, the high-water mark of English verse; and then—the pity of it—he resigns his place among poets, gives himself up to politics, and for nearly twenty years suffers his lyre to hang mute and rusty in the temple of the Muses.

Travels in Italy; close of the first period in his life.

The composition of *Lycidas* may be assigned to the year 1637. In the spring of the next year Milton started for Italy. He had long made himself a master of Italian, and it was natural that he should seek inspiration in the land where many English poets, from Chaucer to Shelley, have found it. Milton remained abroad some fifteen months. Originally he had intended to include Sicily and Greece in his travels, but news of the troubles in England hastened his return. He was brought face to face with the question whether or not he should bear his part in the coming struggle; whether without self-reproach he could lead any longer this life of learning and indifference to the public weal. He decided as we might have expected that he would decide, though some good critics see cause to regret the decision. Milton puts his position very clearly. "I considered it," he says, "dishonourable to be enjoying myself at my ease in foreign lands, while my countrymen were striking a blow for freedom." And again: "Perceiving that the true way to liberty followed on from these beginnings, inasmuch also as I had so prepared myself from my youth that, above all things, I could not be ignorant what is of Divine and what of human right, I resolved, though I was then meditating certain other matters, to transfer into this struggle all my genius and all the strength of my industry."

Cause of his return to England.

The second period, 1639—1660. Milton abandons poetry.

The summer of 1639 (July) found Milton back in England. Immediately after his return he wrote the *Epitaphium Damonis*, the beautiful elegy in which he lamented the death of his school friend, Diodati. *Lycidas* was the last of the English lyrics: the *Epitaphium*, which should be studied in close connection with *Lycidas*, the last of the long Latin poems. Thenceforth, for a long spell, the rest was silence, so far as concerned poetry. The period which for all men represents the strength and maturity of manhood, which in the cases of other poets produces the best and most characteristic work, is with Milton a blank. In twenty years he composed no more than a bare handful of Sonnets, and even some of these are infected by the taint of political *animus*. Other interests filled his thoughts—the question of Church-reform, education, marriage, and, above all, politics.

Pamphlets on the Church and Education.

Milton's first treatise upon the government of the Established Church (*Of Reformation touching Church-Discipline in England*) appeared in 1641. Others followed in quick succession. The abolition of Episcopacy was the watchword of the enemies of the Anglican Church—the great rallying-cry of Puritanism, and no one enforced the point with greater eloquence than Milton. During 1641 and 1642 he wrote five pamphlets on the subject. Meanwhile he was studying the principles of education. On his return from Italy he had undertaken the training of his nephews[1]. This led to consideration of the best educational methods; and in the *Tractate on Education*, 1644, Milton assumed the part of educational theorist.

Marriage.

In the previous year, May, 1643, he married[2]. The marriage proved, at the time, unfortunate. Its immediate outcome was the pamphlets on

[1] Edward and John Phillips, sons of Milton's only sister. Both subsequently joined the Royalist party. To Edward Phillips we owe a memoir of the poet.

[2] His wife (who was only seventeen) was Mary Powell, eldest daughter of Richard Powell, of Forest Hill, a village some little distance from Oxford. She went to stay with her father in July 1643, and refused to return to Milton; why, it is not certain. She was reconciled to her husband in 1645, bore him four children, and died in 1652, in her twenty-seventh year.

Divorce. Clearly he had little leisure for literature proper.

The finest of Milton's prose works, *Areopagitica*, a plea for the free expression of opinion, was published in 1644. In 1645[1] he edited the first collection of his poems. In 1649 his advocacy of the anti-royalist cause was recognised by the offer of a post under the newly appointed Council of State. His bold vindication of the trial of Charles I., *The Tenure of Kings*, had appeared earlier in the same year. Milton accepted the offer,

Political Pamphlets. Appointment to Latin Secretaryship.

No doubt, the scene in *Paradise Lost* x. 909—946, in which Eve begs forgiveness of Adam, reproduced the poet's personal experience, while many passages in *Samson Agonistes* must have been inspired by the same cause.

[1] i.e. old style. The volume was entered on the registers of the Stationers' Company under the date of October 6th, 1645. It was published on Jan. 2, 1646, with the following title-page:

"*Poems of Mr. John Milton, both English and Latin, compos'd at several times. Printed by his true Copies. The Songs were set in Musick by Mr. Henry Lawes, gentleman of the King's Chappel, and one of His Majesties private Musick.*

'———*Baccare frontem*
Cingite, ne vati noceat mala lingua futuro.' VIRG. *Ecl.* 7.

Printed and publish'd according to Order. London, Printed by Ruth Raworth, for Humphrey Moseley, and are to be sold at the signe of the Princes Arms in Pauls Churchyard. 1645."

From the prefatory Address to the Reader it is clear that the collection was due to the initiative of the publisher. Milton's own feeling is expressed by the motto, where the words "*vati futuro*" show that, as he judged, his great achievement was yet to come. The volume was divided into two parts, the first containing the English, the second the Latin poems. *Comus* was printed at the close of the former, with a separate title-page to mark its importance.

becoming Latin[1] Secretary to the Committee of Foreign Affairs. There was nothing distasteful about his duties. He drew up the despatches to foreign governments, translated state-papers, and served as interpreter to foreign envoys. Had his duties stopped here his acceptance of the post would, I think, have proved an unqualified gain. It brought him into contact with the first men in the state[2], gave him a practical insight into the working of national affairs and the motives of human action; in a word, furnished him with that experience of life which is essential to all poets who aspire to be something more than "the idle singers of an empty day." But unfortunately the secretaryship entailed the necessity of defending at every turn the past course of the revolution and the present policy of the Council. Milton, in fact, held a perpetual brief as advocate for his party. Hence the endless and unedifying controversies into which he drifted; controversies which wasted the most precious years of his life, warped, as some critics think, his nature, and eventually cost him his eyesight.

The advantage of the post.

Its disadvantage.

Between 1649 and 1660 Milton produced no less than eleven pamphlets. Several of these arose out of the publication of the famous *Eikon Basilike*. The book was printed in 1649 and created so great an impression in the king's favour that Milton was asked to reply to it. This he did with

Milton's writings on behalf of the Commonwealth.

[1] A Latin Secretary was required because the Council scorned, as Edward Phillips says, "to carry on their affairs in the wheedling, lisping jargon of the cringing French." Milton's salary was £288, in modern money about £900.

[2] There is no proof that Milton ever had personal intercourse with Cromwell, and Mr Mark Pattison implies that he was altogether neglected by the foremost men of the time. Yet it seems unlikely that the Secretary of the Committee should not have been on friendly terms with some of its members, Vane, for example, and Whitelocke.

Eikonoklastes, introducing the wholly unworthy sneer at Sidney's *Arcadia* and the awkwardly expressed reference to Shakespeare[1]. Controversy of this barren type has the inherent disadvantage that once started it may never end. The Royalists commissioned the Leyden professor, Salmasius, to prepare a counterblast, the *Defensio Regia*, and this in turn was met by Milton's *Pro Populo Anglicano Defensio*, 1651, over the preparation of which he lost what little power of eyesight remained[2]. Salmasius retorted, and died before his second collection of scurrilities was issued: Milton was bound to answer, and the *Defensio Secunda*

His blindness.

[1] See *L'Al.* 133—134, note. It would have been more to the point to remind his readers that the imprisoned king must have spent a good many hours over La Calprenède's *Cassandre.*

[2] Perhaps this was the saddest part of the episode. Milton tells us in the *Defensio Secunda* that his eyesight was injured by excessive study in boyhood: "from the twelfth year of my age I scarce ever left my lessons and went to bed before midnight. This was the first cause of my blindness." Continual reading and writing must have increased the infirmity, and by 1650 the sight of the left eye had gone. He was warned that he must not use the other for book-work. Unfortunately this was just the time when the Commonwealth stood most in need of his services. If Milton had not written the first *Defence* he might have retained his partial vision. The choice lay between private good and public duty. He repeated in 1650 the sacrifice of 1639. "In such a case I could not listen to the physician, not if Æsculapius himself had spoken from his sanctuary; I could not but obey that inward monitor, I know not what, that spoke to me from heaven......I concluded to employ the little remaining eyesight I was to enjoy in doing this, the greatest service to the common weal it was in my power to render" (*Second Defence*). By the Spring of 1652 Milton was quite blind. He was then in his forty-fourth year. The allusion in *Paradise Lost*, III. 21—26, leaves it doubtful from what disease he suffered, whether cataract or amaurosis. Throughout *Samson Agonistes* there are frequent references to his affliction.

appeared in 1654. Neither of the combatants gained anything by the dispute; while the subsequent development of the controversy in which Milton crushed the Amsterdam pastor and professor, Morus, goes far to prove the contention of Mr Mark Pattison, that it was an evil day when the poet left his study at Horton to do battle for the Commonwealth amid the vulgar brawls of the market-place:

> "Not here, O Apollo,
> Were haunts meet for thee."

The Restoration releases Milton from politics. Return to poetry.

Fortunately this poetic interregnum in Milton's life was not destined to last much longer. The Restoration came, a blessing in disguise, and in 1660 the ruin of Milton's political party and of his personal hopes, the absolute overthrow of the cause for which he had fought for twenty years, left him free. The author of *Lycidas* could once more become a poet[1].

Should Milton have kept apart from political life?

Much has been written upon this second period, 1639—1660, and a word may be said here. We saw what parting of the ways confronted Milton on his return from Italy. Did he choose aright? Should he have continued upon the path of learned leisure? There are writers who argue that Milton made a mistake. A poet, they say, should keep clear of political strife: fierce controversy can benefit no man: who touches pitch must expect to be, certainly will be, defiled: Milton sacrificed twenty of the best years of his life, doing work which an underling could have done and which was not

One reply to this question.

[1] We have not attempted to trace the growth of Milton's political and religious opinions: "Through all these stages," Mr Mark Pattison writes, "Milton passed in the space of twenty years—Church-Puritan, Presbyterian, Royalist, Independent, Commonwealth's man, Oliverian." To illustrate this statement would need many pages.

worth doing: another *Comus* might have been written, a loftier *Lycidas:* that literature should be the poorer by the absence of these possible masterpieces, that the second greatest genius which England has produced should in a way be the "inheritor of unfulfilled renown," is and must be a thing entirely and terribly deplorable. This is the view of the purely literary critic. Mr Mark Pattison writes very much to this effect.

The opposite view.

There remains the other side of the question. It may fairly be contended that had Milton elected in 1639 to live the scholar's life apart from "the action of men," *Paradise Lost*, as we have it, could never have been written[1]. Knowledge of life and human nature, insight into the problems of men's motives and emotions, grasp of the broader issues of the human tragedy, all these were essential to the author of an epic poem; they could only be obtained through commerce with the world; they would have remained beyond the reach of a recluse. Dryden complained that Milton saw nature through the spectacles of books: we might have had to complain that he saw men through the same medium. Fortunately it is not so: and it is not so because at the age of twenty-two he threw in his fortunes with those of his country; like the diver in Schiller's ballad he took the plunge which was to cost him so dear. The mere man of letters will never move the world. Æschylus fought at Marathon: Shakespeare was practical to the tips of his fingers; a better business man than Goethe there was not within a radius of a hundred miles of Weimar.

Milton's own opinion.

This aspect of the question is emphasised by Milton himself. The man, he says, "who would not be frustrate of his hope to write well hereafter in laudable things, ought himself to be a true poem, that is, a composition and pattern of the best and honour-

[1] This is equally true of *Samson Agonistes*.

ablest things, ***not***[1] *presuming to sing high praises of heroic men or famous cities, unless he have within himself the experience and the practice of all that which is praiseworthy.*" Again, in estimating the qualifications which the writer of an epic such as he contemplated should possess, he is careful to include "insight into all seemly and generous arts and *affairs*[2]."

How politics may have influenced the poet.

Truth usually lies half-way between extremes: perhaps it does so here. No doubt, Milton did gain very greatly by breathing awhile the larger air of public life, even though that air was often tainted by impurities. No doubt, too, twenty years of unrest and controversy must have left their mark even on Milton. In one of the very few places[3] where he "abides our question," Shakespeare writes:

"O! for my sake do you with Fortune chide,
The guilty goddess of my harmful deeds,
That did not better for my life provide,
Than public means, which public manners breeds:
Thence comes it that my name receives a brand;
And almost thence my nature is subdu'd
To what it works in, like the dyer's hand."

Milton's genius was subdued in this way. If we compare him, the Milton of the great epics and of *Samson Agonistes*, with Homer or Shakespeare—and none but the greatest can be his parallel—we find in him a certain want of humanity, a touch of narrowness. He lacks the large-heartedness, the genial, generous breadth of Shakespeare; the tolerant sympathy with his fellow men that even in *Troilus and Cressida* or *Timon of Athens* is there for those who have eyes wherewith to see it. Milton reflects many of the less gracious aspects of

1 The italics are not Milton's.

2 *Reason of Church Government*, *P. W.* II. 481.

3 *Sonnet* CXI.

Puritanism, its intolerance, want of humour, one-sided intensity. He is stern and austere, and it seems natural to assume that this narrowness was to a great extent the price he paid for many years of ceaseless special pleading and dispute. The real misfortune of his life lay in the fact that he fell on evil, angry days when there was no place for moderate men. He had to be one of two things: either a controversialist or a student: there was no *via media*. Probably he chose aright; but we could wish that there had been no necessity to make the choice.

From the Restoration to Milton's death.

The last part of Milton's life, 1660—1674, passed quietly. At the age of fifty-two he was thrown back upon poetry, and could at length discharge his self-imposed obligation. The early poems he had never regarded as a fulfilment of the debt due to his Creator; even when the fire of political strife burned at its hottest Milton never lost sight of the purpose which had been with him since his boyhood. The main difficulty lay in the selection of a suitable subject. He had weighed themes drawn from the Scriptures and others taken from the history of his own country. For a time he was evidently inclined to choose the Arthurian story[1], the only cycle of events in British history or legend which seems to lend itself naturally to epic treatment. Had he done so we should have lost the *Idylls of the King*. The rough drafts of his projected schemes, now among the Milton

His great work; the subject and treatment.

[1] This project is not mentioned among the schemes enumerated in the Trinity MSS. But cf. the *Epitaphium Damonis*, 162—178, and the poem *Mansus*, 80—84. See also *Comus*, 826—842, *Lycidas*, 160 (note). Among Milton's prose works was a *History of Britain*, written for the most part about 1649, but not printed till 1670. In it he used the materials collected for his abandoned epic on the story of King Arthur.

MSS. at Trinity College[1], shew that exactly ninety-nine possible themes occupied his thoughts from time to time; but even as early as 1641 the story of the lost Paradise began to assume prominence. Still, even when the subject was definitely chosen, the question of its treatment—dramatic or epic—remained. Milton contemplated the former. He even commenced work upon a drama of which Satan's address to the sun in the fourth book of *Paradise Lost*[2] formed the exordium. These lines were written about 1642. Milton recited them to his nephew Phillips at the time of their composition. Possibly, had Milton not been distracted and diverted from poetry by political and other interests, he might from 1642 onwards have continued this drama, and thus produced a dramatic masterpiece akin to *Samson Agonistes*. As things fell out, the scheme was dropped, and never taken up again. When he finally addressed himself to the composition of *Paradise Lost* he had decided in favour of the epic or narrative form.

Paradise Lost begun.

Following Aubrey (from Aubrey and Phillips most of our information concerning Milton is derived) we may assume that Milton began to write *Paradise Lost* about 1658. He worked continuously at the epic for some five years. It was finished in 1663, the year of his third[3] marriage. Two more years, however,

[1] They include the original drafts of *Arcades*, *Comus*, *Lycidas*, and some of the minor poems, together with Milton's notes on the design of the long poem he meditated composing, and other less important papers. The MSS. were presented to Trinity by a former member of the college, Sir Henry Newton Puckering, who died in 1700. It is not known how they originally came into his possession.

[2] Bk. IV. ll. 32 *et seq.*

[3] Milton's second marriage took place in the autumn of 1656, i.e. after he had become blind. His wife died in February, 1658. Cf. the *Sonnet*, "Methought I saw my late espoused

were spent in the necessary revision, and in 1665 Milton placed the completed poem in the hands of his friend Thomas Ellwood[1]. In 1667 *Paradise Lost* was issued from the press[2]. Milton received £5. Before his death he was paid a second instalment, £5. Six editions of the poem had been published by the close of the century.

The poem published.

When Ellwood returned the MS. of *Paradise Lost* to Milton he remarked: "Thou hast said much here of *Paradise Lost*, but what hast thou to say of Paradise found?" Possibly we owe *Paradise Regained* to these chance words; or the poem, forming as it does a natural pendant to its predecessor, may have been included in Milton's original design. In any case he must have commenced the second epic about the year 1665. *Samson Agonistes* appears to have been written a little later. The two poems were published together in 1671.

Paradise Regained: Samson Agonistes.

In giving this bare summary of facts it has not been

saint," the pathos of which is heightened by the fact that he had never seen her.

[1] Cf. the account given in Ellwood's *Autobiography:* "after some common discourses had passed between us, he called for a manuscript of his; which, being brought, he delivered to me, bidding me take it home with me and read it at my leisure, and, when I had so done, return it to him with my judgment thereupon. When I came home, and had set myself to read it, I found it was that excellent poem which he intituled *Paradise Lost.*"

[2] The delay was due to external circumstances. Milton had been forced by the Plague to leave London, settling for a time at Chalfont St Giles in Buckinghamshire, where Ellwood had taken a cottage for him. On his return to London, after "the sickness was over, and the city well cleansed," the Great Fire threw everything into disorder; and there was some little difficulty over the licensing of the poem. For these reasons the publication of *Paradise Lost* was delayed till the autumn of 1667 (Masson).

our purpose to offer any criticism upon the poems. It would take too much space to show why *Samson Agonistes* is in subject-matter the poet's threnody over the fallen form of Puritanism, and in style the most perfectly classical poem in English literature; or again, why some great writers (among them Coleridge and Wordsworth) have pronounced *Paradise Regained* to be in point of artistic execution the most consummate of Milton's works—a judgment which would have pleased the author himself since, according to Phillips, he could never endure to hear *Paradise Regained* "censured to be much inferior to *Paradise Lost*." The latter speaks for itself in the rolling splendour of those harmonies which Tennyson has celebrated and alone in his time equalled.

Close of Milton's life.

In 1673 Milton brought out a reprint of the 1645 edition of his *Poems*, adding most of the sonnets[1] written in the interval. The last four years of his life were devoted to prose works of no

[1] The number of Milton's sonnets is twenty-three (if we exclude the piece on "The New Forcers of Conscience"), five of which were written in Italian, probably during the time of his travels in Italy, 1638—9. Ten sonnets were printed in the edition of 1645, the last of them being that entitled (from the *Cambridge* MS.) "To the Lady Margaret Ley." The remaining thirteen were composed between 1645 and 1658. The concluding sonnet, therefore (to the memory of Milton's second wife), immediately preceded his commencement of *Paradise Lost*. Four of these poems (XV. XVI. XVII. XXII.) could not, on account of their political tone, be included in the edition of 1673. They were first published by Edward Phillips at the end of his memoir of Milton, 1694. The sonnet on the "Massacre in Piedmont" is usually considered the finest of the collection, of which the late Rector of Lincoln College edited a well-known edition, 1883. The sonnet inscribed with a diamond on a window pane in the cottage at Chalfont where the poet stayed in 1665 is (in the judgment of a good critic) Miltonic, if not Milton's (Garnett's *Life of Milton*, p. 175).

particular interest to us[1]. He continued to live in London. His third marriage had proved happy, and he enjoyed something of the renown which was rightly his. Various well-known men used to visit him—notably Dryden[2], who on one of his visits asked and received permission to dramatise *Paradise Lost.*

His death.

Milton died in 1674, November 8th. He was buried in St Giles's Church, Cripplegate. When we think of him we have to think of a man who lived a life of very singular purity and devotion to duty; who for what he conceived to be his country's good sacrificed—and no one can well estimate the sacrifice—during twenty years the aim that was nearest to his heart and best suited to his genius; who, however, eventually realised his desire of writing a great work *in gloriam Dei.*

[1] The treatise on *Christian Doctrine* is valuable as throwing much light on the theological views expressed in the two epic poems and *Samson Agonistes.*

[2] The lines by Dryden which were printed beneath the portrait of Milton in Tonson's folio edition of *Paradise Lost* published in 1688 are too familiar to need quotation; but it is worth noting that the younger poet had in Milton's lifetime described the great epic as "one of the most noble, and most sublime poems which either this age or nation has produced" (prefatory essay to *The State of Innocence*, 1674). Further, tradition assigned to Dryden (a Roman Catholic and a Royalist) the remark, "this fellow (Milton) cuts us all out and the ancients too."

COMUS.

Comus was probably written in the spring of 1634. There can be no doubt that its composition was due to Milton's intimate friend Henry Lawes, the musician. Among Lawes's pupils were the family of the Earl of Bridgewater, son-in-law of the Countess of Derby, in whose honour *Arcades* was written.

Why written, and when.

In July 1631 the Earl of Bridgewater was made Lord-Lieutenant of the counties on the Welsh border and of North and South Wales—a viceregal post similar to the Lord-Lieutenancy of Ireland. For some reason the Earl's formal entry on his duties was delayed till the autumn of 1634. To celebrate the event great festivities were held at his official residence, Ludlow Castle. The first performance of *Comus* was part of these festivities. It took place on Michaelmas night, 1634. Doubtless Lawes, as music-master to the Earl's family, and as a practised writer of Masque-music, had been asked to undertake the provision of an entertainment suitable to the occasion, and had applied to Milton for help. With the Puritan Milton of later years, who in *Paradise Lost*, IV. 764, decried "mixed dance or wanton masque," the petition would have fared ill. But at this time there could be nothing distasteful in it. Milton showed himself in *L'Allegro* friendly to the stage, admitting "masque and antique pageantry" among the legitimate delights that Mirth might offer. Further, there was the desire to do a service to his friend Lawes. Milton accepted the commission, and *Comus* was the outcome.

Date of "Comus."

Probably he wrote the piece early in 1634. It had to be ready by the autumn; and time would be required for the setting of the music, and for all the preparations incidental to the representation of an unusually long Masque. The spring therefore of 1634 may be received with some confidence as the date of the composition of *Comus*.

Whether the play was successful at its representation we do not know. Many of Lawes's friends evidently appreciated it. Some were present in the Hall at Ludlow Castle on that September evening; others, perhaps, heard the songs afterwards sung by Lawes himself or his pupils. They realised that there was in England a poet of rare promise and exquisite performance. Copies of *Comus* were asked for; it became "much desired[1]." At last, to save himself the trouble of making these transcripts, Lawes published an edition of *Comus*, probably from the MS. which had been used as the acting-version. This, the first edition of *Comus*, was issued in 1637. The title-page describes the poem as "A Maske presented at Ludlow Castle, 1634, on Michaelmasse Night, before the Right Honourable John, Earle of Bridgewater, Viscount Brackley, Lord President of Wales, and one of his Majestie's most honourable Privy Counsell.

The first edition of "Comus."

> '*Eheu quid volui misero mihi! floribus Austrum*
> *Perditus*—'"

It will be observed that Milton's name is omitted. The motto, however (from Vergil, *Eclogue*, II. 58, 59), shows that his consent to the publication had been obtained: "Alas! what have I been about in my folly! On my flowers I have let in the sirocco (i.e. the hot south-east wind), infatuate as I am." The last words imply that Milton had some doubt as to the expediency of printing the volume. Had Lawes issued the imprint against the wishes of Milton, the motto chosen would have been pointless. It reminds us of the reluctance to break his silence "before the mellowing year" which he expressed at the beginning of *Lycidas* in that same year,

[1] See p. 3.

1637. That at least one competent and discerning critic was ready to welcome the new voice in English verse we may judge from Sir Henry Wotton's complimentary letter to Milton[1].

Later editions of "Comus."

Editions of Milton's minor poems appeared in 1645 and 1673. *Comus*, of course, was printed in each. In neither, however, did he describe the poem by the name it has long borne. The title in the 1645 edition reads thus: "A Mask of the Same Author, Presented at Ludlow Castle, 1634, before the Earl of Bridgewater, then President of Wales: Anno Dom. 1645." The title of the later edition is almost identical. A more definite designation being desirable, the Masque was named *Comus* after its chief character.

The Text.

The basis of the text of *Comus* is supplied by the three above-mentioned editions—that of Lawes, 1637, and those of Milton, 1645 and 1673. Milton's original draft of the poem is among the MSS.[2] at Cambridge; and the Bridgewater manuscript, supposed to be the stage-copy from which the actors learned their parts, and believed to be in Lawes's handwriting, also survives. All the differences between these five authorities—on the whole, not inconsiderable differences—we have not attempted to record. A careful comparison of them was given by Todd, and it is instructive to note the unerring instinct with which Milton, like Tennyson, always corrected his work for the better. Perhaps the last of the editions published during Milton's life has the most weight. It gives us *Comus*, not as the Masque originally left Milton's hands—for that we must turn to the Cambridge MS.—but in the finally revised form which he wished it to assume. There is a single passage where one is fain to believe that the Cambridge manuscript is right, and the printed copies

[1] See p. 4.

[2] *i.e.* the Milton MSS. at Trinity College; see p. xxii.

wrong. This is line 553. Milton's blindness necessarily introduces a slight uncertainty as to the text of his poems published in the latter part of his life.

Such, in brief, is the external history of *Comus*. Something must be said about the poem itself—the sources from which Milton drew, the undercurrent of idea that runs throughout, the dramatic value of the Masque, its ethical and literary qualities.

In lines 43—45 the Attendant Spirit says:

The sources of "Comus."

> "I will tell you now
> What never yet was heard in tale or song,
> From old or modern bard, in hall or bower."

This claim to absolute originality must not be pressed. Milton was indebted in *Comus*, in some measure, to previous writers. We shall best be able to estimate the debt if we split up the Masque into its chief component parts.

Milton's debt to George Peele (1558—1595).

There is (1) the main story: that of the sister lost in a wood, entrapped by a magician, and rescued by her brothers; with the attendant incidents. This Milton owed, it is almost certain, to the *Old Wives' Tale* (1595) of George Peele, the Elizabethan poet (1558—1598). Warton summarised thus the points of contact between *Comus* and the *Old Wives' Tale*: "This curious piece (i.e. Peele's play) exhibits, among other parallel incidents, two Brothers wandering in quest of their Sister, whom an Enchanter had imprisoned. This magician had learned his art from his mother Meroe, as Comus had been instructed by his mother Circe. The Brothers call out the Lady's name, and Echo replies[1]. The Enchanter had given her a potion which suspends the power of reason, and superinduces oblivion of herself. The Brothers afterwards meet with an Old Man, who is also skilled in magic; and by listening to his soothsayings,

[1] In *Comus* it is the Lady who invokes the Echo.

they recover their lost Sister. But not till the Enchanter's wreath has been torn from his head, his sword wrested from his hand, a glass broken, and a light extinguished."

Warton's abstract of the *Old Wives' Tale* somewhat accentuates the resemblance. It does not strike us quite so forcibly when we read Peele's work. Still the similarity is there, and Milton's indebtedness to Peele is universally admitted.

The traditional account of the origin of "Comus."

The popular tradition, still extant, as to the genesis of *Comus* must also be mentioned. This was to the effect that the young Lady Alice Egerton and her two brothers, Viscount Brackley and Mr Thomas Egerton, were actually overtaken by nightfall in Haywood Forest, near Ludlow: they were returning to the castle from a visit to their relatives, the Egertons, in Herefordshire, and the sister was separated from her brothers. If this ever took place and news of it reached Milton's ears, then he simply dramatised the episode; though part of his debt to Peele, viz. the introduction of the magician, would still remain. But it seems more probable that the legend, which cannot be traced further back than the last century, grew out of the Masque.

The character of Comus, the magician.

(2) The chief character of the piece, Comus, introduces another element in the story. He is in all essentials the creation of Milton. In classical Greek κῶμος signifies 'revel' or 'revelling-band.' The word κῶμος was specially used of the band of revellers[1] at the vintage festivals held in honour of Dionysus the god of wine (=the Roman god Bacchus). Thence naturally arose the personification Comus, i.e. revelling or sensual pleasure regarded as a

[1] The Cambridge MS of *Comus* has the stage-direction "intrant κωμάζοντες" ('they enter in revelling fashion') at line 93. And in the list of possible subjects of Milton's great poem is the entry "*Comazontes*, or The Benjaminites, or The Rioters," with references to *Judges* xix, xx, xxi.

kind of deity; but this is a post-classical conception, known only to later mythology. Apparently this deity Comus is first mentioned by the Greek writer Philostratus the elder, who lived in the third century A.D. and wrote a book on paintings, under the title "Likenesses, Portraits" (*Imagines*). Philostratus describes a fresco in which Comus is represented as a youth ruddy with wine, but the account is too slight to have been of much service to Milton, even if he was familiar with it. More definite is the picture drawn by Ben Jonson in the Masque of *Pleasure Reconciled to Virtue* (1619). Comus is a character in that Masque and described as

"The founder of taste
For fresh meats, or powdered, or pickle, or paste;
Devourer of boiled, baked, roasted or sod;
An emptier of cups."

Obviously this sordid power of dull, "lust-dieted" appetite has not very much in common with Milton's blithe, caressing personification of pleasure, so fatal because outwardly so beautiful; though I do not doubt that Milton knew Ben Jonson's Masque.

The Latin Play, "Comus."

There is also a certain Latin play which may have given suggestions and which from its title deserves to be mentioned. It was called *Comus*. It was written by a Dutchman, Hendrik van der Putten (better known under the name of Erycius Puteanus), sometime professor at Louvain. First printed in 1608, his *Comus* was reissued at Oxford in 1634, a remarkable coincidence. The Comus of Puteanus is a much subtler embodiment of sensuality than the cup-quaffing deity of Ben Jonson; he approximates more to the graceful reveller and enticing magician of Milton, and I should be loath to acquit Milton of all indebtedness to Puteanus. I think that he must have gone through the Latin piece, picking out from the worthless slag an occasional atom of genuine ore.

The extremely appropriate parentage which is assigned to Comus (46—58) was Milton's own invention. It was partly suggested, no doubt, by the association of the word *κῶμος* with Dionysus (Bacchus). Milton's purpose in making Comus the son of Circe and inheritor of her magic powers was to bring out the enticing aspect of sensual pleasure, which seeks to cast its beguiling spells upon men.

Milton's use of the legend of Circe.

(3) The third strand in the material out of which *Comus* is woven is the Circe-myth. In describing the supernatural powers of Comus Milton transfers to the wizard the classical attributes of his mother Circe. Like Vergil and Ovid before him, he lays the *Odyssey* under large contribution: so had Spenser in his account of the enchantress Acrasia in *The Faerie Queene*, II. 12, 55 *et seq.* Browne, too, had made the adventure of Odysseus and his crew at the island of Circe the theme of *The Inner Temple Masque* (1614). Probably each account—certainly Spenser's—was known to Milton, and may have exercised an unconscious influence upon him, *e.g.* in the turn of a phrase or addition of a descriptive detail. Going over the same ground as other writers with whom he is in any degree familiar, a poet can scarcely escape being influenced in some way, even though he is quite unaware of it.

The Story of Sabrina. Milton's indebtedness to Fletcher.

(4) There remains the legend of the river-goddess Sabrina, whose intervention frees the imprisoned lady and brings the Masque to a happy close. The source of this legend, which had been handled by other poets, was the *History* of Geoffrey of Monmouth[1]. In this important part of *Comus* the influence of Fletcher's *Faithful Shepherdess* is unmistakeable. This beautiful pastoral was composed before 1625. It had been acted as a Court-drama, and representations were given in the

[1] See p. 186.

London theatres in 1633 and 1634. The motive of the play is identical with that of *Comus*, viz. the strength of purity; and in Fletcher's heroine must be recognised an elder sister of Milton's Sabrina. Speaking briefly we may say that the last two hundred lines of *Comus*—the disenchantment scene—betray in the conception of the nymph Sabrina, in the incidents, and the lyric movement, the spell which Fletcher's genius exercised on Milton. Milton chose the story of the goddess who swayed the Severn stream in compliment to his audience. It suited the scene and the setting of his Masque; and his treatment of the theme reflects, in no servile spirit of imitation, the graceful example of the poet with whom the name of Shakespeare himself is linked in more than one work.

It is not doing Milton any real service to ignore or deny his indebtedness to these various sources. Absolute, unqualified originality is practically impossible. Literature is a series of echoes, and one of the tests of genius is to take inferior work and tune it to finer issues. Has the artist breathed fresh suggestion into things old? has he added things new? If we can answer 'yes' to each of these questions, his record is clear. We must indeed always try to get a clear idea wherein lies the greatness of a work, what are the qualities that make it immortal. In *Comus* those qualities, surely, are the exquisite music, especially of the lyric portions, the rapt elevation of thought and tone, the distinction of style. These gifts are a poet's own. He does not obtain them from 'sources,' search he never so carefully. And they constitute the 'originality' that is essential.

"Comus" to be judged as a Masque.

It is manifestly unfair to judge any work by tests which do not properly apply to it: we must not condemn a thing for not being what it does not profess to be—a truism which criticism often ignores. So it is beside the mark to say that *Comus* is "deficient as a drama." It does not profess to be a "drama" in the sense that *The Merchant of Venice* or *Hamlet* is. It is a "Masque." Now in a Masque we are not to look for the qualities which are indispensable to an ordinary drama, such as probability of story and logical development of dramatic motive, propriety of construction, studied and consistent character-drawing[1]. These things lie outside the province of the Masque-writer, whose fancy plays unfettered in a land where truth and realism seldom set foot. Consequently *Comus* should not be contrasted with works that belong to a different sphere of art. To estimate its merits aright we should study what Ben Jonson and Fletcher, the ablest of professional Masque-writers, have left us of a like description. We must accord Milton the licence which the composers of such pieces habitually claimed, and test *Comus* by the elementary standard of dramatic propriety recognised in these entertainments. Judged so, it has no cause to fear the objection that its story lacks probability or its construction violates rule.

Its moralising.

On the other hand, there is one objection to *Comus* which we cannot gainsay: as a Masque designed for representation it is overweighted with the moralising element. Magnificent in itself and intensely interesting as a revelation of Milton's character and of his relation towards the peculiar religious and social conditions of his age, this lofty strain of moralising is out of place in a Masque. It fits neither the occasion nor the speakers[2]. You cannot but feel that Milton uses the long speeches of the Lady and the Elder Brother to expound views which he holds especially sacred. All great art teaches, but the teaching is indirect. In *Comus* the didactic purpose is patent; nay, obtrudes. It hampers the movement of the piece, checks the natural

[1] In *Comus* the absence of names for all the characters except Comus should prepare us for the slightness of the characterisation.

[2] Hence the significant omissions, made doubtless by Lawes, at the original performance. See notes on 195—225, 737—755. One passage, 779—806, was an addition.

progress of the story; and worse, it strikes a note alien to the genius of the fanciful Masque and all its festive associations. But this demerit is characteristic of the poet. Milton's one defect, what more than aught else marks him Shakespeare's inferior, is lack of humour. A sense of humour means a keen sense of the incongruous; and a writer with half Milton's genius but more of that sense would have shunned the incongruous element which mars *Comus* as a Masque while increasing its power and beauty as a poem. It is, therefore, as a poem that the piece should be regarded, and the long speeches "must be read as majestic soliloquies" (Macaulay).

"The Miltonic idea" embodied in "Comus."

This didactic element reveals Milton, and that at a point of special interest in his career. It teaches the doctrine nearest to his heart, namely, sobriety of life. There was nothing for which Milton cared more than this. An atmosphere of rare purity breathes in his works. He shows an extraordinarily nice sense of whatsoever things are fair and of good report. There is in him a strong vein of asceticism, and he praises more than once the "cloistered virtue" of abstinence. As a youth he described thus, in a strain of classical allusion, the obligations of those who would touch the highest reaches of poetic art:

"But they, who demi-gods and heroes praise,
And feats performed in Jove's more youthful days,
Who now the counsels of high heaven explore,
Now shades that echo the Cerberean roar,
Simply let these, like him of Samos, live,
Let herbs to them a bloodless banquet give;
In beechen goblets let their beverage shine,
Cool from the crystal spring their sober wine.
Their youth should pass in innocence secure
From stain licentious, and in manners pure,
Pure as the priest, when robed in white he stands,
The fresh lustration ready in his hands.

Thus Linus lived, and thus, as poets write,
Tiresias, wiser for his loss of sight.
Thus exiled Chalcas, thus the bard of Thrace,
Melodious tamer of the savage race.
Thus trained by temperance, Homer led of yore
His chief of Ithaca from shore to shore.
For these are sacred bards, and from above
Drink large infusions from the mind of Jove[1]."

That was his youthful ideal: his works and all that we know of his life show that it was his practice. Professor Masson well sums up the matter in the statement that "the sublime notion and high mystery" of a disciplined life is "*the* Miltonic idea." Nowhere is it more conspicuous than in this Masque.

The Puritans and the Cavaliers.

Under any circumstances the theme would have kindled his muse to eloquence. But now in the year 1634, when the people were slowly separating into hostile camps, the truth was of more than personal import: it had become vitalised with a tragic national intensity. Each day the conflict between the gloom and ungraciousness of Puritanism and the pleasure-seeking carelessness of the Cavalier world grew keener. Extremes produce extremes: for one part of the nation life meant pleasure: the other identified pleasure with sin. When *Comus* was written Milton stood between the two armies. His Puritanism was tempered by Renaissance culture. The life of ideal happiness as pictured in *L'Allegro* is one into which enter all the influences of culture and nature that bring in their train "the joy in widest commonalty spread;" the cheerfulness which should be synonymous with Life, and to which Art should minister. And when in *Il Penseroso* Milton celebrates divinest Melancholy, she is not the bitter power whom Dante punished with the pains of Purgatory; rather, she has something of the kindliness

[1] From the sixth of the Latin *Elegies*, Cowper's translation.

that Shakespeare attributes to his goddess Adversity, whose uses are sweet, and of whom it was happily said that she must be a fourth Grace, less known than the classic Three, but still their sister.

These poems, *L'Allegro*, *Il Penseroso*, and *Comus*, belong to the non-political period in Milton's life. The bare fact that he wrote the last showed that he had not yet gone over to help the party whose unreasoning hatred of all amusement had flashed out in Prynne's *Histriomastix*[1] (1633). As Green says, "the historic interest of *Comus* lies in its forming part of a protest made by the more cultured Puritans against the gloomier bigotry which persecution was fostering in the party at large." On the other hand, the whole tone of *Comus* was opposed to the spirit of the Cavaliers. It sternly rebuked intemperance. The revel-god personified the worst elements of Court-life. In his overthrow Milton allegorically foreshadowed the downfall of those who led that life; just as in *Lycidas*, under the guise of pastoral symbolism, he predicted the ruin of the "corrupted Clergie," and at the end of his life lamented the crash of Puritanism through the mouth of Samson Agonistes. Two hundred and fifty years ago therefore *Comus* was terribly real as a warning against the danger upon which the ship of national life was drifting. But the theme is true yesterday, to-day, and for ever; and the art with which it is enforced remains undimmed, the wisdom unfading.

The lyrical parts of "Comus."

Johnson had fault to find with the songs in *Comus*. He considered them "harsh" and "not very musical." This was the most curious feature of his strange, grudging criticism of

[1] Prynne often refers to Masques, and always in terms of scorn; *e.g.* on page 783 of the *Histriomastix*, "Stage-players, Mũmeries, Masques, and such like heathenish practises," 1633 ed.

the Masque, since the superlative excellence of Milton's lyrics has never been a matter of dispute. In them Milton achieves a style of quintessential beauty, reminding us with Wordsworth that poetry is primarily a matter of inspiration, and proving, like Gray, that it must also be a matter of art. Richness of imagery, epithets that (in Macaulay's words) supply "a text for a canto," single phrases that for their curious felicity are, as Archbishop Trench said, "poems in miniature," evanescent touches that recall to the classical reader the old and happy, far-off things of Athens and Rome—these qualities, that belong mainly to art, are held together and heightened by a perfect genuineness of emotion which is the outcome of sheer inspiration. Above all, Milton gives us what we require most in lyric verse—true melody, and those who are deaf to these sphere-born notes, who find the "numbers" of *Comus* unpleasing, must be left to their displeasure.

Most of us will prefer Mr Saintsbury's verdict: "It is impossible to single out passages, for the whole is golden. The entering address of Comus, the song 'Sweet Echo,' the descriptive speech of the Spirit, and the magnificent eulogy of the 'sun-clad power of chastity,' would be the most beautiful things where all is beautiful, if the unapproachable 'Sabrina fair' did not come later, and were not sustained before and after, for nearly two hundred lines of pure nectar."

It was a happy inspiration which reserved the rhymed parts mainly for the close, where they form a kind of lyric *cadenza* on which the Masque closes. After bearing the heat and burden of the piece, after enforcing with all the power of his eloquence and righteous enthusiasm the moral which *Comus* illustrates, Milton turned to his muse and bade her touch a lighter, festive note. The philosophic strain was dropped: the poet of *L'Allegro* reasserted himself; and *Comus* came to an end with Lawes's music ringing through the Hall.

The stage-history of *Comus* is very slight. The representation at Ludlow appears to be the only one that took place in the seventeenth century. It is interesting to note that part at least of the music written by Lawes for the original performance survives, viz. the five numbers, "From the heavens," "Sweet Echo," "Sabrina fair," "Back Shepherds" and "Now my task." In the last century most of Milton's minor poems were made to supply *libretti* for contemporary musicians. Handel set *L'Allegro* and *Il Penseroso* (1740) to music, and afterwards (1742) made *Samson Agonistes* the basis of his Oratorio. *Comus*, or rather an adaptation of it, fell to the skilful hands of Dr Arne, the composer to whom we owe some of the best known settings of Shakespeare's songs. The adaptation of the Masque was made by the Rev. John Dalton, afterwards Canon of Worcester. He altered it beyond recognition, dividing it into three acts, redistributing the speeches, introducing fresh characters (among them Lycidas) and scenes, and interpolating songs of his own composition. The most curious change occurs in Act III., which commences with twenty-six lines ("But come, thou goddess," line 11) taken from *L'Allegro*, the invocation to Mirth being followed by the appearance on the scene of Euphrosyne.

Stage-history.

This stage-version was produced at Drury Lane theatre in 1738, and was frequently acted and several times printed. On the title-page of the first imprint (1738) are the words "never presented but on Michaelmas Day, 1634."

Geneste in his *Annals of the Stage* mentions later stage-versions with Arne's music, notably one for which Sir Henry Bishop wrote additional airs. Altogether *Comus* seems to have had some vogue on the stage in a quasi-operatic form. The last notable rendering of the Masque was that produced by Macready, who himself played the part of the magician.

LYCIDAS.

Date.

Lycidas was composed in November 1637, and published some time in 1638. It is an *In memoriam* poem, and the circumstances which evoked it were as follows.

Circumstances of its composition.

On August the 10th, 1637, a Fellow of Christ's College, Cambridge, Edward King, was lost at sea. He had been slightly junior to Milton at the University, but there had, no doubt, been some intimacy, possibly some friendship, between them. He seems to have been a scholar of great promise and much beloved; and when the news of his death was known at Cambridge in the ensuing Michaelmas term, his friends decided to publish a collection of elegiac verses as an expression of the University's regret at his early death.

Similar collections of verse.

Such collections were customary in the 17th century. When any event of significance occurred—especially a royal birth, or wedding, or death—the scholars and wits of Oxford and Cambridge invoked the Muses in strains of congratulation or lament. Thus the death of Ben Jonson (in 1637) was marked by the issue in this very year, 1638, of a volume of elegies; and there was a tradition in the last century that Milton's own *Epitaph on the Marchioness of Winchester* was first printed in a Cambridge collection of elegiac poems on her death.

That Edward King should have been honoured by the issue of one of these tributes, usually reserved for greater names, is a proof of the esteem in which he was held at Cambridge.

The memorial poems were published in 1638, in a volume divided into two sections. The first contains twenty-three pieces of Greek and Latin verse. The English portion is composed of thirteen poems, Milton's being the last. It is introduced with the simple title *Lycidas*, and signed with the initials "J. M." This therefore is the first edition of the elegy.

The Cambridge volume.

Besides the poems the volume includes a brief preface in Latin, setting forth the manner of King's death. He had sailed from Chester for Ireland, where most of his relations were settled; he himself had been born at Boyle, county Roscommon, and his father had held office as Secretary for Ireland under Elizabeth and the two succeeding monarchs. Not far from the British coast the vessel struck on a rock, sprang a leak, and sank. The narrative says that while other passengers were trying to save their lives Edward King knelt on the deck, and was praying as the ship went down. Some of those on board must have escaped, else this fact would not have been known. It is curious, I think, that Milton should have made no allusion to an episode so affecting, and for the purposes of the poet so effective. Other contributors to the volume mention it. Probably, however, Milton had not heard full details of the accident. He was living away from Cambridge—at Horton—and may have received no more than a notice in general terms of King's death, and an invitation to join his friends in lamenting the loss to the College and University.

The events of the poem.

For students of Milton the text of *Lycidas* possesses unusual interest. We have the original MS. preserved at Trinity; the Cambridge edition of 1638; a copy of this edition in the University Library, with corrections in Milton's handwriting; and the 1645 edition of Milton's early poems. This last version, almost identical with the issue of 1673, represents the final

Text.

revision of *Lycidas*. It offers a good many differences of reading from the MS. and the first (1638) edition. The changes illustrate what we have already noted in the case of *Comus*, viz. Milton's true instinct for improving his work. The same quality is very marked in Tennyson, the successive editions of whose works show numerous corrections for the better.

Lycidas, it is scarcely necessary to say, represents the pastoral style[1]. No type of poetry is more artificial. With some readers the inherent artificiality of the type is a ground of depreciation of this elegy. They find in it a note of unreality, a falseness of tone.

Is "Lycidas" an expression of personal grief?

"*Lycidas*," writes Johnson, "is not to be considered as the effusion of real passion; for passion runs not after remote allusions and obscure opinions. Passion plucks no berries from the myrtle and ivy, nor calls upon Arethuse and Mincius, nor tells of rough 'Satyrs' and 'Fauns with cloven heel.' Where there is leisure for fiction, there is little grief."

But pastoralism is only an imaginative medium of expression, and it is surely a hard saying that true feeling will not find imaginative vent. We must not apply rigidly the prosaic test of fact to works of fancy, and seek to bind down art to the literal presentment of life. All feeling, when it exceeds the bounds of the barest, briefest self-expression, tends to metaphor and symbol. Grief finds relief in so doing. "She clothes herself in metaphors, and, abstaining from the direct expression of poignant emotion, dwells on thoughts and images that have a beauty of their own for solace." It seems to me therefore a fallacy that the feeling of *Lycidas* must necessarily be unreal because the allegory in which it is prefigured had no actual basis in experience. Pastoral

[1] It will be more convenient to give a brief sketch of the history of pastoral poetry independently; see p. 181.

elegy is one of the recognised vehicles of lament, and the poet who adopts it is bound by literary traditions to do those things which Johnson says that no mourner does in real life. Truth of art is not identical with truth of fact.

Nevertheless, Johnson's remark that *Lycidas* is not to be regarded as "the effusion of real passion" does serve to warn us from a wrong way of looking at the poem. The primary interest of the elegy is artistic, not emotional. It is a study in the pastoral manner; "a highly-wrought piece of art," as Shelley said of his own elegiac poem *Adonais*.

"Lycidas" a 'study.'

Milton knew the Greek pastoral writers and their Latin imitator, Vergil, by heart. He knew, in particular, those poems—the first *Idyl* of Theocritus and the *Lament for Bion* by Moschus—which are models for all time of pastoralism dedicated to the purposes of elegy. And he had doubtless studied modern works, especially Italian, cast in the same vein. Here was an opportunity of weaving this knowledge into an exquisite fabric of learning and literary suggestion and artistic pathos. The outcome was a poem singularly appropriate to the circumstances which evoked it. For what more fitting than that the lament of a University over a gifted student should take the form of a work in which preeminently art and scholarship join hands? As to the kind or degree of personal feeling towards Edward King which *Lycidas* expresses, that will ever remain an open question. To me it seems that the feeling is no more than the sentiment of regret and pity which the premature death of a fellow-student and associate would naturally excite.

Milton and the Church.

There is, however, in *Lycidas* one subject on which Milton lets the reader know what he thought in entirely unambiguous language: namely, the corruption, from his point of view, of the Anglican Church. No one can mistake the drift of lines 118—131, or the spirit that animates them. The passage has been much censured, and from the standpoint of art seems indefensible. First, it is a digression, distracting attention from the main theme of the poem into a wholly different channel: the fact that Edward King had intended to take orders in the Church scarcely justifies the insertion of a long invective against it. Under any circumstances, whatever the style of the poem, an episode of this kind would be objectionable. But here amid bucolic imagery and pagan *dramatis personæ* Christianity can have no place. It would be hard to conceive greater incongruity of effect, and the only defence that can be offered is, that this blending of Christian sentiment and associations with paganism had long been a tradition with pastoral writers.

Christianity introduced into pastoral verse.

It is found in the *Eclogues* of the Carmelite Baptista Spagnola (commonly called Mantuan from the fact that he lived at Mantua), a now forgotten writer whose influence on pastoral verse was considerable, as the *Glosse* to *The Shepheards Calender* shows. It is found also in the Latin elegiac poetry of Italian scholars of the 16th century with whom references to the contemporary Church and State are freely interspersed among pictures of pastoral life painted in the manner of Theocritus and Vergil.

Spenser, again, in the fifth *Eclogue* of *The Shepheards Calender*, twenty-nine lines of which are quoted by Milton in his prose-work the *Animadversions*, shadows forth under the slightest of disguises the ordinary contrast between Roman Catholicism and Protestantism. And Phineas Fletcher in his *Piscatorie Eclogues*, which are cast in an essentially classical, pastoral style, attacks the "corrupted clergy" in the character of fishermen neglectful of their duty. Milton therefore could at least plead the privilege of custom[1], and he took full advantage of it.

[1] See the Globe *Spenser*, pp. 451, 476, 478, for references to Mantuan; Symonds's *Renaissance in Italy* ('Revival of Learning'), II. 486—498, for the Italian writers of pastoral; and Grosart's edition of Fletcher, ii. 274, 276.

Personally I cannot help thinking that our dislike of what we call incongruity in literature, i.e. the mixture of inharmonious associations, is a comparatively late development of taste. Consider for example the combination of Elizabethanism and classical mythology or history in a play like *A Midsummer-Night's Dream* or *Julius Cæsar*.

"The pilot of the Galilæan lake."

We cannot assume that what Milton writes is meant to apply to the whole Church. He limits it to the corrupt elements, though a few years later he seems to have regarded the corruption as universal. Nor is it a reasonable inference from his description of St Peter that he then felt any sympathy with episcopacy, which he afterwards assailed so vehemently. Dramatic propriety required that the Apostle should be invested with all the circumstance and pomp of his office—the mitre and the fateful keys—since by heightening the dignity of those who mourned for Lycidas the poet paid honour to him. Religion and learning alike bent over his tomb, the one symbolised by the head of the Catholic Church, the other by the spokesman of Edward King's University. Truly, he was fortunate in his elegist.

The supposed allusion to contemporary poets.

Once elsewhere in *Lycidas* the personal note interrupts the even monotone of elegy. It is surely not fanciful to detect in lines 64—69 a complaint that poetry had fallen on trifling times when all the qualities which in Milton's view were essential to the poet—sobriety of life, learning, earnestness of thought—counted for nothing in popular esteem. As we read this passage we remember the introduction to the second book of *The Reason of Church Government* (than which Milton's prose works contain nothing more valuable), where he contrasts two types of poets. He shows us there on the one hand "the vulgar amourist" whose inspiration is "the heat of youth, or the vapours of wine." On the other hand, he describes the scholar and seer who gives himself over to study and the mastery of all arts and sciences that illuminate the mind, and "devout prayer to that eternal Spirit, who can enrich with all utterance and knowledge, and sends out his seraphim, with the hallowed fire of his altar, to touch and purify the lips of whom he pleases." It is under this type that he directly classes himself; and to the former that he indirectly assigns in *Lycidas*, 64—69, the Sucklings and Herricks and Cavalier song-writers.

Modern elegies.

An *Introduction* to *Lycidas* cannot well omit mention, however brief, of those modern works which owe something to Milton's elegy, viz. Shelley's *Adonais*, written on the death of Keats, and Matthew Arnold's *Thyrsis*, a lament for his poet-friend and Oxford contemporary, Arthur Hugh Clough. These later elegists drew inspiration from the same classical sources as the author of *Lycidas*. They too revive echoes of the Greek shepherd-music; and apart from such general similarities as we should expect where writers have chosen the same vehicle of expression (in this case the most stereotyped and conventional of methods), each has at least one point of contact with Milton. *Thyrsis*, like *Lycidas*, presents an idealised picture of University-life, and perhaps for sincerity and true feeling begotten of love for the scenes described the advantage rests with the modern poet. In the *Adonais* Shelley's invective against the enemies of Keats (the poet regarded them as his own enemies too) recalls Milton's onslaught on the Church: a subsidiary theme kindled the fire of personal feeling in both poems, and neither can be regarded merely as the consecration of friendship. Of the three elegies, *Lycidas* and *Thyrsis* have most affinity. *Thyrsis* follows the pastoral type much more closely than *Adonais*, and has more of that intensely classical spirit which breathes throughout Milton's poem. Moreover, there is a closer parallel between the circumstances which severally produced *Lycidas* and *Thyrsis*. In each a scholar-poet was moved to lament a fellow-student with whom he had

had ties of kindred pursuits; whereas the intimacy between Keats and Shelley had been slight, and what animated Shelley in writing the *Adonais* was primarily the feeling that he was fighting in this, as in his other works, the battle of fairness and freedom, and in another's wrongs avenging his own. Of Tennyson's *In Memoriam*[1], which is sometimes compared with these elegies, we need not speak. It really stands apart. It is not a pastoral; and it has a philosophic scope far beyond that of any poem of lament. It is Tennyson's verdict on the tendencies and peculiar difficulties of his age, and his chief contribution to our "criticism of life."

[1] Tennyson "liked reading *Lycidas* aloud, but always stopped when he had passed [line 164], saying, 'that is the only bad line Milton ever wrote'." One wonders what he disliked in it (the dolphins?).

METRICAL FEATURES OF THESE POEMS.

To those who desire more insight into the poetic Art of Milton it may be helpful to note a few important points of metre[1]. First as to the blank verse of *Comus*. The typical blank verse is a line of ten syllables forming five feet in which the stresses or accents fall on the even syllables. These feet are commonly termed "iambic[2]," and the rhythm of a line composed of iambic feet is a "rising" rhythm. Here is a typical blank verse from *Comus* (line 30):

The typical blank verse.

"And áll this tráct that frónts the fálling sún."

Blank verse prior to Marlowe, the great Elizabethan dramatist whose work influenced Shakespeare, was modelled strictly on this type. Further, this early blank verse was what is termed "end-stopt": that is to say, there was almost always *some* pause, however slight, in the sense, and consequently in the rhythm, at the close of each line; while the couplet was normally the limit of the sense. As an example of "end-stopt" verse look at *Comus*, 73—77:

"And they, so perfect is their misery,
Not once perceive their foul disfigurement,
But boast themselves more comely than before,
And all their friends and native home forget,
To roll with pleasure in a sensual sty."

[1] The authoritative work is Mr Bridges's book *Milton's Prosody*, on which I have drawn.

[2] An iambus in Greek prosody is a foot of two syllables, short + long, thus ⏑ –. Roughly speaking, stress or accent is the equivalent in English prosody for the "quantity" of classical prosody; i.e. a stressed syllable (ʹ) corresponds with the long syllable (–) of classical verse, and an unstressed syllable with the short (⏑). In "scanning" a passage it is better always to use the term "stress" or "accent" than "long syllable," and the symbol ʹ, not –.

If the whole poem were written in verse of this kind the effect, obviously, would be intolerably monotonous. Blank verse before Marlowe *was* intolerably monotonous, and his great service to metre, carried further by Shakespeare, was to introduce variations into the existing type of the blank decasyllabic measure. In fact, analysis of the blank verse of any writer really resolves itself into a study of his modifications of the purely "iambic," "end-stopt" type.

Milton's chief variations.

The four chief variations employed by Milton[1] in *Comus* are these:

The "overflow."

(1) His use of the "overflow" of the sense from one line to another; what the French call "*enjambement.*"

Put simply, this only means that he makes the sense and rhythm run on from one line to another. A large proportion of his blank verse is "unstopt," not "end-stopt." Take *Comus*, 1—4:

> "Before the starry threshold of Jove's court
> My mansion is, where those immortal shapes
> Of bright aerial spirits live insphered
> In regions mild of calm and serene air."

In those lines there is no pause of sense and consequently none of rhythm at the end of either of lines 1—3: sense and rhythm run on.

Now "unstopt" verse escapes one of the dangers of blank verse: the danger of being stiff and formal, and hampering the sense, as in the early days of the metre, through arrangement in single lines or couplets. But it incurs another danger: it may be loose and formless through want of clearly marked pauses, balance of the parts, and rhythmic cadences—the qualities which should compensate for the absence of rhyme. Blank verse therefore of the "unstopt" type in which the paragraph is the unit, not the single line or couplet, needs an exquisite

[1] Not necessarily peculiar to him.

sense of sound, and of sound harmonised in a complex, elaborate scheme. And this sense was Milton's great gift. Hence his blank verse unites the two qualities so difficult to reconcile, yet essential, namely freedom and form: the freedom which allows an easy, natural expression of the sense and a variety of rhythm that echoes all its shifting inflections; and the form which comes from consummate mastery of pause, balance and cadence. Thus much as to the arrangement of his lines: now as to their internal formation.

"Extra-metrical" syllables.

(2) The second great feature of his blank verse is the use of "extrametrical" syllables. Briefly, he sometimes has eleven or even twelve syllables instead of ten in a line. The extra syllable may come (*a*) at the end of the line, (*b*) about the middle after some pause, or (*c*) in both places. Here are examples (211, 67, 617):

(*a*) "The virtuous mind, that ever walks áttend(ed)."

(*b*) "To quench the drouth of Phœ(bus); which as they taste."

(*c*) "As to make this rela(tion)? Cáre and útmost (shifts)."

Far the commonest of these variations from the typical decasyllabic line is (*a*). It is a great feature of the verse of *Comus* and *Samson Agonistes.* The proportion of such lines as (*a*) is said to be 1 in 9 in *Comus*, 1 in 6 in *Samson Agonistes.* In *Paradise Lost*, on the other hand, this kind of verse is rare. This is the one great difference between Milton's early and late blank verse, and the reason for it is clear. The extra syllable at the end of the line tends to make the rhythm run on into the next line, and therefore gives a rapid movement suitable to the spoken verse of the stage. It characterises thus the dramatic and lyrical pieces, whilst epic narrative like *Paradise Lost* demands a statelier, slower movement.

This extrametrical syllable at the end of a line is commonly called the "double" or "feminine" ending.

Note that it is of two kinds—where the last syllable would naturally bear a stress or accent, and where it would not.

Thus contrast 265

"And she shall be my queen. Hail, foreign wón(dĕr)"

with 633

"Bore a bright golden flower, but not in thís (sóil)."

Illustrations of (*b*) are lines 302, 415, 599, 662, 842.

The other variation (*c*) is also illustrated, I think, by line 407.

"Inversion of rhythm."

(3) Another feature is "inversion of rhythm," i.e. the substitution of "falling" rhythm for "rising" by use of a trochee in place of an iambus, these feet being exact opposites. A trochee is admitted into any of the first four feet of a line. Compare

(*a*) "Stríve to | keep up a frail and feverish being" (8);

(*b*) "Be well | stóck'd with | as fair a herd as grazed" (152);

(*c*) "But to my task. | Néptune | besides the sway" (18);

(*d*) "Benighted in these woods. | Nów to | my charms" (150).

Observe that inversion generally gives some emphasis to the word. Much the commonest inversion is that of the first foot. Indeed, this use of an initial trochee is one of the most characteristic points in Milton's verse. Among many examples take lines 39 ("thréats the"), 46 ("Bácchus"), 47 ("crúsh'd the"), 49 ("coásting"), with 60, 79, 80, 90, 147, 162, 163, 190 etc. In 145 there are two trochees ("bréak off, bréak off"); but I have not observed a similar instance. The trochee is a swift foot, and you will see that in several of the examples just given the sense refers to motion of some sort.

"Weak Stresses."

(4) The last point is the use of weak stresses. Sometimes there are less than five strong stresses in a line. This occurs most often where there is a preposition, and is com-

monest in the first and fourth feet. It gives, by way of compensation, a peculiar heaviness, as of two[1] stressed syllables, to the following foot. Compare these instances:

(*a*) "Before | the star|ry thres|hold ŏf | Jove's court" (1);

(*b*) "With thè | rank va|pours of this sin-worn mould" (17);

(*c*) "Ere morrow wake, | or thè | low-roost|ed lark" (317);

(*d*) "Stĕpped, as | they said, | to thè | next thick|et side" (185).

Observe that the variations (2), (3) and (4) may be used in combination, e.g. we find all three in line 49

"Coásting | the Týr|rhene shóre | as thè | winds líst(ed),"

and in 617

"As tò | make thís | relá(tion)? | Cáre and | útmost (shifts)";

and (3) and (4) in line 185 (quoted just above).

Metre of the lyrics.

The lyrics of *Comus* are simple in structure, cast for the most part in the octosyllabic measure, in "rising" rhythm, much used by Ben Jonson and easily set as musical recitative. They show that Milton exercised very freely the right of using imperfect rhymes. As proof of this Professor Masson aptly refers to the Echo Song. It has fourteen lines, with four consecutive pairs of irregular rhyme; and it is none the less wholly beautiful.

Imperfect rhyme.

Variations in the octosyllabic measure.

Milton varies the eight-syllabled measure (1) by an extra syllable at the end of the line, (2) by lines of only seven syllables in "falling," i.e. trochaic rhythm, with an extra syllable, stressed, at the end, (3) by occasional decasyllabic rhymed couplets.

For (1) compare 999

"Where young Adonis oft repo(ses)";

[1] *i.e.* forming a spondaic foot, the classical spondee being two long syllables (– –).

and for (2), which is by far the most important modification, cf. the following lines:

> "The stár | that bíds | the shép|herd fóld
> Nów the | tóp of | heáv'n doth | hóld;
> And the | gílded | cár of | dáy
> His glów|ing áx|le dóth | alláy."

For (3) see 115, 116, 129–132.

Then, it must be remembered that in all scansion of English poetry two things play a great part, viz. "contraction" and "elision."

Contractions.

"Contractions" may be divided into (1) the abbreviations of everyday speech, "such as the perfect tenses and participles in *ed*, which Milton often writes *t*";

and (2) those of poetical usage, such as the *en*=*n* of the perfect participle, e.g. 'fall'n,' 'chos'n,' 'giv'n'; and *est*='*st* in the 2nd person singular of verbs, e.g. 'think'st,' 'saw'st,' 'gav'st.'

Elision.

By "elision" one means "slurring" a letter or syllable so that it scarcely sounds at all, and metrically does not count. The (1) main principle of elision is that an "open" vowel, i.e. a vowel preceding a vowel, may be "slurred." The commonest instance is with the definite article. Compare line 11

> "Amongst th(e) enthroned gods on sainted seats."

So with words like 'mans(i)on,' 'aer(i)al,' 'reg(i)on,' 'ambros(i)al,' 'imper(i)al,' 'var(i)ous,'—all in the first 30 lines of *Comus*. Also, (2) this principle of elision applies to an unstressed vowel preceding *r* or *n* or *l* in words like 'fev'rish,' 'ev'ry,' 'sev'ral,' 'wand'ring,' 'grov'lling,' 'om'nous,' 'count'nance,' 'advent'rous'; see *Comus*, 8, 19, 25, 39, 61, 68, 79. Many of the elisions roughly grouped under the headings (1) and (2) are such as we use in common speech.

Finally, some allowance must be made for the different

accentuation of some words[1] in Elizabethan and modern English.

Metre: Italian.

There are two noticeable features in the metrical structure of *Lycidas*. The first is Milton's use of lines of irregular length grouped in what Prof. Masson happily terms "free musical paragraphs," where the rhythm and cadence of the verses wait upon and echo the feelings of the speaker. The source whence Milton borrowed this device was pointed out by Johnson. "Milton's acquaintance," he says, speaking of *Lycidas*, "with the Italian writers may be discovered by a mixture of longer and shorter verses, according to the rules of Tuscan poetry." Compare also Landor's words: "No poetry so harmonious (i.e. as *Lycidas*) had ever been written in our language, but in the same free metre both Tasso and Guarini had captivated the ear of Italy." Many years later Milton employed the same artifice ("but O! the heavy change!") in the choruses of *Samson Agonistes*, the preface to which discusses this irregular type of versification, and describes it as 'unfettered' (*Apolelymenon*). It has one great merit (at least in the hands of Milton) that the variations in the length of the metre may be made to reflect the changing passions which the subject inspires. Emotion seems to find its exact equivalent in verbal expression.

Unrhymed lines.

The second feature is the use of occasional unrhymed lines. It seems to me improbable that it was Milton's own device. I think that this also may have been derived from some Italian source, though none, I believe, has ever been pointed out. In answer to a question on this difficult

[1] See *aspect* in the Glossary.

point a scholar writes to me: "It is noticeable that in every case Milton introduces a *new* rhyme where the ear would expect the rhyme, and in two of the cases, 'shroud' (22) and 'Jove' (82), follows with a couplet which makes the ear forget that it is unsatisfied in the other respect. He manages the first instance of all ('more' in line 1) in the same way by the use of a third rhyme 'crude.' And certainly the effect is satisfactory: one feels that if he had rhymed to 'more' it would have stopped the progression of the poem." The writer adds: "I think some of the unrhymed lines are assonances, e.g. in the first paragraph, 'wind' (13) with 'rhyme' (11), and in the 2nd 'well' (15) with 'hill' (23) and 'rill' (24), and below 'bring' (96) with 'winds' (91).

Assonance partially supplies the effect of rhyme.

The unrhymed third line in Fitzgerald's *Omar Khayyám* stanza may be remembered.

COMUS.

"A MASQUE PRESENTED AT LUDLOW CASTLE, 1634."

DEDICATION[1] OF THE ANONYMOUS EDITION OF 1637.

"*To the Right Honourable John, Lord Brackley, son and heir-apparent to the Earl of Bridgewater etc.*"

"MY LORD,

This Poem, which received its first occasion of birth from yourself and others of your noble family, and much honour from your own person in the performance, now returns again to make a final dedication of itself to you. Although not openly acknowledged by the Author, yet it is a legitimate offspring, so lovely and so much desired that the often copying of it hath tired my pen to give my several friends satisfaction, and brought me to a necessity of producing it to the public view, and now to offer it up, in all rightful devotion, to those fair hopes and rare endowments of your much-promising youth, which give a full assurance to all that know you of a future excellence. Live, sweet Lord, to be the honour of your name; and receive this as your own from the hands of him who hath by many favours been long obliged to your most honoured Parents, and, as in this representation your attendant *Thyrsis*, so now in all real expression

Your most faithful and most humble Servant,

H. LAWES."

[1] Reprinted in the edition of 1645: omitted in that of 1673.

"*The Copy*[1] *of a Letter written by Sir Henry Wotton to the Author upon the following Poem.*"

"From the College, this 13 of April, 1638.

Sir,

It was a special favour when you lately bestowed upon me here the first taste of your acquaintance, though no longer than to make me know that I wanted more time to value it and to enjoy it rightly; and, in truth, if I then could have imagined your farther stay in these parts, which I understood afterwards by Mr H., I would have been bold, in our vulgar phrase, to mend my draught (for you left me with an extreme thirst), and to have begged your conversation again, jointly with your said learned friend, over a poor meal or two, that we might have banded together some good Authors of the ancient time; among which I observed you to have been familiar.

Since your going, you have charged me with new obligations, both for a very kind letter from you dated the 6th of this month, and for a dainty piece of entertainment which came therewith. Wherein I should much commend the tragical part, if the lyrical did not ravish me with a certain Doric delicacy in your Songs and Odes, whereunto I must plainly confess to have seen yet nothing parallel in our language: *Ipsa mollities*. But I must not omit to tell you that I now only owe you thanks for intimating unto me (how modestly soever) the true artificer. For the work itself I had viewed some good while before with singular delight; having received it from our common friend Mr R., in the very close of the late R.'s Poems, printed at Oxford: whereunto it was added (as I now suppose) that the accessory might help out the principal, according to the art of Stationers, and to leave the reader *con la bocca dolce*.

Now, Sir, concerning your travels; wherein I may challenge a little more privilege of discourse with you. I suppose you will not blanch Paris in your way: therefore I have been bold to trouble you with a few lines to Mr M. B., whom you shall

[1] Omitted in the reprint of 1673, this letter was given in the edition of 1645.

easily find attending the young Lord S. as his governor; and you may surely receive from him good directions for the shaping of your farther journey into Italy where he did reside, by my choice, some time for the King, after mine own recess from Venice.

I should think that your best line will be through the whole length of France to Marseilles, and thence by sea to Genoa; whence the passage into Tuscany is as diurnal as a Gravesend barge. I hasten, as you do, to Florence or Siena, the rather to tell you a short story, from the interest you have given me in your safety.

At Siena I was tabled in the house of one Alberto Scipioni, an old Roman courtier in dangerous times; having been steward to the Duca di Pagliano, who with all his family were strangled, save this only man that escaped by foresight of the tempest. With him I had often much chat of those affairs, into which he took pleasure to look back from his native harbour; and, at my departure toward Rome (which had been the centre of his experience), I had won his confidence enough to beg his advice how I might carry myself there without offence of others or of mine own conscience. '*Signor Arrigo mio*,' says he, '*i pensieri stretti ed il viso sciolto* will go safely over the whole world.' Of which Delphian oracle (for so I have found it) your judgment doth need no commentary; and therefore, Sir, I will commit you, with it, to the best of all securities, God's dear love, remaining

Your friend, as much to command as any of longer date,

HENRY WOTTON."

Postscript.

"Sir: I have expressly sent this my footboy to prevent your departure without some acknowledgement from me of the receipt of your obliging letter; having myself through some business, I know not how, neglected the ordinary conveyance. In any part where I shall understand you fixed, I shall be glad and diligent to entertain you with home-novelties, even for some fomentation of our friendship, too soon interrupted in the cradle."

THE PERSONS.

THE ATTENDANT SPIRIT, afterwards in the habit of THYRSIS.

COMUS, with his Crew.

THE LADY.

FIRST BROTHER.

SECOND BROTHER.

SABRINA, the Nymph.

The Chief Persons which presented were :—

The Lord Brackley ;
Mr Thomas Egerton, his Brother ;
The Lady Alice Egerton.

COMUS.

The first Scene discovers a wild wood.

The ATTENDANT SPIRIT *descends or enters.*

BEFORE the starry threshold of Jove's court
My mansion is, where those immortal shapes
Of bright aerial spirits live insphered
In regions mild of calm and serene air,
Above the smoke and stir of this dim spot
Which men call Earth, and with low-thoughted care,
Confined and pestered in this pinfold here,
Strive to keep up a frail and feverish being,
Unmindful of the crown that Virtue gives,
After this mortal change, to her true servants
Amongst the enthroned gods on sainted seats.
Yet some there be that by due steps aspire
To lay their just hands on that golden key
That opes the palace of eternity.
To such my errand is; and, but for such,
I would not soil these pure ambrosial weeds
With the rank vapours of this sin-worn mould.
  But to my task. Neptune, besides the sway
Of every salt flood and each ebbing stream,
Took in by lot, 'twixt high and nether Jove,
Imperial rule of all the sea-girt isles
That, like to rich and various gems, inlay

The unadorned bosom of the deep;
Which he, to grace his tributary gods,
By course commits to several government,
And gives them leave to wear their sapphire crowns
And wield their little tridents. But this Isle,
The greatest and the best of all the main,
He quarters to his blue-haired deities;
And all this tract that fronts the falling sun
A noble Peer of mickle trust and power
Has in his charge, with tempered awe to guide
An old and haughty nation, proud in arms:
Where his fair offspring, nursed in princely lore,
Are coming to attend their father's state,
And new-intrusted sceptre; but their way
Lies through the perplexed paths of this drear wood,
The nodding horror of whose shady brows
Threats the forlorn and wandering passenger;
And here their tender age might suffer peril,
But that by quick command from sovran Jove
I was despatched for their defence and guard!
And listen why; for I will tell you now
What never yet was heard in tale or song,
From old or modern bard, in hall or bower.
Bacchus, that first from out the purple grape
Crushed the sweet poison of misused wine,
After the Tuscan mariners transformed,
Coasting the Tyrrhene shore, as the winds listed,
On Circe's island fell. (Who knows not Circe,
The daughter of the Sun, whose charmed cup
Whoever tasted lost his upright shape,
And downward fell into a grovelling swine?)
This nymph, that gazed upon his clustering locks,
With ivy berries wreathed, and his blithe youth,
Had by him, ere he parted thence, a son
Much like his father, but his mother more,

Whom therefore she brought up, and Comus named:
Who, ripe and frolic of his full-grown age,
Roving the Celtic and Iberian fields,
At last betakes him to this ominous wood,
And, in thick shelter of black shades imbowered,
Excels his mother at her mighty art;
Offering to every weary traveller
His orient liquor in a crystal glass,
To quench the drouth of Phœbus; which as they taste
(For most do taste through fond intemperate thirst),
Soon as the potion works, their human countenance,
The express resemblance of the gods, is changed
Into some brutish form of wolf, or bear,
Or ounce, or tiger, hog, or bearded goat,
All other parts remaining as they were.
And they, so perfect is their misery,
Not once perceive their foul disfigurement,
But boast themselves more comely than before,
And all their friends and native home forget,
To roll with pleasure in a sensual sty.
Therefore, when any favoured of high Jove
Chances to pass through this adventurous glade,
Swift as the sparkle of a glancing star
I shoot from heaven, to give him safe convoy,
As now I do. But first I must put off
These my sky-robes spun out of Iris' woof,
And take the weeds and likeness of a swain
That to the service of this house belongs,
Who with his soft pipe, and smooth-dittied song,
Well knows to still the wild winds when they roar,
And hush the waving woods; nor of less faith,
And in this office of his mountain watch
Likeliest, and nearest to the present aid
Of this occasion. But I hear the tread
Of hateful steps; I must be viewless now.

COMUS *enters, with a charming-rod in one hand, his glass in the other; with him a rout of monsters, headed like sundry sorts of wild beasts, but otherwise like men and women, their apparel glistering: they come in making a riotous and unruly noise, with torches in their hands.*

Comus. The star that bids the shepherd fold
Now the top of heaven doth hold;
And the gilded car of day
His glowing axle doth allay
In the steep Atlantic stream;
And the slope sun his upward beam
Shoots against the dusky pole,
Pacing toward the other goal
Of his chamber in the east.
Meanwhile, welcome joy and feast,
Midnight shout and revelry,
Tipsy dance and jollity.
Braid your locks with rosy twine,
Dropping odours, dropping wine.
Rigour now is gone to bed;
And Advice with scrupulous head,
Strict Age, and sour Severity,
With their grave saws, in slumber lie.
We that are of purer fire
Imitate the starry quire,
Who, in their nightly watchful spheres,
Lead in swift round the months and years.
The sounds and seas, with all their finny drove,
Now to the moon in wavering morrice move;
And on the tawny sands and shelves
Trip the pert faeries and the dapper elves.
By dimpled brook and fountain-brim,
The wood-nymphs, decked with daisies trim,

Their merry wakes and pastimes keep:
What hath night to do with sleep?
Night hath better sweets to prove;
Venus now wakes, and wakens Love.
Come, let us our rites begin;
'Tis only daylight that makes sin,
Which these dun shades will ne'er report.
Hail, goddess of nocturnal sport,
Dark-veiled Cotytto, to whom the secret flame
Of midnight torches burns! mysterious dame,
That ne'er art called but when the dragon womb
Of Stygian darkness spets her thickest gloom,
And makes one blot of all the air!
Stay thy cloudy ebon chair,
Wherein thou ridest with Hecate, and befriend
Us thy vowed priests, till utmost end
Of all thy dues be done, and none left out;
Ere the blabbing eastern scout,
The nice Morn, on the Indian steep
From her cabined loop-hole peep,
And to the tell-tale Sun descry
Our concealed solemnity.
Come, knit hands, and beat the ground
In a light fantastic round.

The Measure.

Break off, break off! I feel the different pace
Of some chaste footing near about this ground.
Run to your shrouds within these brakes and trees;
Our number may affright. Some virgin sure
(For so I can distinguish by mine art)
Benighted in these woods! Now to my charms,
And to my wily trains: I shall ere long
Be well stocked with as fair a herd as grazed
About my mother Circe. Thus I hurl

My dazzling spells into the spongy air,
Of power to cheat the eye with blear illusion,
And give it false presentments, lest the place
And my quaint habits breed astonishment,
And put the damsel to suspicious flight;
Which must not be, for that's against my course:
I, under fair pretence of friendly ends,
And well-placed words of glozing courtesy,
Baited with reasons not unplausible,
Wind me into the easy-hearted man,
And hug him into snares. When once her eye
Hath met the virtue of this magic dust,
I shall appear some harmless villager,
Whom thrift keeps up about his country gear.
But here she comes; I fairly step aside,
And hearken, if I may her business hear.

The LADY *enters.*

Lady. This way the noise was, if mine ear be true,
My best guide now: methought it was the sound
Of riot and ill-managed merriment,
Such as the jocund flute or gamesome pipe
Stirs up among the loose unlettered hinds,
When, for their teeming flocks and granges full,
In wanton dance they praise the bounteous Pan,
And thank the gods amiss. I should be loth
To meet the rudeness and swilled insolence
Of such late wassailers; yet, oh! where else
Shall I inform my unacquainted feet
In the blind mazes of this tangled wood?
My brothers, when they saw me wearied out
With this long way, resolving here to lodge
Under the spreading favour of these pines,
Stepped, as they said, to the next thicket-side
To bring me berries, or such cooling fruit

As the kind hospitable woods provide.
They left me then when the gray-hooded Even,
Like a sad votarist in palmer's weed,
Rose from the hindmost wheels of Phœbus' wain.
But where they are, and why they came not back,
Is now the labour of my thoughts; 'tis likeliest
They had engaged their wandering steps too far,
And envious darkness, ere they could return,
Had stole them from me: else, O thievish Night,
Why shouldst thou, but for some felonious end,
In thy dark lantern thus close up the stars
That Nature hung in heaven, and filled their lamps
With everlasting oil, to give due light
To the misled and lonely traveller?
This is the place, as well as I may guess,
Whence even now the tumult of loud mirth
Was rife, and perfect in my listening ear;
Yet nought but single darkness do I find.
What might this be? A thousand fantasies
Begin to throng into my memory,
Of calling shapes, and beckoning shadows dire,
And airy tongues that syllable men's names
On sands and shores and desert wildernesses.
These thoughts may startle well, but not astound
The virtuous mind, that ever walks attended
By a strong siding champion, Conscience.
O, welcome, pure-eyed Faith, white-handed Hope,
Thou hovering angel girt with golden wings,
And thou unblemished form of Chastity!
I see ye visibly, and now believe
That He, the Supreme Good, to whom all things ill
Are but as slavish officers of vengeance,
Would send a glistering guardian, if need were,
To keep my life and honour unassailed—
Was I deceived, or did a sable cloud

Turn forth her silver lining on the night?
I did not err; there does a sable cloud
Turn forth her silver lining on the night,
And casts a gleam over this tufted grove.
I cannot hallo to my brothers, but
Such noise as I can make to be heard farthest
I'll venture; for my new-enlivened spirits
Prompt me, and they perhaps are not far off.

Song.

Sweet Echo, sweetest nymph, that liv'st unseen
Within thy airy shell
By slow Meander's margent green,
And in the violet-embroidered vale
Where the love-lorn nightingale
Nightly to thee her sad song mourneth well:
Canst thou not tell me of a gentle pair
That likest thy Narcissus are?
O, if thou have
Hid them in some flowery cave,
Tell me but where,
Sweet Queen of parley, Daughter of the sphere!
So may'st thou be translated to the skies,
And give resounding grace to all Heaven's harmonies!

Comus. Can any mortal mixture of earth's mould
Breathe such divine enchanting ravishment?
Sure something holy lodges in that breast,
And with these raptures moves the vocal air
To testify his hidden residence.
How sweetly did they float upon the wings
Of silence, through the empty-vaulted night,
At every fall smoothing the raven down
Of darkness till it smiled! I have oft heard
My mother Circe with the Sirens three,
Amidst the flowery-kirtled Naiades,

Culling their potent herbs and baleful drugs;
Who, as they sung, would take the prisoned soul,
And lap it in Elysium: Scylla wept,
And chid her barking waves into attention,
And fell Charybdis murmured soft applause.
Yet they in pleasing slumber lulled the sense,
And in sweet madness robbed it of itself;
But such a sacred and home-felt delight,
Such sober certainty of waking bliss,
I never heard till now. I'll speak to her,
And she shall be my queen.—Hail, foreign wonder!
Whom certain these rough shades did never breed,
Unless the goddess that in rural shrine
Dwell'st here with Pan or Sylvan, by blest song
Forbidding every bleak unkindly fog
To touch the prosperous growth of this tall wood.

Lady. Nay, gentle shepherd, ill is lost that praise
That is addressed to unattending ears:
Not any boast of skill, but extreme shift
How to regain my severed company,
Compelled me to awake the courteous Echo
To give me answer from her mossy couch.

Comus. What chance, good Lady, hath bereft you thus?

Lady. Dim darkness, and this leavy labyrinth.

Comus. Could that divide you from near-ushering guides?

Lady. They left me weary on a grassy turf.

Comus. By falsehood, or discourtesy, or why?

Lady. To seek i' the valley some cool friendly spring.

Comus. And left your fair side all unguarded, Lady?

Lady. They were but twain, and purposed quick return.

Comus. Perhaps forestalling night prevented them.

Lady. How easy my misfortune is to hit!

Comus. Imports their loss, beside the present need?

Lady. No less than if I should my brothers lose.

Comus. Were they of manly prime, or youthful bloom?
Lady. As smooth as Hebe's their unrazored lips.
Comus. Two such I saw, what time the laboured ox
In his loose traces from the furrow came,
And the swinked hedger at his supper sat.
I saw them under a green mantling vine,
That crawls along the side of yon small hill,
Plucking ripe clusters from the tender shoots;
Their port was more than human, as they stood:
I took it for a faery vision
Of some gay creatures of the element,
That in the colours of the rainbow live,
And play i' the plighted clouds. I was awe-strook,
And, as I passed, I worshipped: if those you seek,
It were a journey like the path to Heaven,
To help you find them.
Lady. Gentle villager,
What readiest way would bring me to that place?
Comus. Due west it rises from this shrubby point.
Lady. To find out that, good shepherd, I suppose,
In such a scant allowance of star-light,
Would overtask the best land-pilot's art,
Without the sure guess of well-practised feet.
Comus. I know each lane, and every alley green,
Dingle, or bushy dell, of this wild wood,
And every bosky bourn from side to side,
My daily walks and ancient neighbourhood;
And if your stray attendance be yet lodged,
Or shroud within these limits, I shall know
Ere morrow wake, or the low-roosted lark
From her thatched pallet rouse: if otherwise,
I can conduct you, Lady, to a low
But loyal cottage, where you may be safe
Till further quest.
Lady. Shepherd, I take thy word,

And trust thy honest-offered courtesy,
Which oft is sooner found in lowly sheds,
With smoky rafters, than in tapestry halls
And courts of princes, where it first was named,
And yet is most pretended. In a place
Less warranted than this, or less secure,
I cannot be, that I should fear to change it.
Eye me, blest Providence, and square my trial
To my proportioned strength! Shepherd, lead on.
[*Exeunt.*

Enter the TWO BROTHERS.

Elder Brother. Unmuffle, ye faint Stars; and thou, fair Moon,
Thou wont'st to love the traveller's benison,
Stoop thy pale visage through an amber cloud,
And disinherit Chaos, that reigns here
In double night of darkness and of shades;
Or, if your influence be quite dammed up
With black usurping mists, some gentle taper,
Though a rush-candle from the wicker hole
Of some clay habitation, visit us
With thy long levelled rule of streaming light,
And thou shalt be our star of Arcady,
Or Tyrian Cynosure.
Second Brother. Or, if our eyes
Be barred that happiness, might we but hear
The folded flocks, penned in their wattled cotes,
Or sound of pastoral reed with oaten stops,
Or whistle from the lodge, or village cock
Count the night-watches to his feathery dames,
'Twould be some solace yet, some little cheering,
In this close dungeon of innumerous boughs.
But, Oh, that hapless virgin, our lost sister!
Where may she wander now, whither betake her

From the chill dew, amongst rude burs and thistles?
Perhaps some cold bank is her bolster now,
Or 'gainst the rugged bark of some broad elm
Leans her unpillowed head, fraught with sad fears.
What if in wild amazement and affright,
Or, while we speak, within the direful grasp
Of savage hunger, or of savage heat!
Eld. Bro. Peace, brother: be not over-exquisite
To cast the fashion of uncertain evils;
For, grant they be so, while they rest unknown,
What need a man forestall his date of grief,
And run to meet what he would most avoid?
Or, if they be but false alarms of fear,
How bitter is such self-delusion!
I do not think my sister so to seek,
Or so unprincipled in virtue's book,
And the sweet peace that goodness bosoms ever,
As that the single want of light and noise
(Not being in danger, as I trust she is not)
Could stir the constant mood of her calm thoughts,
And put them into misbecoming plight.
Virtue could see to do what Virtue would
By her own radiant light, though sun and moon
Were in the flat sea sunk. And Wisdom's self
Oft seeks to sweet retired solitude,
Where, with her best nurse, Contemplation,
She plumes her feathers, and lets grow her wings,
That in the various bustle of resort
Were all to-ruffled, and sometimes impaired.
He that has light within his own clear breast
May sit i' the centre, and enjoy bright day:
But he that hides a dark soul, and foul thoughts,
Benighted walks under the mid-day sun;
Himself is his own dungeon.
Second Brother. 'Tis most true

That musing Meditation most affects
The pensive secrecy of dèsert cell,
Far from the cheerful haunt of men and herds,
And sits as safe as in a senate-house;
For who would rob a hermit of his weeds,
His few books, or his beads, or maple dish,
Or do his gray hairs any violence?
But Beauty, like the fair Hesperian tree
Laden with blooming gold, had need the guard
Of dragon-watch with unenchanted eye,
To save her blossoms, and defend her fruit,
From the rash hand of bold Incontinence.
You may as well spread out the unsunned heaps
Of miser's treasure by an outlaw's den,
And tell me it is safe, as bid me hope
Danger will wink on Opportunity,
And let a single helpless maiden pass
Uninjured in this wild surrounding waste.
Of night or loneliness it recks me not;
I fear the dread events that dog them both,
Lest some ill-greeting touch attempt the person
Of our unowned sister.
  Elder Brother. I do not, brother,
Infer as if I thought my sister's state
Secure without all doubt or controversy;
Yet, where an equal poise of hope and fear
Does arbitrate the event, my nature is
That I incline to hope rather than fear,
And gladly banish squint suspicion.
My sister is not so defenceless left
As you imagine; she has a hidden strength,
Which you remember not.
  Second Brother. What hidden strength,
Unless the strength of Heaven, if you mean that?
  Eld. Bro. I mean that too, but yet a hidden strength,

Which, if Heaven gave it, may be termed her own.
'Tis chastity, my brother, chastity:
She that has that is clad in complete steel,
And, like a quivered nymph with arrows keen,
May trace huge forests, and unharboured heaths,
Infamous hills, and sandy perilous wilds;
Where, through the sacred rays of chastity,
No savage fierce, bandite, or mountaineer,
Will dare to soil her virgin purity:
Yea, there where very desolation dwells,
By grots and caverns shagged with horrid shades,
She may pass on with unblenched majesty,
Be it not done in pride, or in presumption.
Some say no evil thing that walks by night,
In fog or fire, by lake or moorish fen,
Blue meagre hag, or stubborn unlaid ghost,
That breaks his magic chains at curfew time,
No goblin, or swart faery of the mine,
Hath hurtful power o'er true virginity.
Do ye believe me yet, or shall I call
Antiquity from the old schools of Greece
To testify the arms of chastity?
Hence had the huntress Dian her dread bow,
Fair silver-shafted queen for ever chaste,
Wherewith she tamed the brinded lioness
And spotted mountain-pard, but set at nought
The frivolous bolt of Cupid; gods and men
Feared her stern frown, and she was queen o' the woods.
What was that snaky-headed Gorgon shield
That wise Minerva wore, unconquered virgin,
Wherewith she freezed her foes to congealed stone,
But rigid looks of chaste austerity,
And noble grace that dashed brute violence
With sudden adoration and blank awe?

So dear to Heaven is saintly chastity,
That, when a soul is found sincerely so,
A thousand liveried angels lackey her,
Driving far off each thing of sin and guilt,
And in clear dream and solemn vision
Tell her of things that no gross ear can hear;
Till oft converse with heavenly habitants
Begin to cast a beam on the outward shape,
The unpolluted temple of the mind,
And turns it by degrees to the soul's essence,
Till all be made immortal. But when lust,
By unchaste looks, loose gestures, and foul talk,
But most by lewd and lavish act of sin,
Lets in defilement to the inward parts,
The soul grows clotted by contagion,
Imbodies, and imbrutes, till she quite lose
The divine property of her first being.
Such are those thick and gloomy shadows damp
Oft seen in charnel-vaults and sepulchres,
Lingering and sitting by a new-made grave,
As loth to leave the body that it loved,
And linked itself by carnal sensualty
To a degenerate and degraded state.

Second Brother. How charming is divine Philosophy!
Not harsh and crabbed, as dull fools suppose,
But musical as is Apollo's lute,
And a perpetual feast of nectared sweets,
Where no crude surfeit reigns.

Elder Brother. List! list! I hear
Some far-off hallo break the silent air.

Sec. Bro. Methought so too; what should it be?

Elder Brother. For certain,
Either some one, like us, night-foundered here,
Or else some neighbour woodman, or, at worst,
Some roving robber calling to his fellows.

Second Brother. Heaven keep my sister! Again, again, and near!
Best draw, and stand upon our guard.
Elder Brother. I'll hallo.
If he be friendly, he comes well: if not,
Defence is a good cause, and Heaven be for us!

Enter the ATTENDANT SPIRIT, *habited like a shepherd.*

That hallo I should know. What are you? speak.
Come not too near; you fall on iron stakes else.
Spirit. What voice is that? my young Lord? speak again.
Sec. Bro. O brother, 'tis my father's Shepherd, sure.
Eld. Bro. Thyrsis! whose artful strains have oft delayed
The huddling brook to hear his madrigal,
And sweetened every musk-rose of the dale.
How camest thou here, good swain? hath any ram
Slipped from the fold, or young kid lost his dam,
Or straggling wether the pent flock forsook?
How couldst thou find this dark sequestered nook?
Spirit. O my loved master's heir, and his next joy,
I came not here on such a trivial toy
As a strayed ewe, or to pursue the stealth
Of pilfering wolf; not all the fleecy wealth
That doth enrich these downs is worth a thought
To this my errand, and the care it brought.
But, Oh! my virgin Lady, where is she?
How chance she is not in your company?
Elder Brother. To tell thee sadly, Shepherd, without blame
Or our neglect, we lost her as we came.
Spirit. Ay me unhappy! then my fears are true.
Elder Brother. What fears, good Thyrsis? Prithee briefly shew.
Spirit. I'll tell ye; 'tis not vain or fabulous,

(Though so esteemed by shallow ignorance)
What the sage poets, taught by the heavenly Muse,
Storied of old in high immortal verse
Of dire Chimeras and enchanted isles,
And rifted rocks whose entrance leads to Hell;
For such there be, but unbelief is blind.
Within the navel of this hideous wood,
Immured in cypress shades, a sorcerer dwells,
Of Bacchus and of Circe born, great Comus,
Deep skilled in all his mother's witcheries;
And here to every thirsty wanderer
By sly enticement gives his baneful cup,
With many murmurs mixed, whose pleasing poison
The visage quite transforms of him that drinks,
And the inglorious likeness of a beast
Fixes instead, unmoulding reason's mintage
Charactered in the face. This have I learnt
Tending my flocks hard by i' the hilly crofts
That brow this bottom glade; whence night by night
He and his monstrous rout are heard to howl
Like stabled wolves, or tigers at their prey,
Doing abhorred rites to Hecate
In their obscured haunts of inmost bowers.
Yet have they many baits and guileful spells
To inveigle and invite the unwary sense
Of them that pass unweeting by the way.
This evening late, by then the chewing flocks
Had ta'en their supper on the savoury herb
Of knot-grass dew-besprent, and were in fold,
I sat me down to watch upon a bank
With ivy canopied, and interwove
With flaunting honeysuckle, and began,
Wrapt in a pleasing fit of melancholy,
To meditate my rural minstrelsy,
Till fancy had her fill; but ere a close

The wonted roar was up amidst the woods,
And filled the air with barbarous dissonance;
At which I ceased, and listened them a while,
Till an unusual stop of sudden silence
Gave respite to the drowsy-flighted steeds
That draw the litter of close-curtained Sleep.
At last a soft and solemn-breathing sound
Rose like a steam of rich distilled perfumes,
And stole upon the air, that even Silence
Was took ere she was ware, and wished she might
Deny her nature, and be never more,
Still to be so displaced. I was all ear,
And took in strains that might create a soul
Under the ribs of Death: but, Oh! ere long
Too well I did perceive it was the voice
Of my most honoured Lady, your dear sister.
Amazed I stood, harrowed with grief and fear;
And 'O poor hapless nightingale,' thought I,
'How sweet thou sing'st, how near the deadly snare!'
Then down the lawns I ran with headlong haste,
Through paths and turnings often trod by day,
Till, guided by mine ear, I found the place
Where that damned wizard, hid in sly disguise
(For so by certain signs I knew), had met
Already, ere my best speed could prevent,
The aidless innocent lady, his wished prey;
Who gently asked if he had seen such two,
Supposing him some neighbour villager.
Longer I durst not stay, but soon I guessed
Ye were the two she meant; with that I sprung
Into swift flight, till I had found you here;
But further know I not.
Second Brother. O Night and Shades,
How are ye joined with hell in triple knot
Against the unarmed weakness of one virgin,

Alone and helpless! Is this the confidence
You gave me, brother?

Elder Brother. Yes, and keep it still;
Lean on it safely; not a period
Shall be unsaid for me. Against the threats
Of malice or of sorcery, or that power
Which erring men call Chance, this I hold firm:
Virtue may be assailed, but never hurt,
Surprised by unjust force, but not enthralled;
Yea, even that which Mischief meant most harm
Shall in the happy trial prove most glory.
But evil on itself shall back recoil,
And mix no more with goodness, when at last,
Gathered like scum, and settled to itself,
It shall be in eternal restless change
Self-fed and self-consumed: if this fail,
The pillared firmament is rottenness,
And earth's base built on stubble. But come, let's on!
Against the opposing will and arm of Heaven
May never this just sword be lifted up;
But, for that damned magician, let him be girt
With all the griesly legions that troop
Under the sooty flag of Acheron,
Harpies and Hydras, or all the monstrous forms
'Twixt Africa and Ind, I'll find him out,
And force him to return his purchase back,
Or drag him by the curls to a foul death,
Cursed as his life.

Spirit. Alas! good venturous youth,
I love thy courage yet, and bold emprise;
But here thy sword can do thee little stead:
Far other arms and other weapons must
Be those that quell the might of hellish charms;
He with his bare wand can unthread thy joints,
And crumble all thy sinews.

Elder Brother. Why, prithee, Shepherd,
How durst thou then thyself approach so near
As to make this relation?
Spirit. Care and utmost shifts
How to secure the Lady from surprisal
Brought to my mind a certain shepherd lad,
Of small regard to see to, yet well skilled
In every virtuous plant and healing herb
That spreads her verdant leaf to the morning ray:
He loved me well, and oft would beg me sing;
Which when I did, he on the tender grass
Would sit, and hearken even to ecstasy,
And in requital ope his leathern scrip,
And show me simples of a thousand names,
Telling their strange and vigorous faculties.
Amongst the rest a small unsightly root,
But of divine effect, he culled me out;
The leaf was darkish, and had prickles on it,
But in another country, as he said,
Bore a bright golden flower, but not in this soil:
Unknown, and like esteemed, and the dull swain
Treads on it daily with his clouted shoon;
And yet more med'cinal is it than that Moly
That Hermes once to wise Ulysses gave.
He called it Hæmony, and gave it me,
And bade me keep it as of sovran use
'Gainst all enchantments, mildew blast, or damp,
Or ghastly Furies' apparition.
I pursed it up, but little reckoning made,
Till now that this extremity compelled:
But now I find it true; for by this means
I knew the foul enchanter, though disguised,
Entered the very lime-twigs of his spells,
And yet came off. If you have this about you
(As I will give you when we go) you may

Boldly assault the necromancer's hall;
Where if he be, with dauntless hardihood
And brandished blade rush on him: break his glass,
And shed the luscious liquor on the ground,
But seize his wand; though he and his curst crew
Fierce sign of battle make, and menace high,
Or, like the sons of Vulcan, vomit smoke,
Yet will they soon retire, if he but shrink.
Eld. Bro. Thyrsis, lead on apace; I'll follow thee;
And some good angel bear a shield before us!

The Scene changes to a stately palace, set out with all manner of deliciousness: soft music, tables spread with all dainties. COMUS *appears with his rabble, and* THE LADY *set in an enchanted chair; to whom he offers his glass, which she puts by, and goes about to rise.*

Comus. Nay, Lady, sit: if I but wave this wand,
Your nerves are all chained up in alabaster,
And you a statue, or as Daphne was,
Root-bound, that fled Apollo.
Lady. Fool, do not boast:
Thou canst not touch the freedom of my mind
With all thy charms, although this corporal rind
Thou hast immanacled, while Heaven sees good.
Comus. Why are you vexed, Lady? why do you frown?
Here dwell no frowns, nor anger; from these gates
Sorrow flies far. See, here be all the pleasures
That fancy can beget on youthful thoughts,
When the fresh blood grows lively, and returns
Brisk as the April buds in primrose season.
And first behold this cordial julep here,
That flames and dances in his crystal bounds,

With spirits of balm and fragrant syrups mixed.
Not that Nepenthes which the wife of Thone
In Egypt gave to Jove-born Helena
Is of such power to stir up joy as this,
To life so friendly, or so cool to thirst.
Why should you be so cruel to yourself,
And to those dainty limbs, which Nature lent
For gentle usage and soft delicacy?
But you invert the covenants of her trust,
And harshly deal, like an ill borrower,
With that which you received on other terms,
Scorning the unexempt condition
By which all mortal frailty must subsist,
Refreshment after toil, ease after pain,
That have been tired all day without repast,
And timely rest have wanted; but, fair virgin,
This will restore all soon.
Lady. 'Twill not, false traitor!
'Twill not restore the truth and honesty
That thou hast banished from thy tongue with lies.
Was this the cottage and the safe abode
Thou told'st me of? What grim aspects are these,
These ugly-headed monsters? Mercy guard me!
Hence with thy brewed enchantments, foul deceiver!
Hast thou betrayed my credulous innocence
With vizored falsehood and base forgery?
And wouldst thou seek again to trap me here
With lickerish baits, fit to ensnare a brute?
Were it a draught for Juno when she banquets,
I would not taste thy treasonous offer: none
But such as are good men can give good things;
And that which is not good is not delicious
To a well-governed and wise appetite.
Comus. O foolishness of men! that lend their ears
To those budge doctors of the Stoic fur,

And fetch their precepts from the Cynic tub,
Praising the lean and sallow Abstinence!
Wherefore did Nature pour her bounties forth
With such a full and unwithdrawing hand,
Covering the earth with odours, fruits, and flocks,
Thronging the seas with spawn innumerable,
But all to please and sate the curious taste?
And set to work millions of spinning worms,
That in their green shops weave the smooth-haired silk,
To deck her sons; and, that no corner might
Be vacant of her plenty, in her own loins
She hutched the all-worshipped ore and precious gems,
To store her children with. If all the world
Should in a pet of temperance feed on pulse,
Drink the clear stream, and nothing wear but frieze,
The All-giver would be unthanked, would be unpraised,
Not half his riches known, and yet despised;
And we should serve him as a grudging master,
As a penurious niggard of his wealth,
And live like Nature's bastards, not her sons,
Who would be quite surcharged with her own weight,
And strangled with her waste fertility:
The earth cumbered, and the winged air darked with plumes,
The herds would over-multitude their lords;
The sea o'erfraught would swell, and the unsought diamonds
Would so emblaze the forehead of the deep,
And so bestud with stars, that they below
Would grow inured to light, and come at last
To gaze upon the sun with shameless brows.
List, Lady; be not coy, and be not cozened
With that same vaunted name, Virginity.
Beauty is Nature's coin; must not be hoarded,
But must be current; and the good thereof

Consists in mutual and partaken bliss,
Unsavoury in the enjoyment of itself:
If you let slip time, like a neglected rose
It withers on the stalk with languished head.
Beauty is Nature's brag, and must be shown
In courts, at feasts, and high solemnities,
Where most may wonder at the workmanship:
It is for homely features to keep home,
They had their name thence; coarse complexions
And cheeks of sorry grain will serve to ply
The sampler, and to tease the huswife's wool.
What need a vermeil-tinctured lip for that,
Love-darting eyes, or tresses like the morn?
There was another meaning in these gifts;
Think what, and be advised; you are but young yet.
Lady. I had not thought to have unlocked my lips
In this unhallowed air, but that this juggler
Would think to charm my judgment, as mine eyes,
Obtruding false rules pranked in reason's garb.
I hate when Vice can bolt her arguments
And Virtue has no tongue to check her pride.
Impostor! do not charge most innocent Nature,
As if she would her children should be riotous
With her abundance; she, good cateress,
Means her provision only to the good,
That live according to her sober laws,
And holy dictate of spare Temperance.
If every just man that now pines with want
Had but a moderate and beseeming share
Of that which lewdly-pampered Luxury
Now heaps upon some few with vast excess,
Nature's full blessings would be well-dispensed
In unsuperfluous even proportion,
And she no whit encumbered with her store;
And then the Giver would be better thanked,

His praise due paid: for swinish gluttony
Ne'er looks to Heaven amidst his gorgeous feast,
But with besotted base ingratitude
Crams, and blasphemes his Feeder. Shall I go on?
Or have I said enow? To him that dares
Arm his profane tongue with contemptuous words
Against the sun-clad power of chastity,
Fain would I something say;—yet to what end?
Thou hast nor ear, nor soul, to apprehend
The sublime notion and high mystery
That must be uttered to unfold the sage
And serious doctrine of Virginity;
And thou art worthy that thou shouldst not know
More happiness than this thy present lot.
Enjoy your dear wit, and gay rhetoric,
That hath so well been taught her dazzling fence;
Thou art not fit to hear thyself convinced:
Yet, should I try, the uncontrolled worth
Of this pure cause would kindle my rapt spirits
To such a flame of sacred vehemence,
That dumb things would be moved to sympathize,
And the brute Earth would lend her nerves, and shake,
Till all thy magic structures, reared so high,
Were shattered into heaps o'er thy false head.
Comus. She fables not. I feel that I do fear
Her words set off by some superior power;
And, though not mortal, yet a cold shuddering dew
Dips me all o'er, as when the wrath of Jove
Speaks thunder and the chains of Erebus
To some of Saturn's crew. I must dissemble,
And try her yet more strongly.—Come, no more!
This is mere moral babble, and direct
Against the canon laws of our foundation;
I must not suffer this; yet 'tis but the lees
And settlings of a melancholy blood:

But this will cure all straight; one sip of this
Will bathe the drooping spirits in delight
Beyond the bliss of dreams. Be wise, and taste . . .

The BROTHERS *rush in with swords drawn, wrest his glass out of his hand, and break it against the ground: his rout make sign of resistance, but are all driven in. The* ATTENDANT SPIRIT *comes in.*

Spirit. What! have you let the false enchanter scape?
O ye mistook; ye should have snatched his wand,
And bound him fast: without his rod reversed,
And backward mutters of dissevering power,
We cannot free the Lady that sits here
In stony fetters fixed and motionless.
Yet stay: be not disturbed; now I bethink me,
Some other means I have which may be used,
Which once of Melibœus old I learnt,
The soothest shepherd that e'er piped on plains.
There is a gentle nymph not far from hence,
That with moist curb sways the smooth Severn stream:
Sabrina is her name: a virgin pure;
Whilom she was the daughter of Locrine,
That had the sceptre from his father Brute.
She, guiltless damsel, flying the mad pursuit
Of her enraged stepdame, Guendolen,
Commended her fair innocence to the flood
That stayed her flight with his cross-flowing course.
The water-nymphs, that in the bottom played,
Held up their pearled wrist, and took her in,
Bearing her straight to aged Nereus' hall;
Who, piteous of her woes, reared her lank head,
And gave her to his daughters to imbathe
In nectared lavers strewed with asphodil,
And through the porch and inlet of each sense

Dropt in ambrosial oils, till she revived,
And underwent a quick immortal change,
Made goddess of the river. Still she retains
Her maiden gentleness, and oft at eve
Visits the herds along the twilight meadows,
Helping all urchin blasts, and ill-luck signs
That the shrewd meddling elf delights to make,
Which she with precious vialed liquors heals:
For which the shepherds at their festivals
Carol her goodness loud in rustic lays,
And throw sweet garland wreaths into her stream
Of pansies, pinks, and gaudy daffodils.
And, as the old swain said, she can unlock
The clasping charm, and thaw the numbing spell,
If she be right invoked in warbled song;
For maidenhood she loves, and will be swift
To aid a virgin, such as was herself,
In hard-besetting need: this will I try,
And add the power of some adjuring verse.

Song.

Sabrina fair,
  Listen where thou art sitting
Under the glassy, cool, translucent wave,
  In twisted braids of lilies knitting
The loose train of thy amber-dropping hair;
  Listen for dear honour's sake,
  Goddess of the silver lake,
    Listen and save!
Listen and appear to us,
In name of great Oceanus,
By the earth-shaking Neptune's mace,
And Tethys' grave majestic pace;
By hoary Nereus' wrinkled look,
And the Carpathian wizard's hook;

By scaly Triton's winding shell,
And old soothsaying Glaucus' spell;
By Leucothea's lovely hands,
And her son that rules the strands;
By Thetis' tinsel-slippered feet,
And the songs of Sirens sweet;
By dead Parthenope's dear tomb,
And fair Ligea's golden comb,
Wherewith she sits on diamond rocks
Sleeking her soft alluring locks;
By all the nymphs that nightly dance
Upon thy streams with wily glance;
Rise, rise, and heave thy rosy head
From thy coral-paven bed,
And bridle in thy headlong wave,
Till thou our summons answered have.
Listen and save!

SABRINA *rises, attended by Water-nymphs, and sings.*

By the rushy-fringed bank,
Where grows the willow and the osier dank,
My sliding chariot stays,
Thick set with agate, and the azurn sheen
Of turkis blue, and emerald green,
That in the channel strays:
Whilst from off the waters fleet
Thus I set my printless feet
O'er the cowslip's velvet head,
That bends not as I tread.
Gentle swain, at thy request
I am here!

Spirit. Goddess dear,
We implore thy powerful hand
To undo the charmed band

Of true virgin here distressed,
Through the force and through the wile
Of unblessed enchanter vile.
Sabrina. Shepherd, 'tis my office best
To help ensnared chastity:
Brightest Lady, look on me.
Thus I sprinkle on thy breast
Drops that from my fountain pure
I have kept of precious cure;
Thrice upon thy finger's tip,
Thrice upon thy rubied lip:
Next this marbled venomed seat,
Smeared with gums of glutinous heat,
I touch with chaste palms moist and cold.
Now the spell hath lost his hold;
And I must haste ere morning hour
To wait in Amphitrite's bower.

SABRINA *descends, and* THE LADY *rises out of her seat.*

Spirit. Virgin, daughter of Locrine,
Sprung of old Anchises' line,
May thy brimmed waves for this
Their full tribute never miss
From a thousand petty rills,
That tumble down the snowy hills:
Summer drouth or singed air
Never scorch thy tresses fair,
Nor wet October's torrent flood
Thy molten crystal fill with mud;
May thy billows roll ashore
The beryl and the golden ore;
May thy lofty head be crowned
With many a tower and terrace round,
And here and there thy banks upon

With groves of myrrh and cinnamon.
  Come, Lady, while Heaven lends us grace,
Let us fly this cursed place,
Lest the sorcerer us entice
With some other new device.
Not a waste or needless sound
Till we come to holier ground;
I shall be your faithful guide
Through this gloomy covert wide;
And not many furlongs thence
Is your Father's residence,
Where this night are met in state
Many a friend to gratulate
His wished presence, and beside
All the swains that there abide
With jigs and rural dance resort;
We shall catch them at their sport,
And our sudden coming there
Will double all their mirth and cheer.
Come, let us haste; the stars grow high,
But Night sits monarch yet in the mid sky.

The Scene changes, presenting Ludlow Town and the President's Castle: then come in Country Dancers; after them the ATTENDANT SPIRIT, *with the two* BROTHERS *and* THE LADY.

Song.

  Spirit. Back, shepherds, back! enough your play,
Till next sun-shine holiday:
Here be, without duck or nod,
Other trippings to be trod
Of lighter toes, and such court guise
As Mercury did first devise

With the mincing Dryades
On the lawns and on the leas.

This second Song presents them to their Father and Mother.

Noble Lord, and Lady bright,
I have brought ye new delight;
Here behold so goodly grown
Three fair branches of your own:
Heaven hath timely tried their youth,
Their faith, their patience, and their truth,
And sent them here through hard assays
With a crown of deathless praise,
To triumph in victorious dance
O'er sensual folly and intemperance.

The dances ended, the SPIRIT *epiloguizes.*

Spirit. To the ocean now I fly,
And those happy climes that lie
Where day never shuts his eye,
Up in the broad fields of the sky;
There I suck the liquid air,
All amidst the gardens fair
Of Hesperus, and his daughters three
That sing about the golden tree.
Along the crisped shades and bowers
Revels the spruce and jocund Spring;
The Graces and the rosy-bosomed Hours
Thither all their bounties bring;
There eternal Summer dwells,
And west winds with musky wing
About the cedarn alleys fling
Nard and cassia's balmy smells.

Iris there with humid bow
Waters the odorous banks, that blow
Flowers of more mingled hue
Than her purfled scarf can shew;
And drenches with Elysian dew
(List, mortals, if your ears be true)
Beds of hyacinth and roses,
Where young Adonis oft reposes,
Waxing well of his deep wound
In slumber soft, and on the ground
Sadly sits the Assyrian queen:
But far above in spangled sheen
Celestial Cupid, her famed son advanced,
Holds his dear Psyche sweet entranced,
After her wandering labours long,
Till free consent the gods among
Make her his eternal bride,
And from her fair unspotted side
Two blissful twins are to be born,
Youth and Joy; so Jove hath sworn.
But now my task is smoothly done:
I can fly, or I can run,
Quickly to the green earth's end,
Where the bowed welkin slow doth bend,
And from thence can soar as soon
To the corners of the moon.
Mortals, that would follow me,
Love Virtue: she alone is free;
She can teach ye how to climb
Higher than the sphery chime;
Or if Virtue feeble were,
Heaven itself would stoop to her.

LYCIDAS.

LYCIDAS.

"*In this Monody the author bewails a learned Friend, unfortunately drown'd in his passage from Chester on the Irish Seas,* 1637; *and by occasion foretells the ruine of our corrupted Clergie then in their height.*"

YET once more, O ye laurels, and once more,
Ye myrtles brown, with ivy never sere,
I come to pluck your berries harsh and crude,
And with forced fingers rude
Shatter your leaves before the mellowing year.
Bitter constraint, and sad occasion dear,
Compels me to disturb your season due;
For Lycidas is dead, dead ere his prime,
Young Lycidas, and hath not left his peer.
Who would not sing for Lycidas? he knew
Himself to sing, and build the lofty rhyme.
He must not float upon his watery bier
Unwept, and welter to the parching wind,
Without the meed of some melodious tear.
  Begin then, Sisters of the sacred well,
That from beneath the seat of Jove doth spring;
Begin, and somewhat loudly sweep the string.
Hence with denial vain and coy excuse;
So may some gentle Muse

With lucky words favour my destined urn,
And as he passes turn,
And bid fair peace be to my sable shroud.
For we were nursed upon the self-same hill,
Fed the same flock, by fountain, shade and rill:
Together both, ere the high lawns appeared
Under the opening eyelids of the Morn,
We drove a-field, and both together heard
What time the gray-fly winds her sultry horn,
Battening our flocks with the fresh dews of night,
Oft till the star that rose at evening bright
Toward heaven's descent had sloped his westering wheel.
Meanwhile the rural ditties were not mute,
Tempered to the oaten flute;
Rough Satyrs danced, and Fauns with cloven heel
From the glad sound would not be absent long,
And old Damœtas loved to hear our song.
But, O the heavy change, now thou art gone,
Now thou art gone, and never must return!
Thee, Shepherd, thee the woods and desert caves,
With wild thyme and the gadding vine o'ergrown,
And all their echoes mourn.
The willows, and the hazel copses green,
Shall now no more be seen
Fanning their joyous leaves to thy soft lays.
As killing as the canker to the rose,
Or taint-worm to the weanling herds that graze,
Or frost to flowers that their gay wardrobe wear,
When first the white-thorn blows:
Such, Lycidas, thy loss to shepherd's ear.
Where were ye, Nymphs, when the remorseless deep
Closed o'er the head of your loved Lycidas?
For neither were ye playing on the steep
Where your old bards, the famous Druids, lie,
Nor on the shaggy top of Mona high,

Nor yet where Deva spreads her wizard stream.
Ay me! I fondly dream,
Had ye been there—for what could that have done?
What could the Muse herself that Orpheus bore,
The Muse herself, for her enchanting son,
Whom universal Nature did lament,
When, by the rout that made the hideous roar,
His gory visage down the stream was sent,
Down the swift Hebrus to the Lesbian shore?
Alas! what boots it with uncessant care
To tend the homely slighted shepherd's trade,
And strictly meditate the thankless Muse?
Were it not better done, as others use,
To sport with Amaryllis in the shade,
Or with the tangles of Neæra's hair?
Fame is the spur that the clear spirit doth raise
(That last infirmity of noble mind)
To scorn delights, and live laborious days;
But the fair guerdon when we hope to find,
And think to burst out into sudden blaze,
Comes the blind Fury with the abhorred shears,
And slits the thin-spun life. "But not the praise,"
Phœbus replied, and touched my trembling ears:
"Fame is no plant that grows on mortal soil,
Nor in the glistering foil
Set off to the world, nor in broad rumour lies,
But lives and spreads aloft by those pure eyes,
And perfect witness of all-judging Jove;
As he pronounces lastly on each deed,
Of so much fame in Heaven expect thy meed."
O fountain Arethuse, and thou honoured flood,
Smooth-sliding Mincius, crowned with vocal reeds,
That strain I heard was of a higher mood:
But now my oat proceeds,
And listens to the herald of the sea,

That came in Neptune's plea:
He asked the waves, and asked the felon winds,
What hard mishap hath doomed this gentle swain?
And questioned every gust of rugged wings
That blows from off each beaked promontory.
They knew not of his story;
And sage Hippotades their answer brings:
That not a blast was from his dungeon strayed,
The air was calm, and on the level brine
Sleek Panope with all her sisters played.
It was that fatal and perfidious bark,
Built in the eclipse, and rigged with curses dark,
That sunk so low that sacred head of thine.
  Next Camus, reverend sire, went footing slow,
His mantle hairy, and his bonnet sedge,
Inwrought with figures dim, and on the edge
Like to that sanguine flower inscribed with woe.
"Ah! who hath reft" (quoth he) "my dearest pledge?"
Last came, and last did go,
The Pilot of the Galilean Lake;
Two massy keys he bore of metals twain
(The golden opes, the iron shuts amain);
He shook his mitred locks, and stern bespake:
"How well could I have spared for thee, young swain,
Enow of such as for their bellies' sake
Creep, and intrude, and climb into the fold!
Of other care they little reckoning make
Than how to scramble at the shearers' feast,
And shove away the worthy bidden guest.
Blind mouths! that scarce themselves know how to hold
A sheep-hook, or have learnt aught else the least
That to the faithful herdman's art belongs!
What recks it them? What need they? They are sped;
And when they list, their lean and flashy songs
Grate on their scrannel pipes of wretched straw;

The hungry sheep look up, and are not fed,
But swoln with wind, and the rank mist they draw,
Rot inwardly, and foul contagion spread;
Besides what the grim wolf with privy paw
Daily devours apace, and nothing said;
But that two-handed engine at the door
Stands ready to smite once, and smite no more."
  Return, Alpheus, the dread voice is past
That shrunk thy streams; return, Sicilian Muse,
And call the vales, and bid them hither cast
Their bells, and flowrets of a thousand hues.
Ye valleys low, where the mild whispers use
Of shades, and wanton winds, and gushing brooks,
On whose fresh lap the swart star sparely looks,
Throw hither all your quaint enamelled eyes,
That on the green turf suck the honied showers,
And purple all the ground with vernal flowers.
Bring the rathe primrose that forsaken dies,
The tufted crow-toe, and pale jessamine,
The white pink, and the pansy freaked with jet,
The glowing violet,
The musk rose, and the well-attired woodbine,
With cowslips wan that hang the pensive head,
And every flower that sad embroidery wears;
Bid amaranthus all his beauty shed,
And daffadillies fill their cups with tears,
To strew the laureate hearse where Lycid lies.
For so to interpose a little ease,
Let our frail thoughts dally with false surmise;
Ay me! whilst thee the shores and sounding seas
Wash far away, where'er thy bones are hurled;
Whether beyond the stormy Hebrides,
Where thou perhaps, under the whelming tide,
Visit'st the bottom of the monstrous world;
Or whether thou, to our moist vows denied,

Sleep'st by the fable of Bellerus old,
Where the great Vision of the guarded mount
Looks toward Namancos and Bayona's hold:
Look homeward, Angel, now, and melt with ruth;
And, O ye dolphins, waft the hapless youth.
Weep no more, woeful shepherds, weep no more,
For Lycidas, your sorrow, is not dead,
Sunk though he be beneath the watery floor;
So sinks the day-star in the ocean bed,
And yet anon repairs his drooping head,
And tricks his beams, and with new-spangled ore
Flames in the forehead of the morning sky:
So Lycidas sunk low, but mounted high,
Through the dear might of Him that walked the waves,
Where, other groves and other streams along,
With nectar pure his oozy locks he laves,
And hears the unexpressive nuptial song,
In the blest kingdoms meek of joy and love.
There entertain him all the saints above,
In solemn troops and sweet societies,
That sing, and singing in their glory move,
And wipe the tears for ever from his eyes.
Now, Lycidas, the shepherds weep no more;
Henceforth thou art the Genius of the shore,
In thy large recompense, and shalt be good
To all that wander in that perilous flood.

Thus sang the uncouth swain to the oaks and rills,
While the still Morn went out with sandals gray;
He touched the tender stops of various quills,
With eager thought warbling his Doric lay:
And now the sun had stretched out all the hills,
And now was dropt into the western bay;
At last he rose, and twitched his mantle blue:
To-morrow to fresh woods, and pastures new.

NOTES.

LAWES'S DEDICATION OF THE FIRST EDITION OF COMUS.

Henry Lawes, 1595—1662, sometime a "Gentleman of the Chapel Royal" (i.e. one of the royal choir). and a member of the king's "private music" (orchestra), was the chief composer of his age. He was specially noted as a composer of incidental music for Masques and of songs. He composed in 1633 part of the music for Shirley's great Masque *The Triumph of Peace*, and all the music for Carew's equally famous *Cœlum Britannicum*. He wrote the music for *Comus* (and probably for *Arcades*), acted the part of "the Attendant Spirit" when the piece was first performed at Ludlow Castle in 1634, and was responsible for the publication of the first edition in 1637. He seems to have been one of Milton's earliest and most intimate friends, thanks, no doubt, to their common love of music.

Milton addressed the following Sonnet to him.

"TO MR H. LAWES ON HIS AIRS.

HARRY, whose tuneful and well-measured song
First taught our English music how to span
Words with just note and accent, not to scan
With Midas' ears, committing short and long,
Thy worth and skill exempts thee from the throng,
With praise enough for Envy to look wan;
To after age thou shalt be writ the man
That with smooth air couldst humour best our tongue.

Thou honour'st verse, and verse must lend her wing
 To honour thee, the priest of Phœbus' quire,
 That tunest their happiest lines in hymn or story.
Dante shall give Fame leave to set thee higher
 Than his Casella, whom he wooed to sing,
 Met in the milder shades of Purgatory."

This Sonnet appeared as an introduction to a volume of "Choice Psalmes, put into Musick for three Voices: composed by Henry and William Lawes, Brothers, and Servants to his Majestie: 1648." The date of the composition of the Sonnet was Feb. 1646, as we learn from the Cambridge MS. Its familiar tone shows that the intimacy between the poet and the musician had not been affected by political differences, though Lawes, like his brother (who fell fighting for the king at Chester in 1645), was an ardent Royalist, and the volume of *Psalms* to which Milton's poem was prefixed was dedicated to Charles. After 1648 we do not hear of Lawes in connection with Milton, so that the force of circumstances may have driven them apart. It is significant that Lawes's dedication of *Comus*, which was reprinted in the 1645 edition of the poem, was omitted from the 1673 edition; though the omission may have been due to another cause.

The first four lines of the Sonnet, which should be compared with *Comus*, 86—88 and 494—496, give a very precise and musicianly description of Lawes's songs. He was content to make his music subordinate to the words, preserving their rhythm and accent with fidelity; so that the poetry, not the music (very often, a kind of recitative), was the chief element. This quality explains his great popularity with the poets of the period, many of whom, e.g. Herrick, Cartwright, Waller, had songs set to music by him. See Grove's *Dictionary of Music*.

Lord Brackley. The second Earl of Bridgewater, born in 1622; he succeeded his father in 1649, and died in 1686. This dedication was omitted (as we have said) from the edition of 1673; not unnaturally, since the Earl and the poet had taken opposite sides in the civil troubles. The former was arrested in 1651 on suspicion of being a Royalist. Milton's polemical tract *Pro Populo Anglicano Defensio* appeared in that year, and Todd says that the Earl of Bridgewater wrote on the title-page of his copy "Liber igne, author furca dignissimi" (i.e. 'the book well deserves burning and the author hanging'). For the rest he seems to have been a genial, learned man, who patronised literature and "delighted much in his library." See the *National Dictionary of Biography*. Of the younger brother, Mr Thomas Egerton, who took part in the Masque, little is known. The sister, Lady Alice, married Richard Vaughan, Earl of Carberry.

SIR HENRY WOTTON'S LETTER.

This letter is interesting as one of the earliest extant testimonies to Milton's genius. That he valued it much and thought that it would be a weighty recommendation of *Comus* is shown by his causing it to be prefixed to the 1645 edition of the poem. And in the *Second Defence* he says: "On my departure for Italy, the celebrated Henry Wotton gave me a signal proof of his regard, in an elegant letter which he wrote, not only breathing the warmest friendship, but containing some maxims of conduct which I found very useful in my travels" (*P. W.* I. 255).

Sir Henry Wotton, 1568—1639, was a man of some note in diplomacy and literature. He represented the English Court at Venice for some years; and afterwards (1625) became Provost of Eton, and took orders in the Church. He was a friend of Isaac Walton, who wrote his life. Wotton's chief work was published posthumously in 1651, under a title which explains its miscellaneous contents: "*Reliquiæ Wottonianæ;* or, a Collection of Lives, Letters, Poems, with Characters of sundry Personages, and other incomparable Pieces of Language and Art: By the curious Pencil of the ever-memorable Sir Henry Wotton, Knt., late Provost of Eaton College, 1651."

At least one of his poems ("You meaner beauties of the night") is familiar to lovers of Jacobean verse; and his definition of an ambassador as "an honest man sent to lie abroad for the good of his country" is still fresh. The *équivoque* had more point then than now, because "to lie" was technically used of an ambassador's residence abroad (Hannah). Wotton seems to have had a turn for aphorism. His favourite motto—engraved on his tombstone—was *disputandi pruritus ecclesiarum scabies* ('an itching for discussion is the mania of churches'). Sir

Henry Wotton admirably represents the type of courtier, wit and scholar. A sympathetic account of his career was published by Dr A. W. Ward; and recently his letters have been edited elaborately, with a full *Life*, for the Clarendon Press.

2. Horton being so close to Eton, it is curious that Sir Henry had not met his neighbour between 1632 and 1638.

6. *Mr H.* Commonly identified, and no doubt rightly, with the Broad Church divine John Hales, who was for some years a Fellow of Eton and Canon of Windsor. His learning won for him the title "the ever-memorable." There are allusions to him in Wotton's *Reliquiæ.*

10. *banded,* discussed.

16. *Doric,* i.e. Theocritean. Cf. *Lyc.* 189, "With eager thought warbling his Doric lay." Wotton shows his critical faculty in singling out the lyric portions of *Comus* for special commendation. Contrast Johnson's criticism.

23. *Mr R.* This "common friend" was either John Rouse, of Oriel College, Bodley's Librarian (1620—1652), to whom Milton addressed (1647) an elaborate Latin ode; or Robert Randolph, of Oxford, brother of the poet.

in the very close. Sir Henry Wotton means that a copy of Lawes's edition of *Comus* was inserted at the end of a volume of poems by "the late R": probably the Cambridge poet Thomas Randolph, who died in 1634 and whose poems were published by his brother in 1638. Randolph was one of the ablest of the followers (intellectual "sons," as they called themselves) of Ben Jonson, and wrote several amusing plays. He was contemporary with Milton at Cambridge, and there is some reason for thinking that "Milton was familiar with Randolph's poems before their publication." Thus the speech in *Comus*, 710—742, bears a very close resemblance to one in Randolph's play *The Muses' Looking-Glass*, not known to have been printed before 1638, but probably acted (and possibly printed) at Cambridge during Milton's residence there. (*Times Lit. Sup.*)

26. *con la bocca dolce,* i.e. with a pleasant taste in the mouth. Cf. French *bonne bouche.*

29. *blanch,* omit, pass by. If we used the verb at all we should treat it as intransitive, inserting *from.*

Paris. Milton arrived there in April or May, 1638. He

seems to have stayed some time, not reaching Florence till August.

30. *Mr M. B.* Identified with Michael Branthwaite. Sir Henry Wotton mentions him in the *Reliquiæ* as "heretofore his Majesties Agent in Venice, a gentleman of approved confidence and sincerity," p. 546. This was in 1626. Afterwards Branthwaite became diplomatic agent at Paris.

Page 5, line 1. Lord S., i.e. Lord Scudamore, son of the English ambassador, Viscount Scudamore, who showed Milton much courtesy in Paris; as we learn from his *Second Defence of the People of England.* (This was one of Milton's political treatises, written in Latin to justify the English Civil War, and more especially the execution of Charles I., in the eyes of Europe. Milton's first pamphlet on the subject had elicited violent attacks upon himself, his life and character; in his reply he gave a sketch of his career. The *Second Defence* therefore has very great autobiographical interest.)

governor; we should say 'tutor.'

7. *Marseilles...to Genoa.* The route that Addison took; see his *Travels.* But Milton entered Italy by way of Nice, coasted thence to Genoa, and went on to Florence, the favourite resting-place of English travellers, where he spent some months.

8, 9. *a Gravesend barge.* Cf. Hasted's *History of Kent*, vol. I. p. 450: "King Richard II. granted to the *Abbat* and *Convent* of *St Mary Graces*, that the inhabitants of *Gravesend* and *Milton* should have the sole privilege of carrying passengers by water from hence to *London*, on condition that they should provide boats for that purpose, and carry all passengers either at 2*d.* per head with their bundle, or let the hire of the whole boat at 4*s.* This charter was confirmed several times afterwards by succeeding kings, and under proper regulation by the legislature they still (1778) enjoy the privilege."

12. *At Siena.* This was in the autumn of 1592. "I am here," Sir Henry writes to Lord Zouch from Siena, Oct. 25, 1592, "by the means of certain Persons (to whom I was recommended) gotten into the House of Scipione Alberti, an ancient Courtier of the Popes, and a Gentleman of this Town, at whose Table I live." In a letter dated August 22, 1593, he mentions his Siena host again, and also refers to the Duke of Pagliano—a reference which I cannot explain.

17, 18. *at my departure.* Evidently the story that follows was a favourite with Sir Henry; he tells it in the *Reliquiæ.*

21, 22. *i pensieri* etc. "Your thoughts close and your countenance loose" (literally 'open'), as George Herbert renders the saying in his collection of proverbs entitled *Jacula Prudentum* ('Shafts of the Wise').

In spite of the maxim Milton gave free expression to his strong Protestant views, offending the English Jesuits and others at Rome. See Mark Pattison's *Life of Milton*, pp. 33—38.

23. *Delphian oracle*, i.e. maxim which might have been uttered by the oracle of Apollo at Delphi.

35. *entertain you with home-novelties*, i.e. write news of events in England. No further correspondence between Sir Henry Wotton and Milton is extant.

COMUS.

G. = *Glossary.*

The performance. This took place on Michaelmas night, 1634, in the great Hall of Ludlow Castle, afterwards, says Professor Masson, called 'Comus Hall.' At the end of the room a stage was erected, concealed from the audience by a curtain or screen until the piece began. The Earl and Countess of Bridgewater occupied the Throne of State, the audience filling the rest of the hall. When everything was ready the scene, representing a wood, was disclosed.

THE PERSONS. The Masque contains six characters. We know how four of the parts were filled, viz. that the Lady was represented by the young Lady Alice Egerton, daughter of the Earl of Bridgewater; the two Brothers by her brothers Lord Brackley and Mr Thomas Egerton; and the Attendant Spirit by Lawes. It is likely that all four performers took part in the representation of *Arcades*, while it is known that Lord Brackley and his brother were among the Masquers in Carew's *Cælum Britannicum* acted in the previous February. Probably therefore *Comus* had the advantage of tolerably competent amateur acting. For Sabrina and Comus, no doubt, some relatives or friends of the Bridgewater family appeared.

presented, i.e. represented the characters. Cf. *The Tempest*, IV. 167, "when I presented Ceres"; and Tennyson's *Princess*, I.,

"Remembering how we three presented Maid,
Or Nymph, or Goddess, at high tide of feast,
In masque or pageant at my father's court."

The first Scene. The stage-directions throughout *Comus* are extremely simple. Usually Masque-writers—especially Ben Jonson, Campion, and Shirley—insert very full details as to the arrangement of the scenes, the dresses of the *dramatis personæ*, the music, and so forth.

discovers, reveals; see G.

The ATTENDANT SPIRIT *descends.* Probably the scenery in the background represented a hill; down this the Spirit comes, and at the actual representation of *Comus* his arrival was heralded by music. This we know from the *Bridgewater MS.* (the stage-copy in accordance with which the piece was performed), where the attendant Genius enters with a song. The song consisted of lines 976—1011.

To detach the passage from its context and make it a speech of arrival instead of departure only one slight change was necessary, viz. "*from* the heavens" in line 976 for "*to*." No doubt, Lawes made the change, and we may assume that the details of the performance of *Comus* were arranged by him, not Milton. By introducing music the alteration gave the piece a more effective opening from the stage point of view, but from the literary was objectionable. For having explained in the song that he came from heaven, it was superfluous for the Spirit to add that his mansion lay before the threshold of Jove's palace. Also, spoken as an Epilogue, the verses had a point which they here lose; they were meant to emphasize the moral of *Comus*.

1—9. This introductory speech serves as a prologue, of the type which Euripides employed so much as a way of explaining the purport of a play before any action took place. In the third draft of the scheme of *Paradise Lost*, which he originally intended to treat in the form of a tragedy, Milton gave the outline of a prologue similar to the present: "Moses προλογίζει, recounting how he assumed his true body; that it corrupts not" etc. Then followed a sketch of the drama, divided into five acts. The paper referred to is among the Milton MSS. at Trinity College; see *Introduction*, p. xxii.

2. *those.* Milton often uses the demonstrative, like Lat. *ille*, to mean 'the illustrious,' 'of whom all have heard.'

3. *spirits*, i.e. spiritual beings like himself, and the souls of the "just" (13).

insphered, dwelling in their allotted *sphere*. 'Sphere' is a word which he always uses with some reference to the Ptolemaic idea of the ten spheres or regions of space encircling the Earth, the supposed centre of the Universe. Cf. *Il Penseroso*, 88, 89,

"unsphere
The spirit of Plato,"

i.e. call it down from the sphere which it inhabits. So Shelley in the *Adonais* (XLVI.) represents the soul of Keats ascending upward and being welcomed by his brother-poets:

"'Thou art become as one of us,' they cry;
'It was for thee yon kingless sphere has long
Swung blind in an unascended majesty,
Silent alone amid a Heaven of song.'"

4—11. What Milton has in mind is the classical conception of "the gods who live at ease" (*Par. Lost*, II. 868) in Olympus, the heaven of Greek mythology.

"Not by winds is it shaken, nor ever wet with rain, nor doth the snow come nigh thereto, but most clear air is spread about it cloudless, and the white light floats over it. Therein the blessed gods are glad for all their days," Homer, *Odyssey*, VI. 43—46 (Butcher and Lang's version). Cf. Tennyson's *Œnone* (which is full of Homeric spirit and allusion):

"gods, who have attain'd
Rest in a happy place and quiet seats
Above the thunder, with undying bliss."

serene; scan *sérene* and see note on 273.

5. *smoke and stir;* an echo perhaps of Horace's famous line *fumum et opes strepitumque Romæ* ('the reek and riches and din of Rome'), *Odes*, III. 29. 12. Note how "smoke" is antithetic to "serene" (used in the strict sense of Lat. *serenus*, bright, cloudless), and "stir" to "calm."

dim; carrying on the picture in "smoke."

6. *low-thoughted care*, i.e. anxiety about the material interests of life. Pope borrowed the phrase; cf. *Eloisa to Abelard*, 297, 298:

"O Grace serene! O Virtue heavenly fair!
Divine oblivion of low-thoughted care!"

7. i.e. penned up and shackled, like animals in a pound.

pestered...pinfold; see each in the Glossary.

8. *Strive to keep up;* implying that men do so *too long*, instead of being glad, when death comes, to change this life for a better.

frail, insecure, easily brought to an end, and full of unrest ("feverish") while it does last.

9. *the crown;* that is, the "incorruptible" crown (1 *Corinthians*, ix. 25) of everlasting life (*Revelation*, ii. 10, iii. 11).

10. *mortal change*, change from mortality. Some interpret 'a change brought about by his mortality.'

11. Cf. *Antony and Cleopatra*, I. 3. 28, "Though you in swearing shake the throned gods." Milton, however, is referring not only to this classical idea of the "quiet seats" of "the gods," but also to the Scriptural account of the "four and twenty seats" of the elders "clothed in white raiment; and [having] on their heads crowns of gold" (*Revelation*, iv. 4).

And here note a great feature of Milton's style, namely, the blending of Scriptural and classical associations. His mind was steeped in knowledge of the Bible and the classics, and what he writes is coloured now by one influence, now by the other, and often by both together in a way that seems to us sometimes quite incongruous. Thus in *Comus* and *Lycidas* we are moving in a pagan world where the deities of Greek and Latin mythology reign; nevertheless the Scriptural influence is often, if not always, present. This mixture of alien associations is opposed to modern taste.

the enthroned gods, i.e. the gods enthroned on. Such inversions of the order of words are common; cf. *Par. Lost*, I. 206, "With fixed anchor in his scaly rind." So in *Richard II.* III. 1, 9, "A happy gentleman in blood and lineaments." See Abbott's *Shakespearian Grammar*, p. 308.

12. *be;* see G. Abbott (p. 212) notes that *be* is often used "to refer to a number of persons, considered not individually, but as a kind or class"—as here.

13. *just*, righteous. *that golden key;* a favourite poetic allusion (see *Lyc.* 110, 111, note), variously applied. Ben Jonson in his Masque *The Barriers*, describing the figure of Truth, says:

"Her right hand holds a sun with burning rays,
Her left a curious bunch of golden keys
With which heaven's gates she locketh and displays."

Gray in the *Progress of Poesy* (III. 1) speaks of the Muse giving Shakespeare at his birth the "golden keys" of Comedy and Tragedy:

"Thine too these golden keys, immortal Boy!
This can unlock the gates of Joy;
Of Horror that, and thrilling Fears,
Or ope the sacred source of sympathetic Tears."

And Tennyson speaks of the humble-born genius who rises to high place in the State, "And lives to clutch the golden keys" of office and power (*In Memoriam*, LXIV.). It is instructive to note how great imaginations give a fresh turn to the familiar, putting it in a new light, adding new associations.

15. *but for such*, except on their account, to benefit them.

16. *ambrosial*, heavenly, such as the gods have; see G.

weeds, raiment; see G.

17. The line is commonly explained 'the noisome exhalations of this sin-corrupted earth.' But *mould* has the general sense 'substance, material' in Milton (cf. 244), and I think that it is intended here—implying 'flesh,' the Spirit having assumed a mortal form. Cf. *Par. Lost*, IX. 485, where Adam is described as "Heroic built, though of *terrestrial mould*," which is explained by "formed of earth" (149), "this man of clay" (176).

18—21. For the division of empire cf. *Iliad*, XV. 190 et seq. where Poseidon (the Greek god of the sea = Latin Neptunus) says: "Three brethren are we, and sons of Kronos, whom Rhea bare, Zeus and myself, and Hades is the third, the ruler of the folk in the under-world. And in three lots are all things divided, and each drew a domain of his own, and to me fell the hoary sea, to be my habitation for ever, when we shook the lots: and Hades drew the murky darkness, and Zeus the wide heaven, in clear air and clouds, but the earth and the high Olympus are yet common to all—" *The Iliad, Done into English Prose* by Lang, Leaf and Myers.

19. *every...each.* A favourite variation with Milton; cf. 311 and *Lyc.* 93, 94. Etymologically *ever-y = ever-each.*

20. *Took in*, received as his share. *by lot;* cf. the extract just quoted from *Iliad*, XV. *'twixt;* referring to place, i.e. Neptune's realm lay between Heaven, the dominion of Jove (Gk. Zeus), and the nether world.

Some editors place a comma after *took in*, and explain *by lot 'twixt* = by agreement between.

nether Jove; that is Hades (Lat. Plato), often called 'the infernal Zeus' (καταχθόνιος, literally 'underground,' hence 'belonging to the lower regions').

21—23. Newton thought that the germ of this was Gaunt's famous description of England as "This precious stone set in the silver sea," *Richard II.* II. I. 46. Probably the whole passage was in Milton's mind when he wrote the lines 21—28.

23. *unadorned*, i.e. without other adornment.

24, 25. i.e. Neptune entrusts each island to the government of some particular sea-deity—these inferior rulers all acknowledging him as their supreme lord.

27. *little*, i.e. as compared with the great trident, a three-pronged (Lat. *tridens*) sceptre, of Neptune. Spenser in the dedicatory stanzas of *The Faerie Queene* salutes Elizabeth as "Great Ladie of the greatest Isle."

29. *quarters*, assigns. *blue-haired.* From the stage-directions in other Masques it may be inferred that convention associated hair of this hue with water-deities. It was intended, of course, to symbolise the colour of the waves. Thus in Beaumont and Fletcher's *Masque of the Inner Temple and Gray's Inn* (1612) four Naiads appear on the stage, "with blueish tresses on their heads, garlands of water-lilies." Poetic tradition counts for much in the Masque.

Masson says: "There seems to be some emphasis on the phrase 'blue-haired deities,' as if these were a special section of the 'tributary gods' of line 24. Can there be a recollection of 'blue' as the British colour, inherited from the old times of the blue-stained Britons who fought with Cæsar?"

30. *this tract;* Wales.

31. *noble Peer*, i.e. the Earl of Bridgewater, who was present. Milton in the course of *Comus* pays a compliment to all those who were mainly concerned in the performance of the Masque; cf. 86—88, 244—248, 297—301, 494—496. Personal and flattering allusion of this kind was a marked feature of Masques.

It was no unusual thing for the Elizabethan dramatists to insert pieces of flattery to the Queen when they knew that she would be present at the representation of a play.

mickle, great; see G.

32. *with tempered awe*, with a due mixture of firmness and conciliation. It is said that the new Lord President received particular instructions as to the official course which he should pursue.

33. *nation*, i.e. the Welsh. Milton knew that there would be Welshmen present among his audience. One of Ben Jonson's *Entertainments* fulfils the promise of its title—*For the Honour of Wales*—and pays every possible compliment to the "old and haughty nation, proud in arms."

34. *nursed in princely lore.* "In this phrase some find an allusion to a link with Royalty at a remote point in the pedigree of the Egerton family; others find a reference to the fact that the young people had been a good deal at Court. The more natural meaning, however, is simply 'highly-educated'"—*Masson.*

36. *new-intrusted.* The Earl's appointment dated from the summer of 1631; but he did not formally take up his duties till 1634.

37. *perplexed*, entangled; the Latin sense, as in *Par. Lost*, IV. 176. Cf. Pope, *Messiah*, 73, "Waste sandy valleys, once perplexed with thorn."

38. *horror*, awe-inspiring appearance.

41. Cf. *Arcades*, 44, 45, where the Genius of the Wood proclaims himself the minister of Jove.

43. *I will tell you.* Johnson condemned this address to the audience; "a mode of communication so contrary to the nature of dramatic representation, that no precedents can support it." But *Comus* is a Masque, and a Masque must not be judged in the same way as an ordinary drama.

43—45. A claim to novelty of theme or treatment is one of the conventions of poetry influenced by the classics. Thus at the outset (I. 16) of *Par. Lost* Milton says that his Muse is about to essay "Things unattempted yet in prose or rhyme." Cf. Horace's *carmina non prius audita...canto* ('I sing strains never heard before'), *Odes*, III. 1. 2—4, and IV. 9. 3, 4, where Horace claims for himself the merit of originality of style.

44, 45. Milton has in mind a scene such as Scott depicts in *The Lay of the Last Minstrel.* Some have argued that these "bards" of the middle ages were "honoured guests in the castles of the nobles" to whose service they were attached; others that they were "merely wandering harpers." Perhaps some belonged to the one class, some to the other; until minstrelsy fell upon evil days, and of each of its latest few followers it could be said:

"A wandering Harper, scorn'd and poor,
He begg'd his bread from door to door,
And tuned, to please a peasant's ear,
The harp a king had loved to hear."

hall or bower. A traditional phrase; cf. Spenser's *Astrophel,* 27, 28:

"And he himselfe seemed made for meriment,
Merily masking both in bowre and hall."

"Hall" = the room of State in which the whole household assembled; "bower" = the ladies' private room. Cf. *The Lay of the Last Minstrel,* Canto I. 1, 11; and Wordsworth's Sonnet "Milton, thou shouldst be living."

48. The allusion is to the story of Bacchus, the god of wine, being seized on his way from Icaria to Naxos. "He hired a ship which belonged to *Tyrrhenian* [cf. 49] pirates; but the men, instead of landing at Naxos, steered towards Asia, to sell him there as a slave. Thereupon the god changed the mast and oars into serpents, and himself into a lion; ivy grew round the vessel, and the sound of flutes was heard on every side; the sailors were seized with madness, leaped into the sea, and were *metamorphosed into dolphins*"—Smith's *Classical Dictionary.*

After the mariners transformed; a Latinism (*post nautas mutatos*) such as we get in phrases like *post conditam urbem* ('since the foundation of the city'), where the participle, as it were, does the duty of a noun followed by a genitive case. Milton uses this idiom with 'after' and 'since'; cf. *Par. Lost,* I. 573, "since created Man," i.e. since the creation of.

49. *the Tyrrhene shore,* the coast of Etruria which, roughly speaking, was the same region as the modern Tuscany (cf. "Tuscan" in 48). *listed,* pleased; see G.

50. *Circe*; a famous sorceress, described by Homer in *Odyssey,* x., who dwelt on the island of Aeaea, off the western coast of Italy; daughter of the Sun-god and Perse, one of the daughters of the Ocean. On his wanderings after the Trojan war Odysseus visited her with his companions, some of whom she changed by her magic draughts into animals. By the help of the god Hermes (see 636, 637) Odysseus was able to resist

her enchantments and make her change his companions back again into men. Homer's description has this peculiar interest in the history of literature, that it became the model of all the accounts of fair enchantresses dwelling in palaces which we get in Tasso and Spenser and other writers of romance.

"The bringing of Bacchus to Circe's Island is Milton's own invention, with a view to the parentage he had resolved on for Comus"—*Masson*. The fact is that Milton sometimes *makes his own mythology*.

fell, chanced, came upon, in his voyage.

Who knows not Circe? The repetition of a name or word in the form of a question was a favourite artifice, especially with Spenser. Cf. *The Shepheards Calender*, August:

"A doolefull verse
Of Rosalend (who knows not Rosalend?)."

It is one of the imitations of archaic manner in Matthew Arnold's *Thyrsis*; cf. "I know these slopes; who knows them if not I?"

52, 53. There seems to be the underlying thought that physical uprightness symbolises moral. The poet was himself a very graceful man. Aubrey tells us, "his harmonical and ingenious soul dwelt in a beautiful and well proportioned body."

54. *This nymph*, i.e. Circe.

55. The representations of Bacchus in art differ widely, but the youthful god described here is a recognised type; cf. Dryden's poem *Alexander's Feast*. It was probably the traditional association of ivy with the wine-god that led to the custom of affixing an ivy-bush at the doors of taverns: whence the proverb "good wine needs no bush"; cf. *As You Like It*, *Epilogue*, 4. 6.

56. *parted*; cf. French *partir*, to depart.

57. Comus typifies sensuality, as his name implies, and magical power. In the scene with the Lady (659—813) he represents sensual pleasure. To the Attendant Spirit he appears rather as "a sorcerer" (521), "that damned wizard" (571), "the foul enchanter" (645). Cf. "but [like] his mother *more*." He owes the one character to his father the wine-god; the other to his mother the sorceress, skilled in magic drugs (πολυφάρμακος, as Homer calls her, *Odyssey*, x. 276). The parentage, as we saw, is Milton's own invention; nothing could be more appropriate.

59. *frolic*. German *fröhlich*, 'gay.'

60. i.e. France and Spain. Cf. *Par. Lost*, I. 520, 521:

"Fled over Adria to the Hesperian fields,
And o'er the Celtic roamed the utmost isles."

Iberia; a classical name for Spain.

61. *this;* pointing to the scenery representing a wood. *ominous;* not so much 'threatening,' as 'full of portents or magical appearances.' The wood is peopled with "calling shapes, and beckoning shadows dire," 207. *Ominous* is a dissyllable = *om'nous.*

65. *orient,* bright, lustrous (as described in 673); see G.

66. *the drouth of,* the thirst caused by the sun.

67. *fond,* foolish; see G. The epithet is transferred to the thirst from the thirsty man who indulges it foolishly.

69. An echo of *Genesis* i. 27: "So God created man in his own image, in the image of God created he him"; and *Hebrews* i. 3, "the express image of his person." *express,* exact.

71. *ounce.* Also written *once;* it is a kind of lynx—*felis uncia.* Perhaps from Persian *yúz* (nasalised), a panther, lynx.

72. A departure from Homer's account, which represents Circe's victims as changed entirely into beasts. Newton notes that this partial metamorphosis suited better the purposes of the stage. Each character would wear a mask representing some animal's head, as does Bottom in *A Midsummer-Night's Dream.* Cf. the stage-direction that follows—"headed like sundry sorts of wild beasts, but otherwise like men and women."

73. *perfect,* complete; from completeness comes the idea 'excellence.' French *parfait.*

74. Milton has not followed Homer strictly; cf. *Odyssey,* x. 237 et seq.: "Now when Circe had given them the cup and they had drunk it off, presently she smote them with a wand, and in the styes of the swine she penned them. So they had the head and voice, the bristles and the shape of swine, *but their mind abode even as of old.* Thus were they penned there weeping"—Butcher and Lang's translation (as in the next note). Perhaps Homer's account gives greater pathos: Circe's victims are conscious of the contrast between their present and past; and pathos is largely a matter of self-appreciated contrast. Milton's account emphasizes the completeness of the power of Comus, i.e. the deadliness of the pleasure he has to offer.

76. Cf. *Odyssey,* x. 235, 236: "and Circe mixed harmful

drugs with the food to make them [her victims] utterly forget their own country." The lotus-flower possessed this peculiar power, and Milton, no doubt, has in mind the description of the 'lotus-eaters' (Lotophagi) who dwelt on an island off the Mediterranean coast of Africa, and offered the lotus to all strangers: and "whosoever of them did eat the honey-sweet fruit of the lotus, had no more wish to come back, but there he chose to abide with the lotus-eating men, ever feeding on the lotus, and forgetful of his homeward way"—*Odyssey*, IX. 94—97.

See Tennyson's poem *The Lotos-Eaters*, in which the rhythm and alliteration and verbal effects convey an exquisite sense of listless languid bliss. And turn to the witty 'perversion' of the present passage in the *Dunciad*, IV, where Pope makes the high-priest of Dullness offer to her victims "the cup which causes a total oblivion of all obligations," so that (for example) the man who has won Court-favour quite ignores his past:

"a wizard old his cup extends,
Which whoso tastes forgets his former friends,
Sire, ancestors, himself."

79. *adventurous*; where you are likely to meet with adventures; 'dangerous'.

80. The simile is repeated in *Par. Lost*, I. 745, 746. There, as here, the rhythm of the verses suggests the motion described.

81. *convoy*, escort. Low Lat. *conviare*, to bring on the way (Lat. *via*). The same word as *convey*.

83. i.e. robes dyed in the tints of the rainbow; Iris being the goddess of the rainbow and "many-colour'd messenger" of Juno, *Tempest*, IV. 76. See *Par. Lost*, XI. 244.

85. Alluding to Lawes's connection, as music-master, with the family of the Earl of Bridgewater. So in 493.

86—88. The compliment to Lawes is repeated at 494—496. Milton chooses his epithets, "soft," "smooth-dittied," with careful reference to the qualities of Lawes's music. See p. 48.

87. *Knows to.* For the construction (where we should insert *how*) cf. *Lyc.* 10, 11. The idiom is an obvious classicism, on the model of the infinitive after words like ἐπίσταμαι, *calleo*.

87, 88. Note Milton's favourite form of alliteration, *w...w*, corresponding to the alliterative use of *v* in Latin poetry. Cf. *Lyc.* 13, and compounds like 'wide-wasting' (*Par. Lost*, VI. 253), 'wide-waving' (*Par. Lost*, XI. 121), 'wide-watered' (*Il Pen.* 75).

88. *nor of less faith*, i.e. "not less trustworthy than he is skilled in music"—*Masson*.

90. *Likeliest*, most fitting; so in 2 *Henry IV*. III. 2. 273: "They are your likeliest men, and I would have you served with the best." Not far removed from *likely*=pleasing; as we say, 'a likely lad.'

91, 92. i.e. nearest at hand to lend the help that this occasion requires.

92. *Viewless*, invisible. Cf. *The Passion*, 50. Milton remembered Claudio's "viewless winds," *Measure for Measure*, III. I. 124. The termination *less* is now active, and *viewless* in modern E. would mean 'having no view.' But in the English of Shakespeare and Milton the force of adjectival and participial endings is not stereotyped.

The Attendant Spirit moves from the stage, and Comus appears with his followers. Strictly this was the Anti-masque, or comic interlude, and probably would have been treated as such at greater length by Ben Jonson.

Stage-direction. The stage-direction in the *Cambridge MS*. omits several points here introduced: e.g. there is no mention of torches, which would add greatly to the effectiveness of the scene, nor have the characters "glistering" apparel. When Milton wrote *Comus* he thought chiefly of the poetry and the moral which it enforced; mere scenic details could be left to Lawes, who had been so busy earlier in the year over the production of Shirley's *Triumph of Peace* and Carew's *Cœlum Britannicum*.

Comus would wear a fantastic dress to remind the audience of his supernatural powers; cf. the allusion in line 157 to his "quaint habits." Campion in one of his Masques brings "two enchanters" on the stage—Rumour and Error; the latter dressed "in a skin coat scaled like a serpent, and an antic habit painted with snakes, a hair of curled snakes, and a deformed Vizard"—Bullen's *Campion*, p. 216. Symbolical garb of this kind was much employed, Masques dealing so often with allegory.

his glass; containing his magic potion; cf. 65. *rout*, band.

glistering. Referring, probably, to the cloth of silver and tinsel (see 877), which was used a good deal on the stage.

93. *The star*, the evening-star; "thy folding-star," says Collins in his *Ode to Evening*. Keightley notes that Milton has adapted Shakespeare's converse description of the morning-star,

Measure for Measure, IV. 2. 218, "Look, the unfolding star calls up the shepherd." In the one case the star is Hesperus; in the other, Phosphorus ('the Light-bringer'); cf. Tennyson's *In Memoriam*, CXXI:

"Sweet Hesper-Phosphor, double name
For what is one, the first, the last."

95—97. Some think that Milton refers to the classical belief that the waves of the Atlantic hissed as the fiery wheels of the setting sun's chariot touched them.

96. *allay*, steep, cool.

97. *steep*. Standing on the sea-shore we can verify the accuracy of *steep*. Tennyson gives us the same picture in *The Progress of Spring*, VI., "The slant seas leaning on the mangrove copse." Some interpret 'deep,' like Latin *altus*.

stream; alluding, perhaps, to the Homeric conception of the Ocean as a great river surrounding the earth.

98. *slope*, sinking in the horizon. The whole picture in 98, 99 is amplified in *Par. Lost*, IV. 539—543.

101. The imagery of *Psalm* XIX. 5, "In them hath he set a tabernacle for the sun: which cometh forth as a bridegroom out of his chamber" (Prayer-Book).

105. *rosy twine*, twined roses. An allusion to the classical custom of weaving chaplets of flowers, especially roses, at entertainments, and perfuming the hair with unguents.

106. i.e. diffusing fragrance and moist with wine.

107. *Rigour. Comus* has many of these personified abstractions. The use of them is a characteristic of Milton's early style; cf. the *Nativity Ode*, *L' Allegro*, *Il Penseroso*. In 18th century poetry, e.g. in Gray and Collins, this rather tricky artifice became a mannerism. It was an aspect of the "poetical diction" which Wordsworth denounced in the famous preface to the *Lyrical Ballads*. Usually the noun is accompanied by an adjective—e.g. "pure-eyed Faith."

The influence of the old Morality-plays (which affected the Elizabethan drama much, especially upon its ethical side), and of the Masque itself, had fostered this method of personification.

110 *saws*, maxims. The Justice in *As You Like It*, II. 7. 156 (the "seven ages of man" passage) is "full of wise saws." *Saw*, *say*, *saga* (Icelandic) are allied words.

111. *fire*. Alluding to the old theory that everything is

composed of four elements—earth, water, fire and air: the two last being the lighter elements. "I am fire and air," says Cleopatra (*Antony and Cleopatra*, V. 2. 292), about to die: henceforth she will be free of the substance that clogs her spirit.

113. Cf. "the spheres of watchful fire," *Vacation Exercise*, 40.

114. Milton is fond of likening the motions of the heavenly bodies to a dance; cf. "lead" and perhaps "round" = round dance (see 144), though 'circle, revolution' would also suit. Thus he speaks of the "mystic dance" of the planets, *Par. Lost*, V. 178 (and see also 620—624).

the months and years. Cf. *Par. Lost*, VII. 339—342 (echoing the words of *Genesis* i. 14).

115. *sounds*, straits of sea; see G.

116. *to*, in obedience to,—referring to the influence of the moon on the tides; or perhaps 'to the accompaniment of,' i.e. under the light of.

wavering morrice, i.e. an undulating dance; cf. Keats's *Endymion*, IV., where the four Seasons join in a "floating morris." Another name was *Morisco*, i.e. *Moorish* dance. It is said to have been introduced into England in the reign of Edward III. when John of Gaunt returned from Spain. A morris (the more usual spelling) formed, and in some counties still forms, part of the rustic festivities at Whitsuntide and May-day; cf. *Henry V.* II. 4. 25, "busied with a Whitsun morris-dance"; and *All's Well That Ends Well*, II. 2. 25, "As fit as...a morris for May-day."

117. *tawny*. He wrote *yellow*, and perhaps changed to avoid too obvious comparison with Ariel's song "Come unto these yellow sands," *Tempest*, I. 2. 376. The nymph in *Endymion*, II. ruled over "grotto-sands tawny and gold." The influence of Milton's diction is very marked in Keats's poems.

shelves, banks of streams.

118. *pert*, lively, alert. See the Glossary for *pert*, *faery*.

121. *wakes*. Properly a *wake* = "the feast of the dedication of a church, formerly kept by watching [i.e. keeping *awake*] all night"—*Schmidt:* hence any merry-making kept up late.

127. *dun;* cf. "the dun air," i.e. dusky, of Chaos, *Par. Lost*, III. 72.

122. Comus celebrates the night time in his twofold character of magician and patron of license.

Gray's *Ode* written for the installation of the Duke of Grafton as Chancellor of Cambridge University begins rather curiously:

"Hence! Avaunt! ('tis holy ground)
Comus and his midnight crew."

128—130. *Cotytto*, or Cotys, a Thracian goddess. The Cotyttia, a festival held in her honour, took place at night. These licentious rites were secret; Juvenal (*Satire* II. 91, 92) speaks of their being celebrated with "secret torch" (*secreta tæda*).

131. *ne'er called but when*, i.e. only invoked at night.

dragon. Newton considers this an allusion to the idea that the chariot of the night was drawn by dragons; cf. *Cymbeline*, II. 2. 48, "Swift, swift, you dragons of the night!" *Dragons*, i.e. serpents, were chosen because of their proverbial sharpness of sight, the word (Gk. δράκων) coming from a root 'to see.'

132. *Stygian darkness*, i.e. darkness as of the nether world. "Abhorred Styx, the flood of deadly hate" (*Par. Lost*, II. 577), one of the four rivers of Hades, is a synonym of hell. From Gk. στυγεῖν, 'to hate.'

spets; an obsolete form of *spits*. In *The Merchant of Venice*, I. 3. 113, the Quartos and the 1st Folio have "And spet upon my Jewish gaberdine," changed in modern texts to *spit*.

134. *cloudy*, wrapt in clouds. *ebon*, black as ebony.

135. *Hecate;* the goddess of sorcery and witchcraft and mysterious midnight "rites" (535), as in *Macbeth*, where she is the patroness of the Witches. Scan *Hecat'*, as the original editions read. The scansion is very common; cf. Byron, *Childe Harold*, II. 22, "Alike beheld beneath pale Hecate's blaze."

138—141. These lines are a little mosaic of Shakespearian touches. Cf. 2 *Henry VI.* IV. 1. 1, "The gaudy, blabbing and remorseful day"; a passage (written by Marlowe, I believe, not Shakespeare), upon which Milton draws later (552, 553). For *Indian steep*, see 139 note; for *tell-tale* cf. *Lucrece*, 806, "Make me not object to the tell-tale Day."

139. *nice*, squeamish. Comus sneers at the Morn as too prudish to approve of their rites. See G.

the Indian steep. Cf. *A Midsummer-Night's Dream*, II. 1. 69, "the farthest steep of India" (Folio reading).

Indian, i.e. eastern.

141. *descry*, reveal; as in *The Faerie Queene*, VI. 7. 12.

144. *round*, a country-dance, the favourite one being Sellenger's (St Leger's) Round. Titania invited Oberon to join their round—*A Midsummer-Night's Dream*, II. I. 140. For the epithets cf. *L' Allegro*, 34, "On the light fantastic toe."

The Measure. "Measure denoted any dance remarkable for its well-defined rhythm, but in time the name was applied to a solemn and stately dance of the nature of a Pavan or a Minuet. The dignified character of the dance is proved by the use of the expression to 'tread a measure'; a phrase of frequent occurrence in the works of the Elizabethan dramatists. It is somewhat remarkable that no trace can be found of any special music to which Measures were danced; this circumstance seems to prove that there was no definite form of dance tune for them, but that any stately and rhythmical air was used for the purpose"—Grove's *Dictionary of Music*. *Measure*, however, came to be applied to any sort of dance, and the stage-direction in the *Cambridge MS.* describes the dance here intended as "wild and rude."

145. *Break off*, i.e. cease dancing. This is the "stop of sudden silence" mentioned in 552.

147. *shrouds*, places of shelter; see G.

151. *trains*, allurements; see G.

152, 153. Cf. the notes on 50 and 74. The *Cambridge MS.* adds the direction *They all scatter*.

154. *dazzling*. The *Cambridge MS.* has *powdered;* cf. "magic dust," 165. No doubt as the actor spoke these lines, 153—156 (cf. "Thus"), he scattered some powder in the air. A coloured light too may have been burnt behind the scene to heighten the effect—*Masson*.

spongy, because it seems, like a sponge, to drink in and retain the spells; cf. *Troilus and Cressida*, II. 2. 12, "More spongy to suck in the sense of fear."

155. *blear*, deceptive. To *blear* the eyes is to *blur*, i.e. make them dim. Dimness led easily to the notion of deceiving.

156. *presentments*. Cf. Hamlet's "counterfeit presentment," where 'representation,' 'picture' is the sense required, III. 4. 54.

157. *quaint habits*, i.e. his fanciful magician's dress. Milton has to explain why Comus at his next entry (244) appears as a "gentle shepherd" (271).

160. *ends*, purposes, intentions.

161. *glozing*, flattering; with the idea of falsehood. See G.

162. *not unplausible*, i.e. *very* specious; an instance of the figure of speech called *meiosis* (Gk. μείωσις, 'diminution'), by which you express in *very* moderate language something which you really wish to emphasise, e.g., 'it is no small pleasure to'=it is a very great pleasure to. Another name for this figure of rhetoric is *litotes* ('simplicity,' from the Greek).

163. *Wind me*, i.e. obtain his confidence. Needlessly changed in some editions to *win*. Shakespeare has *wind* with the sense 'to get an unfair advantage over'; e.g. in *King Lear*, I. 2. 106, "seek him out: wind me into him, I pray you."

the easy-hearted man, unsuspicious people.

165. *virtue*, peculiar power; cf. *virtuous*, 621; see G.

167. *gear*, business. Properly *gear*='apparatus,' 'tackle,' as in compounds, *travelling* or *fishing gear*, etc. In Elizabethan English it usually has the wider meaning of 'affair,' 'matter in hand.' Cf. *Romeo and Juliet*, II. 4. 107, "Here's goodly gear," i.e. as we might say colloquially, 'a pretty business.'

166—169. The edition of 1673 differs from that of 1645, by omitting 167, transposing 168, 169, and giving *hear* for *here* in 169. Most editors keep to the text of the earlier edition, except that they substitute *hear* for *here*. Some, however, follow the 1645 ed. in printing "And hearken, if I may, her business *here*," and take *hearken* transitively.

168. *fairly*, softly; cf. "Soft and fair, friar," *Much Ado About Nothing*, V. 4. 72. Comus steps back into the wood.

172. *ill-managed*, disorderly.

173—177. Milton is thinking of a shearing feast and harvest-home, such as Herrick describes in the *Hesperides* (a work from which we learn much about the rural life of Milton's generation). See again 848, *Lyc.* 117, and *L'Allegro*, 91—114.

174. *hinds*, peasants; see G.

175. *granges*, barns, granaries; from Lat. *granum*, corn. Now a poetic word in this sense; cf. Tennyson's *Demeter*, "Rejoicing in the harvest and the grange."

177. *amiss*, i.e. in a wrong way.

178. *swilled*, drunken; a coarse word, applicable to animals but suiting the context here. Cf. the description in *Par. Lost*, I. 502, of revellers "flown with insolence and wine," i.e. flushed with.

179. *wassailers;* see G.

180. *inform*, find guidance for. Cf. *Samson Agonistes*, 335.

181. *blind*, obscure; as in 'blind alley.'

183. *to lodge*, to pass the night.

184. *the spreading favour*, the kindly shelter.

188. *then when;* a favourite emphatic phrase with Milton; cf. *Par. Lost*, IV. 970, "Then, when I am thy captive, talk of chains."

gray-hooded Even; hence Keats's line in *Endymion*, I.:

"She sings but to her love, nor e'er conceives
How tiptoe Night holds back her dark-gray hood."

189. *sad*, sober, serious, without any notion of sorrow; cf. *sadly* in line 509, and see G.

votarist. Used of anyone who had taken a vow (*votum*); here a vow of pilgrimage. Cf. *Timon of Athens*, IV. 3. 27, "I am no idle votarist."

A *palmer* was "one who bore a palm-branch in memory of having been to the Holy Land"—*Skeat.*

The comparison between "the *gray*-hooded Even" and a palmer may be illustrated by one of Greene's lyrics describing Love dressed as a pilgrim:

"Down the valley gan he track,
Bag and bottle at his back,
In a surcoat all of gray;
Such wear palmers on the way,
When with scrip and staff they see
Jesus' grave on Calvary."

So Collins in his *Ode*, "How sleep the brave," stanza 2:

"There Honour comes, a pilgrim gray,
To bless the turf that wraps their clay."

190. i.e. they left her just as the sun was sinking.

193. *engaged*, ventured, committed.

195—225. From "else O thievish Night" down to "tufted grove" (225) is omitted in the *Bridgewater MS.*, i.e. was not acted; perhaps to lighten the part of the young lady; perhaps from motives of delicacy—*Masson.*

195—200. This piece of imagery has been very generally censured as far-fetched and unnatural. The fact is that Milton's early poems do show just a trace of the fault which mars the works of those fantastie contemporary writers, such as Donne and

Crashaw, whom Johnson calls the 'metaphysical' poets (*Life* of Cowley). One of the 'notes' of this school of writers was the use of fantastic imagery, far-fetched metaphors. Cf. the *Nativity Ode*, 229—231:

"So when the sun *in bed*,
Curtained with cloudy red,
Pillows his chin upon an orient wave."

The image there is a mere 'conceit,' which barely escapes the grotesque.

198. *their lamps;* a much used comparison; cf. Shelley's line, "The lamps of Heaven flash with a softer light," *Adonais*, XIX. Shakespeare quaintly compared the stars to candles in *Romeo and Juliet*, III. 5. 9—"Night's candles are burnt out"; and *Macbeth*, II. 1. 5.

203. *perfect in*, perfectly clear to.

204. *single*, total.

205. *what might?* what *could* this be? The original sense of *may* was 'can,' 'be able.'

207—209. Milton was drawing upon popular superstition. Perhaps some of his audience believed in these "calling shapes" and "airy tongues" of which medieval romance is full. Editors cite many illustrations, e.g. the "strange shapes" and "sounds and sweet airs" and "voices" of *The Tempest*, III. 2. 144—149, 3. 18—39.

207. *beckoning shadows dire.* The order of the words—a noun placed between two qualifying words—is a favourite with Milton. The idiom is Greek; in his note on *Lycidas*, 6 Mr Jerram quotes Euripides, *Phœnissæ*, 234, νιφόβολον ὄρος ἱρόν ('snowclad mount divine,' viz. Parnassus). Gray probably borrowed the device from Milton; cf. his *Elegy*, 53, "Full many a gem of purest ray serene." Cf. also Tennyson's early poems, in which the influence of Milton is very noticeable; e.g. *The Lotos-Eaters*, VII., "With half-dropt eyelid still," and *The Palace of Art*, "In diverse raiment strange."

beckoning. Like the ghost in *Hamlet*, I. 4. 58.

208. *airy tongues.* Cf. *Endymion*, IV.:

"No, never more
Shall airy voices cheat me to the shore."

Probably due to *Comus*. *syllable*, i.e. pronounce clearly.

212. *siding*, going by the side; hence 'defending.'

214. *girt with golden wings.* Possibly a reminiscence of *Psalm* lxviii. 13: "yet shall ye be as the wings of a dove covered with silver, and her feathers with yellow gold."

215. *unblemished*, that may not be blemished; see 349, note.

Chastity. A departure from the ordinary Trinity of Faith, Hope and Charity (to keep the Authorised Version of ἀγάπη). *Comus* is an enforcement of the doctrine intensely sacred in Milton's eye—the doctrine of purity; and it is worth noting that the substantive *chastity* occurs seven times in the poem; the adjective *chaste* four times.

216. *ye;* the original distinction between *ye* (nominative) and *you* (objective) was often ignored by Elizabethan writers; we see it in *John* xv. 16, "Ye have not chosen me, but I have chosen you."

217. *Supreme.* Scan *súpreme;* see note on 273. The sense in 217—219 is: 'he who uses all evil powers as agents to execute his displeasure against wicked men would send...'

221. *Was I deceived?* A moment before she had expressed the belief that Providence would, if necessary, interpose to protect her. The rift in the clouds seems an omen: the moonlight is like a "glistering guardian."

223, 224. Milton employs sparingly, but with fine effect, the artifice of verbal repetition. Cf. *Par. Lost*, VII. 25, 26:

"though fallen on evil days,
On evil days though fallen, and evil tongues."

No modern poet uses this device more beautifully than Tennyson. Cf. in *Enoch Arden* the latter part of the great passage that begins "The mountain wooded to the peak."

224. Cf. the proverb "no cloud without a silver lining."

225. *casts.* We should expect *cast* after *does* in 223.

228. *new-enlivened*, i.e. by the favourable sign in the sky.

230. Invocations of Echo, whose reply would be counterfeited behind the scenery, were not uncommon in Masques. It was a pretty, fanciful device appropriate to the fanciful character of the ordinary Masque. Also, it gave an opportunity for the introduction of Music (ever a great feature of Masque-performances).

Echo, a mountain-nymph (Oread, from ὄρος, a mountain) who was changed by Juno into an Echo—"that is, a being with no control over its tongue, which is neither able to speak before anybody else has spoken, nor to be silent when somebody else has spoken. Echo in this state fell desperately in love with Narcissus; but as her love was not returned, she pined away in grief, so that in the end there remained of her nothing but her voice"—*Classical Dictionary.*

231. *airy shell;* some interpret 'the vault of Heaven'= "sphere," 241; others 'a shell with air in it,' lying by the river's side (232).

232. There is said to be no classical authority for this association of Echo and Meander, though we meet with it in Gray's *Progress of Poesy*, 69—72, a reminiscence perhaps of the present passage. It has been suggested, however, that the mention of the Meander in poetry is due to the fact that it was a special resort of the swan, which, like the nightingale, is one of the favourite birds of poets; cf. the legend of the 'swan's song.' Meander is the modern Mendereh, rising in Phrygia. The circuitous course of the river has given us the word *meander.*

241. *Parley*, conversation, dialogue; since an echo seems to keep up a dialogue with the voice.

Daughter of the sphere. Cf. the epithet 'sphere-born' applied to the "harmonious sisters, Voice and Verse," *At a Solemn Music*, 2. There is perhaps an allusion to the notion of "the music of the spheres," which is referred to in 1021; see note there.

242. *So;* see *Lycidas*, 19, note. *translated*, raised aloft.

243. i.e. re-echo the music of heaven. Note that the verse is an Alexandrine (six feet), the only one in the poem. Milton was fond of the metre; see the *Nativity Ode*, or *Death of a Fair Infant.* An Alexandrine rounds off effectively the close of a stanza; cf. the *Odes* of Gray and Collins. The abuse of the artifice excited Pope's ridicule, *Essay on Criticism*, 356, 357:

"A needless Alexandrine ends the song,
That, like a wounded snake, drags its slow length along."

244. In the *Cambridge MS.* the return of Comus to the scene is marked by a stage-direction—*Comus looks in and speaks.* Probably he appears at the side of the stage, not revealing himself to the Lady till 265.

244, 245. The language of the couplet is a little extravagant; but we must remember that it was inserted out of compliment to the composer and the Lady Egerton who had sung the air.

246—248. Probably a reference to the idea, attributed to Pythagoras, that the soul *is* a harmony. Plato in the *Phædo* compares it to a harmony. Cf. *The Merchant of Venice*, v. 63, where Farmer quoted Hooker's *Ecclesiastical Polity*, Bk. v. "Touching musical harmony...so pleasing effects it hath in that very part of man which is most divine, that some have been thereby induced to think, that the soul itself by nature is or hath in it harmony."

247. *moves the vocal air*, fills the air till it becomes vocal (a *proleptic* use of the epithet).

248. *To*, so as to. *his*, its; see G.

249, 250. "Even silence herself was content to convey her mortal enemy, sound, on her wings, so greatly was she charmed with its harmony"—*Warburton.*

251, 252. These lines exemplify Milton's faculty for suggesting by means of metaphor—the quality in which Coleridge among modern poets is eminent. We are to conceive of darkness as being a dusky bird whose ruffled wings cover the earth—imagery which is illustrated by *L'Allegro*, 6, where "brooding Darkness spreads his jealous wings." And on this bird of night falls the spell of harmony, just as in the first Pythian Ode of Pindar the eagle of Zeus was charmed to rest by music; cf. Gray, *The Progress of Poesy*, I. 2:

"Perching on the sceptred hand
Of Jove, thy magic lulls the feather'd king
With ruffled plumes, and flagging wing:
Quench'd in dark clouds of slumber lie
The terror of his beak, and light'ning of his eye."

The raven is chosen as symbolising darkness by its colour. Mrs Gaskell has a happy allusion to this passage: "she was late—that she knew she would be. Miss Simmonds was vexed and cross. That also she had anticipated—and had intended to smooth her raven down by extraordinary diligence"—*Mary Barton*, II. p. 27. Cf. too *In Memoriam*, "Let darkness keep her raven gloss."

251. *fall*, cadence; cf. "That strain again! it had a dying fall," *Twelfth Night*, I. 1. 4. Cf. *close* in 548.

253. *the Sirens;* "sea-nymphs who had the power of charming by their songs all who heard them...According to Homer, the island of the Sirens was situated between Aea

[Circe's isle] and the rock of Scylla [cf. 257], near the S.W. coast of Italy"—*Classical Dictionary*. Strictly the Sirens (Homer says there were two) had nothing to do with Circe.

254. In *Odyssey*, X. 350, 351, Circe is waited upon by four maidens, "born of the wells and of the woods and of the holy rivers, that flow forward into the salt sea." The Naiads were "the nymphs of fresh water, whether of rivers, lakes, brooks, or springs"—*Classical Dictionary*: hence their association with wild-flowers. Cf. *Par. Regained*, II. 355, 356.

flowery-kirtled; "dressed with garlands of flowers for skirts" —*Dr Bradshaw*. Or perhaps, 'flower-decked.'

255. *potent herbs*. Cf. *Æneid*, VII. 19, 20, where Vergil speaks of the victims whom "the cruel goddess Circe had transformed from men into beasts *potentibus herbis*."

256. *prisoned*, i.e. in the body; cf. 385.

257. *lap it in Elysium*, fill it with an intense bliss.

Elysium; the Paradise of Greek mythology; hence a synonym of supreme happiness.

257—259. Homer makes Odysseus sail some distance beyond the island of the Sirens, and out of reach of their song, before he came to Scylla and Charybdis. All through this passage Milton adapts rather than follows Homer's account of the classical figures enumerated.

"*Scylla* and *Charybdis*, the names of two rocks between Italy and Sicily, and only a short distance from one another. In the one of these rocks which was nearest to Italy, there was a cave, in which dwelt Scylla, a fearful monster, barking like a dog. In the opposite rock dwelt Charybdis, who thrice every day swallowed down the waters of the sea, and thrice threw them up again"—*Classical Dictionary*. There was a proverbial line, *incidis in Scyllam cupiens vitare Charybdim*, 'in seeking to avoid Charybdis you fall into Scylla,' i.e. escape one danger only to fall into another.

Editors note that Milton has in mind a passage in Silius Italicus (a late Latin poet, of the 'silver age'), where the two monsters are represented as charmed by the pipe of a shepherd. Milton's figure of Sin in *Par. Lost*, II. 650 et seq. reflects the influence of the classical accounts of Scylla.

barking; cf. *Odyssey*, XII. 85, "therein dwelleth Scylla, yelping terribly (δεινὸν λελακυῖα)." Vergil speaks of a rock surrounded by "barking waves" (*multis circum latrantibus undis* —*Æneid*, VII. 588).

261. *robbed it of itself*, i.e. made it unconscious.

262. *home-felt*, 'keenly felt'; *home* suggesting 'to the full.' As we say, 'pay him home,' 'drive it home.'

263. *sober;* in contrast to "madness" (261), as "waking" to "slumber" (260). *This* (says Comus) is an elevated pleasure which one enjoys with all the faculties keenly awake to it and not soothed into unconsciousness.

265. Cf. Ferdinand's meeting with Miranda, *The Tempest*, I. 2. 425—427:

> "my prime request,
> Which I do last pronounce, is, O you wonder!
> If you be maid or no?"

267, 268. i.e. unless thou art the goddess that dwells here.

268. *Sylvan. Sylvanus*, originally the god of fields and forests (Lat. *silva*, a wood), was in later times identified with Pan, the god of nature in general (Gk. πᾶν, all).

blest song; referring to the strains he has just heard.

269. Cf. *Arcades*, 48, 49.

271. *shepherd*. See 164—167. *ill is lost*, i.e. *male perditur*.

273. *boast of skill*, i.e. boastful desire to show her skill.

extreme shift; scan *éxtreme*, an illustration of the rule that in Shakespeare and Milton words like *obscúre*, *extréme*, *complléte*, throw the accent on to the previous syllable when they are followed immediately by an accented syllable, e.g. a monosyllable like *shift*. Cf. *Lucrece*, 230, "And éxtreme fear can neither fight nor fly." So "sérene air" (4), "cómplete steel" (421).

276. *her mossy couch*, i.e. on the "margent green" (232).

277—290. Note the severely classical style. Even in *Samson Agonistes* (which for Goethe had "more of the antique spirit than any other production of any other modern poet") we do not find a piece of στιχομυθία (i.e. dialogue in alternate lines) so long as the present. The nearest approach is the dialogue between Manoah and the Messenger, 1552 et seq. There are a few examples of the same type of dialogue in Shakespeare's earlier plays; cf. *Richard III*. IV. 4. 343—367, a play written under the influence of his great predecessor Marlowe. Marlowe was a Cambridge man, and, though the general character of his works is essentially romantic, yet he shows the influence of his academic training by several features, e.g. the use of στιχομυθία and numerous classical allusions. Examples of this kind of dialogue might also be given from the English classical tragedies like *Gorboduc*, in which the model of the late Latin tragic writer Seneca is followed. Seneca himself took the Greek tragedians, especially Euripides, as *his* models.

278. *leavy;* so the original editions, as in *Macbeth*, v. 6. 1, "leavy screens." *V* in place of *f* was characteristic of the southern dialects. In the old poem of *The Owl and the Nightingale*, written in Dorsetshire about 1260, we find *vo* for *foe*, *vairer* for *fairer* etc. (Earle). And the same pronunciation may still be heard any day in Somersetshire; *fallow field* is always (from a labourer) *vallow vield*. *labyrinth;* cf. "mazes," 181.

279. *near-ushering*, going just ahead. *usher;* see G.

282. She gave rather a different reason in 185, 186.

283. *side;* cf. the use of *latus* in phrases like *tegere latus alicui* = to walk close by the side of.

285. *prevented*, anticipated; see G.

286. *hit*, guess; the metaphor of shooting at a target.

"But what it is, hard is to say,
Harder to hit"—*Samson Agonistes*, 1013—14.

287. i.e. 'does the loss of them matter much to you, apart from the inconvenience which it causes you just now?' The question is an indirect way of asking who the two are, what is their connexion with the lady.

290. Cf. *L'Allegro*, 29. Hebe (daughter of Zeus), the cup-bearer of the gods, stands for the personification of blooming youth. Cf. Tennyson, *The Gardener's Daughter:*

"Her violet eyes, and all her Hebe bloom."

291, 292. A common and natural way of indicating the time of sunset (cf. 188—190) in pastoral verse. Cf. Homer's βουλυτόνδε, 'towards evening, at eventide'; literally 'the time for unyoking oxen' (from βοῦς, an ox + λύειν, to loose). We must remember that Comus appears as a rustic.

what time, at the time when, *quo tempore*. Cf. *Psalm* lvi. 3, "What time I am afraid, I will trust in thee." See *Lyc.* 28.

loose, i.e. loosed from the plough which is left in the "furrow." Pope borrowed the couplet in his *Pastorals* (III.):

"While labouring oxen, spent with toil and heat,
In their loose traces from the field retreat."

293. *swinked*, weary; see G.

295. *yon.* Pointing to some part of the scenery in the background. In *Lyc.* 40, Milton conveys by a single epithet ('gadding') the same picture of the vine's straggling growth.

296. *Plucking clusters;* cf. what the Lady said, 186.

297—301. Milton says something complimentary about all who were concerned in the production of *Comus*; cf. 31, note.

297. *port*, bearing; frequent in Shakespeare—"Assume the port of Mars," *Henry V.* prologue 6.

299. *creatures of the element.* According to the common medieval belief, there were four kinds of "demons" or spirits, who respectively inhabited and ruled over the four elements of fire, air, water and earth. Cf. *Il Penseroso*, 93, 94:

> "those demons that are found
> In fire, air, flood, or under ground."

They were called Salamanders (spirits of fire), Sylphs (of air), Nymphs (of water), Gnomes (of under ground). Ariel in *The Tempest* is primarily a spirit of air, but is also at home in and has power over the other three elements.

element, air and sky. Cf. "the complexion of the element," i.e. appearance of the sky, *Julius Cæsar*, I. 3. 128.

301. *plighted*, folded; suggesting masses of clouds. Cf. Collins's *Ode to Liberty*, 103, "yon braided clouds." *plighted;* see G. *awe-strook.* Masson notes that Milton usually writes *strook* rather than *struck* both as preterite and past part.

303, 304. The sense has been well explained as "that it would give Comus extreme happiness to accompany the Lady on her quest, with the implication that the quest of such beings [as he has just described] must be a noble one." *Heaven* carries on the idea in "more than human" (297), "creatures of the element" (299).

304. *villager;* cf. 166.

310. *well-practised*, familiar with the wood; not "unacquainted" (180).

311. *each...every;* see 19, note. *alley*, walk, path; see G.

312. *Dingle.* "A hollow between hills: dale"—*Johnson.* *Dimple* and *dingle* are what Skeat calls 'doublets,' from a Norwegian word *depil*='a pool.' The idea is 'something scooped out' so as to leave a hollow place.

313. *bosky bourn*, a stream with shrubs and trees on the banks. See each word in the Glossary.

315. *stray*, who have gone astray. *attendance*, attendants; abstract for concrete.

315, 316. *lodged*, i.e. in some cottage (cf. 320, 339, 346). *shroud*, are sheltering, i.e. in the open air, under some tree or bank.

317, 318. i.e. the lark which has her roosting-place ("ground-nest," as he calls it in *Par. Regained*, II. 280) among grass or stubble such as *thatched* roofs are made of. For a similar vague use of *thatch'd* cf. *The Tempest*, IV. 63, where the sense seems to be 'thick-covered as with a thatch.'

319, 320. *low but loyal*, humble but reliable.

322—326. The sentiment reminds us of the Republican Milton of the Commonwealth days.

322. The derivation—*courtesy* from *court*, 325—is correct. Cf. Greene's *Friar Bacon and Friar Bungay*, III. 67, "His courtesy gentle, smelling of the court"; and George Herbert, *The Church-Porch*, "Courtesie grows in court." See *As You Like It*, III. I. 41, 42.

324. *tapestry*, hung with tapestry.

327. *warranted;* in the general sense 'safe, secure.'

329. *Eye me*, keep your watch over me. *square*, adjust.

331. Cf. Dryden, *Æneid*, III. 767, "The stars were muffled, and the moon was pent." Tennyson in *The Princess* speaks of "A full sea glazed with muffled moonlight," i.e. the light of a moon half hidden by clouds.

332. *wont'st.* The verb *won*, now limited to the participle *wont* or *wonted*, was then still conjugated; cf. "he wont...to sit," i.e. used to, *Nativity Ode*, 10. But as an inflected verb it was commoner in its original sense 'to dwell in,' i.e. be used to a place; cf. *Par. Lost*, VII. 457, "he wons in forest wild." Cf. the cognate Germ. *wohnen* = (1) to dwell, (2) to be wont.

benison; O. F. *beneison;* Lat. *benedictio*, blessing.

333. *Stoop.* Cf. the picture in *Il Penseroso*, 71, 72 of the moon "Stooping through a fleecy cloud"; and *Endymion*, IV.:

> "The moon put forth a little diamond peak,
> Bright signal that she only stooped to tie
> Her silver sandals."

amber; exactly descriptive of the fringe of light round

the moon when shining through a cloud. Cf. Tennyson's *Margaret*, I.:

> "Like the tender amber round,
> Which the moon about her spreadeth,
> Moving thro' a fleecy night."

"Amber" is the tint of the atmosphere in *The Lotos-Eaters*, Choric Song V., and of the sunrise in *L'Allegro*, 61 ("Robed in flames and amber light").

334. *disinherit*, dispossess. *Inherit* in Shakespeare frequently signifies 'to have,' 'possess,' without any notion, as now, of heirship.

Chaos. Cf. the description of the dark realm of Chaos and his consort "ancient *Night*" in *Par. Lost*, II. 959 et seq.

336—341. i.e. if your influence (the moon's) be quite eclipsed, then do thou, Oh gentle taper, from some quarter, visit us, and thou shalt be, etc.

336. *influence*, power; see G.

340. A beautiful instance of the sound echoing the sense. The alliteration (*l. l.*) is clearly meant to suggest the line of light. Cf. Matthew Arnold's *The Scholar-Gipsy*, "The line of festal light in Christ-Church Hall." For *l. l.* suggesting length see *Par. Lost*, VII. 480.

341, 342. A somewhat fanciful way of saying that they will direct their course by the light of the taper as a mariner directs his course by means of the constellations. *star of Arcady* = any star in the constellation of the Great Bear (*Ursa major*). *Cynosure* = the constellation of the Lesser Bear (*Ursa minor*), especially the star at the end of the tail, known as the Pole-star; the name *Cynosure* being due to the constellation's supposed resemblance to the shape of a dog's tail (κυνὸς οὐρά). The story ran that the *Arcadian* nymph Callisto, after being turned into a she-bear by Juno, was changed into a star, the Great Bear, by Jupiter. She was the daughter of Lycaon, king of *Arcadia*: whence Milton's "star of *Arcady*." Arcas, the son of Callisto, was changed into the Lesser Bear. Greek sailors steered by the Great Bear; the Phœnicians (or *Tyrians*) by the Lesser—hence "*Tyrian* Cynosure." For the same reason the Lesser Bear was also called Φοινίκη (the *Phœnician* star). See *Class. Dictionary*.

As *Cynosura* meant literally the star to which sailors looked, *Cynosure* came to signify metaphorically (1) 'a guiding star,'

(2) 'an object on which attention is specially fixed.' For (1) cf. Sylvester's *Du Bartas*, Grosart's ed., vol. I. p. 88:

> "To the bright Lamp which serves for *Cynosure*
> To all that sail upon the sea obscure."

This sense, now obsolete, is required by the present verse in *Comus*. For (2) cf. *L'Allegro*, 80, "The Cynosure of neighbouring eyes."

344. *wattled cotes*, i.e. sheepfolds made with small hurdles. Matthew Arnold borrowed the phrase in *The Scholar-Gipsy*: "Go, shepherd, and untie the wattled cotes"; and Tennyson varied it in the *Ode to Memory*, IV.:

> "Pour round mine ears the livelong bleat
> Of the thick-fleeced sheep from wattled folds."

Wattle='hurdle' is the same word as *wallet*='a bag.'

345. *pastoral reed*, the traditional shepherd's pipe. See 823.

The *oaten* pipe has been accepted by English writers as distinctly symbolical of pastoral music, without, as Mr Jerram points out in his note on *Lyc*. 33, any direct authority in the classics. In Theocritus we have the κάλαμος (i.e. reed) and Pan's pipe, σῦριγξ; in Latin poets *calamus*, *tibia* and *cicuta* (the stem of hemlock). Probably the notion of the "oaten straw" is to be traced to Vergil's *tenui avena*, in the first *Eclogue*, 2. Cf. the *Glosse* to the *Shepheards Calender*, October, "Oaten reedes, Avena." But *avena* could be applied to any stalk.

stops; the small holes in wind instruments like the flute. Cf. *Hamlet*, III. 2. 365–376: "Will you play upon this *pipe*?... 'Tis as easy as lying: govern these *ventages* with your finger and thumb...these are the *stops*." Collins, who imitated Milton very often, began his *Ode to Evening* with the words "If aught of oaten stop, or pastoral song..."

346. *the lodge*, i.e. of the keeper of the wood.

349. *innumerous*, innumerable; L. *innumerus*. Cf. *Par. Lost*, VII. 455, "innumerous living creatures." We find much the same shifting use of adjectival and participial terminations in Shakespeare; e.g. *unvalued*=invaluable, *Richard III*. I. 4. 27; *unavoided*=unavoidable, *Richard II*. II. 1. 268; *unexpressive*=inexpressible, *As You Like It*, III. 2. 10.

356. *amazement*; a rather stronger word then=utter bewilderment.

358. i.e. "the hunger of savage beasts, or the lust of men as savage as they"—*Newton*.

359. *over-exquisite*, too careful; like Lat. *exquisitus*, subtle.

360. *cast*, i.e. conjecture the nature of; perhaps from the metaphor of casting a nativity. For the sentiment cf. Landor:

> "Oh seek not destined evils to divine,
> Found out at last too soon"—*Gebir*, VI.

361. *grant they be so*, grant that they are real evils, not "false alarms" (364).

363. Alluding to the proverb "Do not meet your trouble half-way." Cf. *Much Ado About Nothing*, I. I. 96—98: "Good Signior Leonato, you are come to meet your trouble; the fashion of the world is to avoid cost, and you encounter it."

365. *self-delusion*. Scan the *ion* as *i-ŏn*. Cf. 413, 457. In Shakespeare and in Milton's early poems the termination *-ion*, especially with words ending in *ction*, such as 'perfe*ction*, 'affe*ction*,' 'distra*ction*,' is often treated as two syllables, especially at the end of a line. In Middle English poetry the termination *-ion* was always treated as two syllables.

366. *so to seek*, so ignorant what to do, so much at a loss. The phrase implies incapacity, or want of knowledge; cf. "they do daylie practise and exercise themselves in the discipline of warre...lest they should be to seek in the feate of armes"—*Utopia*, p. 131, Pitt Press ed. We still say that a quality is 'sadly to seek' in a man, meaning that he lacks it.

367. *unprincipled*, unversed in the principles of. Cf. *principled* in *Samson Agonistes*, 760, =instructed.

368. *bosoms*, i.e. the peace which goodness has in its bosom. Cf. *bosom* used as a verb='enclose in the heart,' 'carefully guard,' in *Henry VIII*. I. I. 112, "bosom up my counsel."

369. *single*, mere. *light and noise*. The Elder Brother had spoken of the darkness, the Younger of the silence.

370. i.e. *she* not being; the absolute case with the pronoun omitted, though easily supplied from the context.

371. The alliteration (*c. c. c.*) emphasises the idea of composure. *constant*, firm, not easily disturbed.

373—375. A reminiscence of *The Faerie Queene*, I. I. 12, "Vertue gives her selfe light through darknesse for to wade."

375. *flat*. Cf. "the level brine" in *Lyc*. 98.

Wisdom's self='Wisdom herself' would sound awkward in

modern E.; but the usage was once common; cf. *Coriolanus*, II. 2. 98, "Tarquin's self he met."

Mr Mark Pattison notes that lines 375—380 possess a personal interest. They are as it were a fragment of the poet's autobiography, descriptive of the years he spent at Horton, 1632—1637. Throughout the poems we catch glimpses of Milton the man.

376. *seeks to*, repairs to; cf. 1 *Kings* x. 24, "And all the earth sought to Solomon, to hear his wisdom"; and *Deuteronomy* xii. 5, "unto his habitation shall ye seek."

378. *plumes;* some would change to the more usual word *prune*. "A hawk *prunes* when she picks out damaged feathers, and arranges her plumage with her bill"—*Dyce.*

380. *all to-ruffled*, very much ruffled. Milton's editions have *all to ruffl'd*, i.e. three distinct words, and there is much difference of opinion as to the right reading.

The difficulty lies with *to*. It is the prefix *to-* = asunder (Germ. *zer*, Lat. *dis*) which is compounded with many Middle E. verbs, giving the sense 'to pieces.' Cf. *to-breken*, to break in pieces (literally 'asunder'); *to-fallen*, to fall to pieces; *to-hewen*, to hew to pieces etc. Verbs thus compounded were often strengthened by the adverb *all* preceding them.

Peculiar idioms come gradually to be misunderstood, and variations in their use arise: so with this.

(1) Sometimes *all* and *to* and the verb are separated; cf. the original reading here and *Judges* ix. 53: "And a certain woman cast a piece of a millstone upon Abimelech's head, and all to brake his scull."

(2) Sometimes *all*, *to* and the verb are joined; cf. Bunyan's *Pilgrim's Progress*, II. 48, "she all-to-befooled me."

(3) Sometimes *to* is detached from the verb but united by force of accent with the *all;* cf. *Latimer's Sermons*, 1538, "We be fallen into the dirt, and be all-to dirtied, even up to the ears."

According therefore to popular usage Milton might equally well write *all to ruffled* (as he did); *all-to-ruffled; all-to ruffled;* and *all to-ruffled.* The last is the most correct (since the *to-* should really go with the verb), and seems the best change if we change at all instead of leaving the idiom as in *Judges* ix. 53. Some editors prefer *all-to ruffled*, but it is not what Milton wrote, and it gives surely a less pleasing rhythm; for reading the line alike quickly or slowly we cannot help treating it as a pure iambic verse in which *to* goes closely with the following, not the preceding, word.

To print *all too ruffled* loses the idiom entirely. See the *New English Dictionary* under *all-to*.

381. *light within his breast;* the "inward light" of which he speaks in *Samson Agonistes*, 162, and *Par. Lost*, III. 51—55.

382. *the centre*, i.e. of the earth. Hamlet would find

"Where truth is hid, though it were hid indeed
Within the centre"—II. 2. 157—159.

385. See 256 ("prisoned"); cf. *Samson Agonistes*, 155, 156:

"Thou art become (O worst imprisonment!)
The dungeon of thyself."

385—392. Cf. *Il Penseroso*, 167—174, which paints the ideal close of the studious life, and *Richard II.* III. 3. 147—150:

"I'll give my jewels for a set of beads,
My gorgeous palace for a hermitage,
My gay apparel for an alms-man's gown,
My figured goblets for a dish of wood."

386. *affects*, likes, has affection for.

388. Milton's anticipation of Gray's more felicitous "Far from the madding crowd's ignoble strife" (*Elegy*, 73).

389. *a senate-house*. Milton was thinking of the Roman Senate-house, the *Curia*. Twenty years later Cromwell showed, April 20th, 1653, that the great English Council-chamber was not inviolable.

390. *hermit;* literally one who dwells in a "desert" (387), as did the hermits of old; Gk. ἐρημίτης, from ἐρημία, a desert.

391. *beads*, i.e. of the rosary. Every detail in the description—*cell*, *weeds*, *grey hairs* etc.—reproduces the conventional picture of hermit-life. If Milton had written *Comus* after his return from Italy, we might have thought that in these lines he was simply repainting in words some picture seen in an Italian palace.

Bead originally meant *prayer;* afterwards the perforated balls used by Roman Catholics in counting their prayers were called *beads*. The verb *bid*=to pray (distinct from *bid*=to command) is extant in '*bidding*-prayer.' Cf. Germ. *gebet*, prayer.

393—396. Alluding to the golden apples which Ge (the Earth) gave to Hera (Juno) on her marriage with Zeus. They grew in "gardens fair" (981) on an island in the far West, and were watched by the nymphs called the Hesperides (982), who were assisted in their watch by the "dragon" (395) Ladon. To slay the dragon and obtain the apples was one of the labours of Hercules. See *Par. Lost*, III. 568 ("those Hesperian Gardens famed of old") and IV. 250. There is a hitherto unpublished poem on the *Hesperides* by Tennyson in his *Life*.

394, 395. i.e. would need dragons to watch over her with eyes that cannot be enchanted, in order to save etc.

398. *unsunned*, i.e. secret.

401. *wink on*, be blind to. Cf. *Macbeth*, I. 4. 51, 52:

> "Let not light see my black and deep desires:
> The eye wink at the hand,"

i.e. let not the eye perceive what the hand is doing. This seems to suit our text. 'Danger' is not to see its opportunity, and, not seeing, is to let the maiden pass unmolested; a thing, argues the brother, for which we cannot hope. But the personification of Danger is strained. *Desire* would be simpler.

Opportunity. Cf. *Lucrece*, 876 et seq.:

> "O Opportunity! thy guilt is great:
> 'Tis thou that executest the traitor's treason."

King John put the same truth differently, IV. 2. 219, 220:

> "How oft the sight of means to do ill deeds
> Makes ill deeds done."

404. *recks*. Cf. *Lyc*. 122. The verb is not often impersonal.

407. *unowned*, lonely.

408. *Infer*, argue.

409. *without*, beyond; cf. 2 *Corinthians* x. 13, "things without our measure." Cf. the adverb *without*=outside.

410—412. i.e. where the chances seem equally balanced, there being as much reason for hope as for fear, I incline to hope.

411. *arbitrate the event*, decide the issue (=Lat. *eventus*).

413. *squint*, i.e. which does not look at things in a fair, straightforward manner.

418. As Masson observes, we have here, up to 475, the most continuous exposition that *Comus* contains of its central doctrine. The idea is never absent from Milton's thoughts; but in no other part of the poem is it treated at such length.

419. *if*, even if.

420—424. Probably Milton was thinking of the description of Parthenia in Phineas Fletcher's *Purple Island*, x. 27—32:

> "A warlike maid,
> Parthenia, all in steel and gilded arms."

(*Parthenia*=the Maiden, from Gk. παρθένος, a virgin.)

421. Scan *cómplete;* see 273, note, and cf. *Hamlet*, I. 4. 51—53:

> "What may this mean,
> That thou, dead corse, again in *cómplete* steel
> Revisit'st thus the glimpses of the moon?"

422. *a quivered nymph;* such as those who attended on Diana (see 441).

423. *trace*, pass, wander, through; cf. *A Midsummer-Night's Dream*, II. 1. 25, "to trace the forests wild."

unharboured, i.e. unharbouring='yielding no *shelter*,' the proper sense of *harbour*. Cf. Tennyson's *Geraint and Enid*, "O friend, I seek a harbourage for the night." See G.

424. *Infamous hills*. Cf. "And now he haunts th'infamous woods and downs," Phineas Fletcher, *Piscatorie Eclogues*, I. 14. *Infamous*='of evil name,' a Latinism; cf. Horace's *infāmes scopulos*, *Odes*, I. 3. 20.

The (Latin) accentuation, *infámous*, occurs in the *Death of a Fair Infant*, 12: "Thereby to wipe away the infámous blot."

426. *bandite;* "so spelt in Milton's editions, and probably rather a new word about Milton's time"—*Masson*. From Ital. *bandito*, literally a man placed under the *ban*, i.e. excommunicated by proclamation of the Church.

mountaineer. An opprobrious term, as always in Shakespeare; cf. "call'd me traitor, mountaineer," *Cymbeline*, IV. 2. 120. People who lived in mountain-districts might naturally be taken as types of savage un-civilization.

428. *very*, utter. In Shakespeare *very* is oftener adjective than adverb, being used, as here, to emphasise the noun.

429. *shagged;* cf. *Lyc*. 54. *with horrid shades*, i.e. *horrentibus umbris*. Poets in whom the classical influence is strong use *horrid* of woods because the Latin *horridus* (=shaggy) is a favourite epithet of woodland scenery.

430. *unblenched*, unfaltering: "if he but blench I know my course," says Hamlet (II. 2. 626). Akin to *blanch*.

431. *Be it not*, provided that it be not.

432. *Some say;* a convenient phrase by which he can mention a popular superstition or theory without committing himself to belief in it. Cf. *Par. Lost*, x. 575, 668, 671.

walks. The regular term; see note on 435.

433. *fire*, i.e. a false flame (*ignis fatuus*) such as was supposed to attend malicious spirits like Will-o'-the-Wisp and Jack-o'-the-Lanthorn, who loved to "Mislead the amazed night-wanderer from his way" (*Par. Lost*, IX. 640). See *L'Allegro*, 104.

lake or fen. In Ben Jonson's *Masque of Queens* eleven witches appear,

"From the lakes, and from the fens,
From the rocks, and from the dens";

and the author, who was very learned in all pertaining to witchcraft and the like, explains in a footnote that "these places, in their own nature dire and dismal, are reckoned up as the fittest from whence such persons should come."

434. *Blue*='livid, haggard,' was a traditional epithet of witches and hags. Cf. "*blue*-eyed hag" (the witch Sycorax, mother of Caliban), i.e. with dark circles under the eyes, such as come from exhaustion or weeping (*The Tempest*, I. 2. 269). *meagre*, lean, F. *maigre*.

stubborn, because refusing to be exorcised or 'laid.' Cf. *Cymbeline*, IV. 2. 278, "*Ghost unlaid* forbear thee!" It was thought that the only tongue in which a spirit could be addressed with effect was Latin; cf. *Hamlet*, I. 1. 42.

435. *magic chains.* Cf. "each fettered ghost," *Nativity Ode*, 234. *curfew time*, usually eight o'clock; cf. *Il Penseroso*, 74. The "foul fiend" in *Lear*, III. 4. 121, "begins at curfew, and walks till the first cock"; and the spirits in *The Tempest*, V. 39, 40, "rejoice to hear the solemn curfew." See G.

436. *goblin;* see G. *swart;* cf. *Lyc.* 138. *faery.* Rarely used, as here, of a malignant power; cf. *The Comedy of Errors*, IV. 2. 35, "A fiend, a fairy, pitiless and rough"; where, however, many editors change to *fury.*

of the mine. It was an old superstition that mines were inhabited by spirits (i.e. the 'demons' of earth—see note on 299). Collins refers to it in his *Ode to Fear*, speaking of the eve,

"When goblins haunt, from fire or fen,
Or mine, or flood, the walks of men";

and Keats in *Lamia:* "Empty the haunted air and gnomèd mine," i.e. mine where gnomes (sprites) dwell.

438—440. Shall I appeal to the works of Greek philosophers for testimony to the power of purity?

schools, i.e. of philosophy. For *school*=a sect professing a special doctrine, cf. *Samson Agonistes*, 297, "For of such doctrine never was there school."

441. *Dian*, Diana, the maiden goddess of the chase, type of virginity. Cf. Ben Jonson's pretty lines "Queen and huntress, chaste and fair."

443. *brinded*, striped, streaked; see G.

444. *mountain-pard*, a kind of wild-cat, usually called *cat-o'-mountain*, as in *The Tempest*, IV. 1. 262.

445. *bolt of Cupid*, i.e. arrow; cf. the famous passage (one of the most exquisite pieces of flattery in all literature) in *A Midsummer-Night's Dream*, II. 1. 155—168), where "Cupid all arm'd" takes his vain aim at the "fair vestal" of the West, i.e. Queen Elizabeth. Cupid was said to have two kinds of darts, one with a golden, the other with a leaden tip; the former to cause, the latter to repel, love.

447—452. Milton points the moral; and we may here note how he has taken two old-world, seemingly outworn legends and has invested them with an entirely new significance. It is Plato's method. Plato will often select some popular expression and apply it in a novel, metaphysical sense; or some popular belief, and read into it a fresh meaning, thereby raising superstition to the higher plane of philosophy.

447. The *Gorgoneion* or head of Medusa, whom Perseus had slain, was fixed upon the ægis or shield of Athene (=Lat. Minerva). Cf. *Iliad*, V. 738—741: "about her shoulders cast she (viz. Athene) the tasselled ægis terrible......and therein is the dreadful monster's Gorgon head, dreadful and grim, portent of ægis-bearing Zeus."

snaky-headed, because Medusa's hair had been changed into serpents by Athene; whence her head became so terrible that all who looked on it were turned to stone. There were three Gorgons, monstrous beings, sisters, of whom Medusa is most mentioned in classical writers.

449. *freezed.* The weak form of the preterite was not uncommon in contemporary writers. The strong verbs

suffer perpetually from the incursions of the weak conjugation.

freezed her foes; note the agreement of sense and sound, the alliteration and sibilants suggesting a petrifying shudder and horror. For the scansion *cóngealed* see again the note on 273.

451. *dashed*, put out of countenance, confounded; cf. *Par. Lost*, II. 114.

452. *blank*, utterly dismayed; this use of the adj. is somewhat colloquial. For *blank* as a verb = to make to turn pale, literally 'white' (F. *blanc*),—in fact, to *blench*—cf. *Samson Agonistes*, 471, "And with confusion blank his worshippers."

453. "The language of mythological allusion now ceases, and the speaker passes, in his own name, into a strain of Platonic philosophy tinged with Christianity"—*Masson*.

454. *sincerely*, entirely. Cf. *sincere* = pure, without alloy (L. *sincerus*) in 1 *Peter* ii. 2, "desire the sincere milk of the word." *so*, i.e. chaste.

455. *liveried*, i.e. in all their celestial array; cf. the description of the six pairs of wings and "feathered mail" of the archangel Raphael in *Par. Lost*, V. 277—285. *liveried;* see G.

lackey, attend. *Lackeying* is Theobald's fine emendation in *Antony and Cleopatra*, I. 4. 46, where the Folios read *lacking*— "Goes to and back, lackeying the varying tide." The word has deteriorated somewhat.

This idea of the Guardian Angel watching over men is a favourite with Milton. See 658 and *Par. Lost*, II. 1033. In his theological treatise *The Christian Doctrine* he devotes a section (IX.) to the ministry on earth of angelic beings.

457. *dream...vision*. Cf. Cowley's *Essays:* "I fell at last into this vision; or if you please to call it but a dream, I shall not take it ill, because the father of poets Homer tells us, even dreams too are from God"; where Dr Lumby's note (Pitt Press ed. p. 197) is:

"In *visions* a higher degree of revelation was supposed to be imparted than in *dreams*. Cf. *Select Discourses of John Smith*, p. 184: 'The Jews are wont to make a vision superior to a dream, as representing things more to the life.'" The same distinction is seen in Bacon's *Advancement of Learning*, I. 3. 3.

459—463. This fine conception of self-perfectibility, "till body up to spirit work," is developed in *Par. Lost*, V. 469—503;

see especially 496—499, where Raphael tells Adam that if he and his descendants live pure, sinless lives then perhaps

"Your bodies may at last turn all to spirit,
Improved by tract of time, and wing'd ascend
Ethereal, as we."

459. *converse.* In the three passages in Shakespeare where *converse*='intercourse' occurs the stress falls, as here, on the second syllable—*convérse.* Cf. *Othello*, III. 1. 40.

461. *temple of the mind.* Scriptural imagery; cf. *John* ii. 21, "He spake of the temple of his body."

463—469. Milton passes to the converse of the previous idea. As the body may by self-discipline become soul, the soul by the self-indulgence of its possessor may become body.

466. "Thou desirest truth in the inward parts," *Psalm* li. 6.

468. i.e. grows fleshly and brutish. Cf. *Par. Lost*, IX. 166, 167, "This essence to incarnate and imbrute!"

469. *property*, essential character, Lat. *proprius*, own.

470—475. Milton here adapts a well-known passage in Plato's *Phædo*, 81, which Professor Jowett renders:

"But the soul which has been polluted...and is the companion and servant of the body always, and is in love with and fascinated by the body......do you suppose that such a soul will depart pure and unalloyed?

That is impossible, he replied.

She is engrossed by the corporeal, which the continual association and constant care of the body have made natural to her.

Very true.

And this, my friend, may be conceived to be that heavy, weighty, earthy element of sight by which such a soul is depressed and dragged down again into the visible world, because she is afraid of the invisible and of the world below—*prowling about tombs and sepulchres*, in the neighbourhood of which, as they tell us, are seen certain *ghostly apparitions of souls* which have not departed pure, but are cloyed with sight and therefore visible." *Dialogues of Plato*, vol. I. p. 429.

It was, no doubt, belief in the continued association of body and soul after death, and the durability of the former, that led to the yearly offering of meat and drink, and even clothes, at tombs—*Thucydides*, III. 58. Many popular superstitions as to the attachment which the soul feels for its corporeal tenement might be instanced; e.g. the old Bohemian idea that the *anima* of a dead man took the form of a bird and perched upon a tree near to the spot where the body was being burnt. When the latter was consumed the soul flitted away.

470. *gloomy shadows damp.* Plato's phrase is ψυχῶν σκιοειδῆ φαντάσματα. For the word-order cf. 207, note.

471. i.e. περὶ τὰ μνήματά τε καὶ τοὺς τάφους κυλινδουμένη, as Plato says of the soul; see the words italicised in extract above.

473. *it;* properly *they*, "gloomy shadows" being the subject; but *it* is more vivid, drawing the eye of imagination to some particular dim shadow.

474. *sensualty;* so the original editions, to suit the metre.

478. Cf. Biron's description of love in *Love's Labour's Lost*, IV. 3. 342—343:

> "Subtle as Sphinx; as sweet and musical
> As bright Apollo's lute."

There is a certain humour in transferring the phrase to philosophy. The editors cite Milton's *Tractate of Education* (1644): "I shall detain you now no longer in the demonstration of what we should not do, but straight conduct you to a hill-side, where I will point you out the right path of a virtuous and noble education; laborious indeed at the first ascent, but else so smooth, so green, so full of goodly prospect, and melodious sounds on every side, that the harp of Orpheus was not more charming."

479. *nectared*, sweet as nectar, the drink of the gods.

480. *crude*, i.e. undigested, =Lat. *crudus;* see *Lyc.* 3.

483. *night-foundered*, overtaken by, or plunged in, night; cf. *Par. Lost*, I. 204, "The pilot of some small night-foundered skiff."

486. *Again, again!* i.e. the shout.

487. *draw*, i.e. their swords.

489. Cf. the sentiment of the king in 2 *Henry VI.* III. 2. 233: "Thrice is he armed that hath his quarrel just."

habited, dressed. *like a shepherd;* cf. 84—91.

490. *That hallo.* The Elder Brother called out, 487, and the Attendant Spirit answered. His reply is marked in the stage-direction of Lawes's edition, 1637. In line 490, therefore,

"that" refers to the answer given by Thyrsis before he appears on the stage.

491. i.e. they present their swords.

494. *Thyrsis.* A traditional shepherd name as far back as Theocritus; cf. his first *Idyl*, and Vergil's seventh *Eclogue*. In the *Epitaphium Damonis*, 4, the pastoral Latin elegy in which he laments the death of his friend Diodati under the guise of one shepherd mourning for another, Milton speaks of himself as Thyrsis. Matthew Arnold's Monody (*Thyrsis*) on Clough lent the name new life and associations.

The lines, 494—496, are an intentional compliment to Lawes, and a more delicate compliment than the other (86—88), which was placed in Lawes's own mouth—*Newton*.

495—512. Note the rhyme and Masson's explanation, viz. that having mentioned the word *madrigal* in 495 Milton wished to carry on for a moment the idea of pastoral poetry which *madrigal* (see G.) suggests. The heroic couplet had been much associated with pastoral verse; e.g. in a considerable portion of *The Shepheards Calender*. Ben Jonson in the *Sad Shepherd* gives us the same combination of blank verse, rhymed decasyllabic couplets, and periodic lyrics.

495. *huddling;* because the waters stop in their course to listen, and thus crowd together; some, however, interpret 'hastening, pressing onward,' i.e. so as to listen. Milton refers to the classical stories how the music of the golden lyre of Orpheus enchanted all nature, "delaying (says Horace, *Odes*, I. 12. 9, 10) even the swift-flowing streams."

501. *his next joy*, i.e. the Second Brother.

502. *toy*, trifle; see G.

506. *to*, compared to; from the idea 'in relation to.' Cf. "Hyperion to a satyr," *Hamlet*, I. 2. 140.

the care it brought, the anxiety which I brought on my errand.

507. Strictly the question is unnecessary. Thyrsis knew that the Lady was in the power of Comus; cf. 571—578. But the enquiry leads up to the explanation that follows.

508. *How chance?* The verb-construction 'how does it chance that?' is influenced by the noun-phrase 'by what chance?' Cf. "How chance the roses there do fade so fast?"—*A Midsummer-Night's Dream*, I. 1. 129. See Abbott's *Shakespearian Grammar*, p. 40.

509. *sadly*, seriously; cf. *Romeo and Juliet*, I. I. 207, "But sadly tell me who." See *sad* in the Glossary.

without blame; i.e. without any fault of ours.

511, 512. Observe the rhyme, *true* and *shew*, proving that the pronunciation of the latter has entirely changed. Cf. 994—997, and Sonnet II., where *youth* and *shew'th* rhyme.

513. *fabulous*, mere matter of fable, legend (Lat *fabula*).

515. *the sage poets;* meaning Homer and Vergil; Tasso (familiar to Elizabethans in the fine translation of Fairfax) and Ariosto; and Spenser—especially Spenser, who influenced Milton greatly. Cf. the publisher's preface to the 1645 ed. of Milton's poems: "I shall deserve of the age by bringing into the light as true a birth as the Muses have brought forth since our famous Spenser wrote; whose poems in these...are as rarely imitated as sweetly excelled." Cf. the reference to "our admired Spenser" in the *Animadversions* (*P. W.* III. 84, 85), where Milton quotes at some length from *The Shepheards Calender*, Maye. Spenser is the "*sage* and serious poet" of the *Areopagitica*, *P. W.* II. 68, where *The Faerie Queene*, II. 7, is in Milton's thoughts. In the preface to his *Fables* (translations from Chaucer and Boccacio) Dryden writes: "Milton was the poetical son of Spenser...... Milton has acknowledged to me that Spenser was his original."

taught by the heavenly Muse. Repeated in *Par. Lost*, III. 19:

"I sung of Chaos and eternal Night,
Taught by the Heavenly Muse."

This claim to direct inspiration is common with poets influenced by the classics. Milton is so great, and so justly conscious of his greatness, that coming from him the words have no trace of boastful egotism.

516. *Storied*, narrated. Cf. *Venus and Adonis*, 1013, 1014.

517. Cf. *Par. Lost*, II. 628, "Gorgons, and Hydras, and Chimæras dire." Milton's poetry is full of these verbal echoes; partly because he so often employs traditional epithets, taken straight from the classics. For the Chimæra cf. *Iliad*, VI. 181: πρόσθε λέων, ὄπιθεν δὲ δράκων, μέσση δὲ χίμαιρα, i.e. it was a monster resembling a lion in its fore part, a dragon in its hind part, and a goat in the middle.

enchanted isles. Referring primarily, we can scarcely doubt, to the "Wandring Islands" of *The Faerie Queene*, II. 12. 11 et seq. Spenser followed Tasso's account of the isle of Armida.

518. *rifted*, i.e. rocks with yawning chasms. *Rift*=to split, closely akin to *rive*, occurs in *The Winter's Tale*, v. 1. 66.

520. *navel*, centre; an imitation of the similar use of Gk. ὄμφαλος, a navel, and Lat. *umbilicus*. Byron coined a participle *navelled*=set in the midst of; cf. "Nemi navelled in the woody hills," *Childe Harold*, IV. 173.

521. *cypress;* the gloomiest of shade, hence appropriate to the scene of the horrid "rites" (535) of the magician and his "monstrous rout."

522—530. Cf. 46—77.

526. *murmurs*, i.e. incantations spoken over the potion as it was being brewed, such as those of the Witches in *Macbeth*, IV. 1. For *murmur*=spell, cf. *Arcades*, 60, "With puissant words, and murmurs made to bless."

529, 530. i.e. destroying the emblem of reason which is stamped in the human countenance. George Herbert says in *The Church-Porch*, "Wine above all things doth God's stamp deface."

529. *reason;* for Milton, the chief faculty of the soul (*Par. Lost*, v. 100—102); the embodiment of those higher qualities of intellect which separate men from the brute creation.

530. *Charactered*, stamped; a continuation of the metaphor in *unmoulding* (i.e. breaking up the pattern) and *mintage*. See G., and for the accentuation cf. *The Two Gentlemen of Verona*, II. 7. 3, 4:

"the table wherein all my thoughts
Are visibly *charácter'd* and engraved."

531. *croft*. "A little close [i.e. enclosure] adjoining to a house, and used for corn or pasture"—*Johnson*.

532. *That brow this bottom glade*, i.e. that skirt the top of the wood which slopes down to the valley. In some dialects (e.g. the New Forest) *bottom* is still in use for a valley, glade.

533. *mònstrous rout*, herd of monsters; an instance of the adjective doing the duty of the first part of a compound noun; cf. *Lyc.* 158. *Monster-rout* would sound awkward. German has a distinct advantage over English in this respect.

534. Perhaps *stabled*= 'which have got inside the sheep-fold (Lat. *stabulum*),' and, as we know from Vergil, *Eclogue* III. 80, *triste lupus stabulis* ('a wolf is no pleasant thing for sheepfolds').

But Milton may only mean 'wolves in their haunts'; cf. *Par. Lost*, XI. 752, where the verb *stable*=to have a lair.

535. *Doing rites;* Lat. *sacra facere*, Gk. ἱερὰ ῥέζειν.

abhorred, detest*able*, horrible; for the termination *ed*=*able* see the note on 349. *Hecate;* see 135, note.

537. *yet*, i.e. though they themselves are "monstrous" and therefore repulsive, and their "rites" horrible, *yet* they have means to attract people.

539. Milton, like Spenser, uses *unweeting*, not *unwitting*. The *ee* represents better the long *i* of A.-S. *witan*, to know.

540. *by then*, by the time that. Cf. *by this*='by this time'; "And I do know, by this, they stay for me," *Julius Cæsar*, I. 3. 125.

542. *knot-grass*. There is a stock joke in the dramatists that short people have eaten knot-grass (*Polygonum aviculare*), whose special property it was to stop growth. Cf. *A Mid-summer-Night's Dream*, III. 2. 329 ("*hindering* knot-grass").

546. *pleasing...melancholy*. Not gloomy dejection, but the serious, meditative mood celebrated in *Il Penseroso* (see 175, "these *pleasures*" etc.); what Gray in a letter calls "white Melancholy, or rather *Leucocholy*." Gk. λευκός=white.

547. i.e. to play on my shepherd's pipe. See *Lyc.* 66.

548. *her fill;* now a somewhat vulgar phrase, but not then; cf. Sonnet XIV. 14, "And drink thy fill of pure immortal streams." See *Leviticus* XXV. 19.

ere a close; "i.e. before he had finished the song he had begun on his pipe"—*Masson*. Possibly *close* has its musical sense 'cadence,' i.e. before he reached a cadence in his song. Cf. *Richard II.* II. I. 12, "music at the close." A musician himself, Milton uses musical terms often, with a musician's accuracy.

549. *wonted;* cf. "night by night" (532).

was up, had begun. The 'Hunt's up' was the title of an old ballad-tune, referred to in *Romeo and Juliet*, III. 5. 34.

551. *Listen* is transitive in *Much Ado About Nothing*, III. I. 12, "listen our purpose" (=hear our conversation, F. *propos*).

552. *an unusual stop*, i.e. at line 145 ("break off").

553. *respite*, i.e. "from the trouble the noise had been causing them"—*Masson*.

drowsy-flighted; so the *Cambridge MS.*, except that the

words are not hyphened. The original editions (1637, 1645, 1673) all have *drowsie frighted*, which must mean, 'the drowsy steeds of night which had been frighted by the noise of Comus and his crew.' Though this reading has the better authority, it seems in itself much inferior to *drowsy-flighted*. For *drowsy-flighted* gives a more picturesque conception; it is in form an *essentially* Miltonic compound—cf. "flowery-kirtled" (254), "rushy-fringed" (890); and it harmonises with the passage in 2 *Henry VI.* IV. I. 3—6, which Milton must have had in his mind's eye:

"And now loud-howling wolves arouse the jades
That drag the tragic melancholy night;
Who with their *drowsy, slow and flagging wings*
Clip dead men's graves."

We have, surely, in the third line of this quotation the germ of *drowsy-flighted*, and it appears most improbable that Milton should have changed the line so manifestly for the worse. Further, *drowsy frighted* is an awkward combination of opposite ideas. I suppose then that *frighted* was simply an error in the 1637 edition which escaped Milton's notice and, not being corrected by him, was of course reproduced by the printer in the later editions. Newton first adopted *flighted* from the *Cambridge MS.* and Masson accepts it. The attempt to make *frighted=freighted* (with the sense 'the steeds of night heavy with sleep') is impossible.

554. *litter*, chariot. *close-curtained Sleep*. We cannot help remembering Macbeth's "curtain'd sleep," II. I. 51; and Juliet's "Spread thy close curtain, night," *Romeo*, III. 2. 5.

555—562. Referring of course to the Lady's Song (230—243), in the same complimentary manner as before (244). Gray (*Progress of Poesy*, I. 2) addresses the power of music:

"Oh! Sovereign of the willing soul,
Parent of sweet and solemn-breathing airs."

556. *stream of perfume*. The edition of 1673 spoils the metaphor by substituting *stream*. Todd quotes a beautiful parallel from Bacon's *Essays* (XLVI.): "Because the breath of flowers is farre sweeter in the aire, where it comes and goes like the warbling of music." Cf. Tennyson, *The Lotos-Eaters*:

"they find a music centred in a doleful song
Steaming up."

Note in 555—557 the effect of the alliteration (*s...s* and *st*).

557, 558. So when the nightingale sang "Silence was pleased" (*Par. Lost*, IV. 604). *that*, so that. *took*, charmed; see G.

559, 560. i.e. cease to exist, if she could always be displaced or banished in the same way. *still*, ever, always.

560. *all ear;* now a rather colloquial phrase, but not then; cf. *The Tempest*, IV. 59, "No tongue! all eyes! be silent!"

562. *the ribs of Death;* a conventional description. Warburton thought that it might have been suggested by some allegorical representation of Death as a "bare-ribbed" skeleton in a popular *Book of Emblems*. "Bare-ribbed" is the epithet applied to Death in *King John*, V. 2. 177. Contrast the shadowy, more awe-inspiring conception of Death in *Par. Lost*, II. 666—673.

565. *Amazed;* see 356, note.

568. *lawns*, glades, open spaces in the forest; see G.

571. *in sly disguise*, i.e. as a "villager," 166; cf. 576.

575. We are to suppose that he was present, though invisible, at part of the interview between the Lady and Comus. *such two*, i.e. as she described. Cf. "two such I saw," 291.

584. *You gave me.* Referring to 418—458.

585. *period*, sentence.

586. *for me*, as far as I am concerned.

591. i.e. that which mischief intended to be most harmful.

592. *happy trial*, trial of happiness; or the adjective might have what is called a proleptic (or anticipatory) force—'the trial which proves virtue happy.'

593—597. Slowly separating from the good the evil element preys upon itself, just as the figure of Sin in *Par. Lost*, II, 798—800 is gnawed by the whelps of her own womb.

594. *when*, till.

595. *settled;* like liquid; the metaphor in "scum."

597. *if this fail;* if what I have said prove false.

598. Cf. *Par. Regained*, IV. 455, "the pillared frame of heaven," where Mr Jerram's note is: "The (supposed) solid dome of the sky requires pillars for its support." He refers to *Job* xxvi. 11, "the pillars of heaven tremble...at his reproof."

603. *legions.* Scan as a trisyllable. *griesly;* see G.

604. *Acheron.* Strictly one of the four rivers of the lower

world round which the shades of the dead hover, as in *Par. Lost*, II. 578:

"Abhorred Styx, the flood of deadly hate;
Sad Acheron, of sorrow, black and deep":

then put for the lower world itself; cf. the use of *Stygian*, 132. From ἄχος, pain, sorrow + ῥέειν, to flow.

605. *Harpies;* the 'robbers' or 'spoilers,' from Gk. ἁρπάζειν, to seize. They were hideous, winged female monsters with hooked claws, who swooped upon Æneas and his followers as they were feasting in one of the Ionian islands and carried off their food (*Æneid*, III. 225—228). One of the most vivid descriptions of the Harpies in English poetry is in William Morris's *Jason*, V. 219 et seq.

Hydra; literally 'a water serpent' (Gk. ὕδωρ, water); specially used of the *Lernean Hydra*, a nine-headed serpent, the slaying of which was one of the 'labours' of Hercules. When he cut off one head two fresh heads sprang in its stead, till at last he discovered how to deal with the monster.

606. *Twixt Africa and Ind*, i.e. from one end of the world to the other—west to east. *Ind* or *Inde* is a common poetic form of India; cf. *Par. Lost*, II. 2.

608. In Ben Jonson's Masque *Pleasure Reconciled to Virtue*, Comus has "his head crown'd with roses and other flowers, his hair curled." In Elizabethan times curling the hair was a mark of effeminacy and affectation; see *King Lear*, III. 4. 88.

609. *purchase*, prize, booty; see G.

610. *yet*, nevertheless, i.e. though he has just said "alas!" It is vain courage, but he cannot help admiring it.

bold emprise; a frequent Spenserian phrase, with an Italian ring; cf. the first line of Ariosto's *Orlando Furioso*: "Le cortesie, l' audaci imprese, io canto." Also in *Par. Lost*, XI. 642.

611. *stead*, service; cf. the verb in *The Merchant of Venice*, I. 3. 7, "May you stead me?" i.e. Can you help me? To do a thing in the *stead*, i.e. place, of a man is to help him.

612. *other*, i.e. mightier. For the repetition cf. *Lyc.* 174.

614, 615. There are resemblances to *The Tempest;* cf. I. 2. 469—473 (Prospero's first meeting with Ferdinand), IV. 259.

bare, mere. *wand;* the usual symbol of magical power; cf. Prospero's "staff" (V. 54). *unthread*, take out of their sockets, dislocate. *crumble*, cause to shrivel up.

617. *As to make*, i.e. as to be able to make.

relation, report; cf. the verb 'to *relate*.'

618. *surprisal;* an echo of 590.

619—628. Probably a reference to Milton's school-friend Diodati, whose premature death in 1638 inspired the *Epitaphium Damonis*. Lines 150—154 of that poem mention Diodati's knowledge of botany and habit of imparting it to Milton.

620. *to see to*. An obsolete expression = to behold; cf. *Ezekiel* xxiii. 15: "Girded with girdles upon their loins, exceeding in dyed attire upon their heads, all of them princes to look to," and *Joshua* xxii. 10, "a great altar to see to."

skilled, i.e. versed in the lore of. *Skill* was a word of wider scope then. Among the synonyms of it given and illustrated by quotation in Schmidt's *Shakespeare Lexicon* are 'discernment,' 'sagacity,' 'mental power,' 'knowledge of any art.'

621. *virtuous*, possessed of medicinal properties.

626. *scrip*, bag. "Orig. sense 'scrap,' because made of a scrap of stuff"—*Skeat*. Cf. *Luke* xxii. 35.

627. *simples*. A *simple* was a single (i.e. *simple*) ingredient in a compound, especially in a compounded medicine. Its association with medicine led to the common meaning 'medicinal herb'; once in current use, as it occurs so often in Shakespeare—"*culling* of simples," *Romeo and Juliet*, v. 1. 40. Cf. 630.

630—633. In point of style this passage, with its accumulation of *buts*, seems the most awkward in *Comus*.

634. *like*, i.e. correspondingly: 'as unknown, so unesteemed.'

635. *clouted*, patched, mended; see G.

636, 637. *that*, the famous; cf. 2. *Moly;* the mysterious plant which Hermes (Lat. Mercury) gave Odysseus as a safeguard against the charms of Circe (*Odyssey*, x. 281—306). In poetry it is the flower of ideal lands. Tennyson's Lotos-Eaters lie "Propt on beds of amaranth and moly"; and Shelley associates the same plants in *Prometheus Unbound*, II. 4:

"folded Elysian flowers,
Nepenthe, Moly, Amaranth, fadeless blooms."

637. *wise*. Homer's constant epithet for Odysseus (= Ulysses) is πολύμητις = of many counsels, i.e. ever ready with some wise scheme. This conception of him as the man of wonderful knowledge and thought and experience is brought out most strikingly in Tennyson's *Ulysses*.

638. *Hæmony.* The name is Milton's invention and commonly explained as a reference to *Hæmonia*, an old name of Thessaly, the land of magic in classical writers (e.g. Horace, *Odes*, I. 27. 21, 22). So we may call it 'the Thessalian plant.'

639. *sovran*, most efficacious; see G.

640. *mildew blast*, i.e. the hurtful power of mildew sent by .vil spirits. Cf. *King Lear*, III, 4. 120, 123, "This is the foul fiend...he mildews the white wheat."

641. *Furies*, evil fairies. Scan *appariti-ón.*

642. i.e. I put it away in my purse, but never thought much about it. See *Lyc.* 116.

644. *it*, i.e. what the shepherd had said about the plant.

644—647. Warton points out that it was a recognised expedient in medieval tales for a warrior of the type of the Red Crosse Knight to carry a charm, often a herb, as a protective against evil influences.

650, 651. Probably an echo of *Odyssey*, X. 294, 295, where Hermes says to Odysseus, "when it shall be that Circe smites thee with her long wand, then draw thou thy sharp sword from thy thigh, and spring on her, as one eager to slay her."

651, 652. So in *The Faerie Queene*, II. 12. 57, when the sorceress Acrasia offered to Guyon the enchanted cup which she was wont to present to strangers, he flung it down, "And with the liquor stained all the land."

653. *seize his wand;* which the brothers fail to do.

curst crew. Cf. *Par. Lost*, VI. 806. In his epics Milton repeatedly applies *crew* to Satan and the rebellious angels.

655. *Vulcan*, the Roman god of fire, and master of the arts, such as working in metals, which need the aid of fire. Hence his "sons" might be expected to "vomit smoke," as did the giant Cacus (one of the "sons"), *Æneid*, VIII. 252, 253.

The Scene changes. Probably a screen, called a *traverse* or *travers*, was put forward while the alteration of the scene was being made. Cf. Ben Jonson's *Entertainment at Theobalds*, 1607, "The King and Queen, being entered into the gallery, after dinner there was seen nothing but a *traverse* of white across the room: which suddenly drawn, was discovered a gloomy obscure place." See Nares's *Glossary*.

soft music. Wanting in the *Cambridge MS.* Doubtless the addition of music was due to Lawes. The idea of tempting by means of a banquet (cf. *The Tempest*, III. 3) meets us in medieval romances of virtue assailed by evil powers. I believe that it is the basis of the scene of temptation in *Par. Regained*, II. 337.

enchanted chair; because "smeared with gums," 917.

puts by, refuses. So Cæsar (I. 2. 230) rejected the crown: "Ay, marry...he put it by thrice." *goes about*, tries.

659—813. Dramatically the most effective part of *Comus*.

660. i.e. your sinews (Lat. *nervi*) will all be turned to alabaster, and you will become a statue, or rooted to the spot, as was Daphne.

For *nerve* in its Latin sense cf. the Sonnet to Vane, where he calls money the "nerves" of war, i.e. sinews, as we say.

are; a vivid present to suggest immediate effect.

alabaster; a sulphate of lime; the pure white variety was much used in images and monuments: hence "statue" in 661. Cf. *The Merchant of Venice*, I. 1. 83, 84:

"Why should a man, whose blood is warm within,
Sit like his grandsire cut in alabaster?"

and "smooth as monumental alabaster" in *Othello*, V. 2. 5.

661. *Daphne.* The story of Daphne the nymph who fled from Apollo and was changed into a laurel-tree at her own petition is told by Ovid, *Metamorphoses*, I. 660 et seq.

664. *corporal rind*, bodily covering.

665. *while*, so long as (and only so long).

668. A reminiscence, perhaps, of *Isaiah* xxxv. 10, "they shall obtain joy and gladness, and sorrow and sighing shall flee away."

670. *returns*, i.e. circulates *again* (as though it had been dormant during the winter).

672. *julep.* Properly rose-water; then any bright drink, as here; finally often used to signify a syrup medicine. Persian *gul*, a rose + *áb*, water.

673. Cf. *Samson Agonistes*, 543—546:

"Nor did the dancing ruby,
Sparkling outpoured, the flavour or the smell,
Or taste that cheers the hearts of gods and men,
Allure thee from the cool crystalline stream."

674. *balm;* implying that which soothes.

675, 676. See *Odyssey*, IV. 219—229, where Menelaus and

Helen entertain Telemachus at Sparta; and "Helen, daughter of Zeus, presently cast a drug into the wine whereof they drank, a drug to lull all pain and anger, and bring forgetfulness of every sorrow. Whoso should drink a draught thereof, when it is mingled in the bowl, on that day he would let no tear fall down his cheeks, not though his father and mother died......... Medicines of such virtue (φάρμακα μητιόεντα) had the daughter of Zeus, which Polydamna, the wife of Thon, had given her, a woman of Egypt" (Butcher and Lang).

Properly Nepenthes, or Nepenthe, (Gk. νηπενθής, without pain) meant the drug itself (perhaps opium)—or herb whence it was extracted—which had this power of lulling sorrow for the day on which it was drunk: hence any deliciously soothing liquor. See *The Faerie Queene*, IV. 3. 43.

679. Cf. *Samson Agonistes*, 784, and Shakespeare's first Sonnet, "Thyself thy foe, to thy sweet self too cruel." In the translation of More's *Utopia* we read, "When nature biddeth the (i.e. *thee*) to be good and gentle to other, she commaundeth the not to be cruell and ungentle to the selfe," p. 107, Pitt Press ed. Probably the idea was suggested by *Proverbs* xi. 17, "The merciful man doeth good to his own soul: but he that is cruel troubleth his own flesh."

680. *Nature lent.* Cf. Shakespeare's fourth Sonnet, 3: "Nature's bequest gives nothing, but doth lend," i.e. nature never gives anything to man for his absolute possession, but always regards him as holding her gifts on "trust."

685. *unexempt condition*, terms from which no one can be exempt. Observe how the metaphor of trusteeship runs through 680—685; cf. "covenants," "trust," "terms," etc.

686. *mortal frailty*, weak human nature.

688. *That.* The antecedent must be "you" in 682.

693, 694. Cf. 319—321.

695. *aspects*, objects, appearances. Scan *aspécts* and see G.

696. *brewed enchantments*, i.e. the draught in his crystal cup "with many murmurs mixed" (526). Cf. *Samson Agonistes*, 934, "Thy fair enchanted cup, and warbling charms."

698. *vizored*, masked, disguised. *forgery*, deceit.

700. *lickerish*, dainty; see G.

702, 703. Cf. Euripides, *Medea*, 618, κακοῦ γὰρ ἀνδρὸς δῶρ' ὄνησιν οὐκ ἔχει ('for the gifts of a bad man bring no advantage');

in the same way 'an enemy's gifts do not profit'—*ἐχθρῶν ἄδωρα δῶρα κοὐκ ὀνήσιμα*, Sophocles, *Ajax*, 665.

706—709. i.e. foolish are those who adopt the doctrines of Stoicism or Cynicism and practise rigid, morose abstinence.

707. *budge;* the name of a fur, perhaps goat-skin; see G. Budge-row in the City was so called because most of the London furriers lived in it; the Skinners' Company's Hall is still there. This fur seems to have been specially employed in the ornamentation of academic dress. Todd quotes a regulation of the University of Cambridge issued in 1414 with reference to the dress of graduates, and budge is one of the furs mentioned as proper for hoods. In a tract against the Presbyterian elders at Belfast Milton refers to their wearing "budge-gowns" (*Observations on the Articles of Peace*). It looks then as if Milton, perhaps with a recollection of budge-trimmed hoods seen at Cambridge, used 'budge' to suggest a learned professor, very much as we use 'ermine' in special association with the judges. I think that we must paraphrase in some such way as 'those teachers whose furred gowns mark them as professors in the school of Stoicism.' There was an adjective *budge* = stiff, formal, solemn-looking; but its use cannot be traced as far as 1634. Moreover, "Stoic *fur*" shows that Milton meant the noun *budge* (= fur), not this adjective. See *New English Dict.*

708. *the Cynic tub.* Referring to Diogenes (B.C. 412—323) the Cynic philosopher, famous for his life of extreme austerity and moroseness at Athens. "He wore coarse clothing, lived on the plainest food, slept in porticoes or in the street, and finally, according to the common story, took up his residence in a tub"—*Classical Dict.* The *Cynics* were so called "from their *dog-like* neglect of all forms and usages of society." Gk. *κύων*, a dog, whence *κυνικός*, dog-like. The founder of the sect was Antisthenes, a pupil of Socrates.

710—742. See p. 50.

711. *unwithdrawing*, bounteous, holding back nothing.

714. *But all to*, except to. *curious*, dainty, critical. Cf. Shakespeare, Sonnet 38, 13, "If my slight Muse do please these curious days." Lat. *cura*, care.

716. *shops*, workshops; meaning on mulberry trees.

719. *hutched*, enclosed, shut up; see G. *ore*, metal; see 233, *Lyc.* 170.

721. Cf. *Daniel* i. 12: "Prove thy servants, I beseech thee, ten days; and let them give us pulse to eat, and water to drink." Cf. *Par. Regained*, II. 278, "Or as a guest with Daniel at his pulse" (=beans, peas). *a pet of*, a foolish craze for.

722. *frieze*, or *frize*; coarse woollen cloth, made chiefly in Wales; originally however, from *Friesland*. For cloths named after the country whence they were first imported, cf. *Cambric* from *Cambray* in Flanders, *calico* from *Calicut*.

724. *yet despised*. Men would be despising the rich gifts of which they foolishly made no use and therefore could form no just opinion. Cf. 634.

727. "If ye be without chastisement, whereof all are partakers, then are ye bastards, and not sons," *Hebrews* xii. 8.

like bastards, because the illegitimate have not the same rights as regards their parents that legitimate "sons" have; thus they have no claim to a parent's property at death. But *we* (says Comus) should enjoy the full rights of sonship in relation to our parent Nature.

728, 729. This idea, expanded in the next lines, occurs in *Par. Lost*, V. 318—320.

surcharged; F. *surchargé*, overladen with. *weight*, i.e. of crops, herds etc. *waste*, wasted.

731. *o'er-multitude*, i.e. grow too numerous for their shepherds and keepers to manage.

732. *o'erfraught*, i.e. overfull of fish; cf. 713.

the unsought diamonds. Cf. 881, where Milton speaks of "diamond rocks." These "rocks" might well be said to "stud" and "emblaze" (i.e. make brilliant) the surface ("forehead") of the sea. The argument seems to be that men should quarry them and take away their diamonds, not leave them there "unsought." Todd argued that the lines were designedly fanciful, and were meant to harmonise "with the character of the 'wily' speaker" (Comus) and "to expose that ostentatious sophistry by which a bad cause is generally supported."

733. Cf. 21—23.

734. *they below*, i.e. the inhabitants and creatures of the deep, such as mermen, fishes. Some say 'men on earth,' *οἱ κάτω*.

735. *inured;* see G.

737, 738. Note the contemptuous effect of the alliteration, especially of *c*, *c*.; so again in 749, 750. *cozened;* see G.

737—755. The whole passage from "List, lady," 737, down to 755, though extant in the *Cambridge MS.*, is wanting in the Bridgewater copy. This shows that the lines were not spoken at the actual performance. The omission was certainly a great advantage from the point of view of good taste.

738. Cf. Fairfax, translation of Tasso, XIV. 63, "Virtue itself is but an idle name." The line occurs in Tasso's famous description of the isle of Armida; Milton probably had the passage in mind both here and in *Par. Lost*, IV. 272, 273.

739—742. Many parallels, as regards both the sentiment and the language, might be quoted from Elizabethan poets, e.g. Shakespeare's Sonnets, 1—17 (especially 4 and 6 where the metaphor resembles Milton's, viz. money lent at interest); Ben Jonson's *Cynthia's Revels*, I. 1 (the latter part of Echo's speech "His name revives"); and Drayton's *Legend of Matilda*.

741. *mutual*, shared with others.

743, 744. Cf. *A Midsummer-Night's Dream*, I. 1. 76—78.

745. *Nature's brag*, i.e. that of which nature boasts justly.

748. Much the same jingle as "Home-keeping youth have ever homely wits," *The Two Gentlemen of Verona*, I. 1. 2.

749, 750. i.e. those who have coarse complexions may be content to ply—that is all very well for *them*, not for you.

complexions. Scan as four syllables. *sorry*, poor, unattractive. *grain;* probably 'hue,' not 'texture' (already implied in "coarse"). See G.

751. *sampler*, a piece of wool-work in which patterns (i.e. *samples*) were designed, especially the alphabet. Lat. *exemplar*, a copy.

to tease, to comb out. In the art of cloth-manufacture *teasing* is the process by which the surface of the cloth is smoothed and roughnesses taken away.

752. *vermeil-tinctured*, red; as if dipped in *vermilion* (from Lat. *vermiculus*, a little worm, used of the cochineal insect).

"Vermeil" as applied to the face represents what has been called "poetic diction," i.e. it is the sort of picturesque description that one poet hands on to another. Cf. Gray, *Ode on Vicissitude*:

> "With vermeil-cheek and whisper soft
> She woos the tardy spring."

and Keats, *Endymion*, IV.:

"O Sorrow,
Why dost borrow
The natural hue of health from vermeil lips?"

753. *Love-darting eyes.* Cf. Sylvester's translation (in exceedingly Spenserian verse) of the French poet Du Bartas: "Whoso beholds her sweet, love-darting eyes" (Grosart's ed. I. 205). This translation was very popular; Milton certainly studied it in his youth and was influenced by Sylvester's diction. Dryden confessed that he once preferred Sylvester to Spenser.

tresses like the morn; an echo of Homer's phrase "the fair-tressed morn," ἐϋπλόκαμος Ἠώς. Cf. Spenser, *Virgil's Gnat*, IX., "And fayre Aurora, with her rosie heare"(=hair). See Shelley's *Adonais*, XIV.

756—761. Spoken aside.

to have unlocked. Elizabethan writers often use this perfect infinitive "after verbs of *hoping*, *intending*, or verbs signifying that something *ought* to *have* been done but was not...The same idiom is found in Latin poetry after verbs of *wishing* and *intending*" (Abbott). Cf. *Par. Lost*, I. 40, "He trusted to have equalled the Most High."

759. *obtruding*, thrusting before me. *pranked*, decked. A common word in old writers; see G. Shelley has it more than once, e.g. in *The Question*, "There grew broad flag flowers, purple pranked with white."

760. *bolt;* probably a metaphor from the preparation of flour, in which to *bolt* (more correctly *boult*) is to sift the meal from the bran. Cf. the description of Coriolanus (III. I. 322, 323) as a rough warrior not schooled

"In bolted language; meal and bran together
He throws without distinction."

Having this sense 'to refine, to sift,' the verb came by a natural metaphor to be used of subtle arguing. So we might paraphrase: 'I hate to see Vice picking out her subtle arguments while Virtue is tongue-tied and unable to check her proud enemy.'

Some take *bolt*='to dart, shoot like a bolt,' i.e. arrow; cf. 445.

766, 767. Cf. *Il Penseroso*, 46, "Spare Fast, that oft with gods doth diet." Comus had ridiculed sobriety of living as a mere freak—cf. "pet of temperance," 721; she replies that temperance is a holy, beneficent power.

767—774. Milton has in mind Gloucester's argument in

favour of practical socialism, *King Lear*, IV. I. 73, 74, viz. that Providence should make "the *superfluous* man" (cf. 773), i.e. him who has more wealth than he needs, give up part of it to his poor neighbours:

"So distribution should undo excess,
And each man have enough."

Lear expresses the same thought earlier, III. 4, 33—36.

Throughout this speech the real speaker is obviously Milton himself. Much of it is inappropriate in the mouth of a young girl. It should be observed that lines 779—806 (from "Shall I go on" to "more strongly") are wanting in the *Cambridge* and *Bridgewater MSS.*, i.e. the passage was added by Milton to bring out the moral of the Masque. He may have thought that there was no likelihood of *Comus* being *acted* again, and that the incongruity between the youthful speaker and her speech would be less apparent in reading the poem.

773. *unsuperfluous*, not superabundant.

774. Understand *would be*. *store*, abundance. She is answering Comus's argument in 728—731; cf. "cumbered," 730.

781. *contemptuous words;* cf. 737, 738. She deals with Comus's points in turn: first temperance, then Nature's excess, then chastity.

782. *sun-clad*, radiant, lustrous; cf. 425. There is perhaps a glance at *Revelation* xii. 1: "And there appeared a great wonder in heaven; a woman clothed with the sun."

784—787. Editors quote Milton's description in the *Apology for Smectymnuus* of his early studies: "Thus, from the laureat fraternity of poets, riper years and the ceaseless round of study and reading led me to the shady spaces of philosophy; but chiefly to the divine volumes of Plato, and his equal Xenophon: where, if I should tell ye what I learnt of chastity and love, I mean that which is truly so, whose *charming cup is* only virtue, which she bears in her hand to those who are worthy; (the rest are cheated with *a thick intoxicating potion, which a certain sorceress, the abuser of love's name, carries about;*) and how the first and chiefest office of love begins and ends in the soul, producing those happy twins of her divine generation, knowledge and virtue: with such abstracted sublimities as these, it might be worth your listening, readers," *P. W.* III. 119—121. So in the same treatise: "Having had the doctrine of Holy Scripture, unfolding those chaste and *high mysteries* with timeliest care infused, that 'the body is for the Lord'." The verbal resemblances indicate that Milton in writing these sentences recollected his earlier vindication of the "serious doctrine of Virginity." Cf. also 525, 526.

784. *Thou hast nor ear.* Cf. 997. Comus cannot hear, or hearing will not understand, her praise of purity, just as in *Arcades*, 72, 73, "the gross unpurged ear" of humanity may not catch the sound of the music from the spheres.

785. *notion*, idea, or perhaps doctrine.

mystery; used in its Scriptural sense of a truth specially revealed to men (=Gk. μυστήριον). Cf. 1 *Cor.* ii. 7, "we speak the wisdom of God in a mystery, even the hidden wisdom."

788. *art worthy*, dost deserve, in a bad sense. A rare use, but cf. *The Winter's Tale*, II. 3. 109, "worthy to be hanged."

790. *dear*, i.e. to Comus—of which he is so proud.

gay, i.e. in appearance ('showy') rather than in spirit; cf. "dazzling," 791.

791. *fence;* cf. the phrases 'to fence with a question,' and 'to parry' it, i.e. not answer it straightforwardly.

792. *convinced*, proved to be in the wrong, refuted. Cf. *Job* xxxii. 12, "behold, there was none of you that convinced Job, or that answered his words."

793. *uncontrolled*, uncontrollable, i.e. irresistible; cf. "uncontrolled tide," *Lucrece*, 645. See note on 349.

794. *rapt;* see G.

797. *brute*, dull, unsympathising; the *bruta tellus* of Horace, *Odes*, I. xxxiv. 9. Cf. Tennyson, *In Memoriam*, CXXVII., "The brute earth lightens to the sky."

her nerves, her strength; the sinews (see 660, note) being regarded as the seat of strength.

798. *thy magic structures;* Comus's "stately palace."

801. *set off;* properly 'shown to the best advantage,' as a jewel by its setting: hence 'improved by,' and so 'made more forcible,' as here.

800—806. An aside.

802—805. i.e. a shudder of horror comes upon me, though not mortal, like that which comes upon Saturn's followers when Jove thunders in his wrath and dooms them to be chained in the lowest hell.

803. *the wrath of Jove*, the wrathful Jove; an abstract turn of phrase imitated from the Latin.

804. *Speaks thunder and chains;* another classical turn of phrase, the verb being used literally with the first noun (='thunders') and figuratively with the second (='sentences them to imprisonment'). This double use of a verb is the figure of speech called *zeugma* ('a joining').

Erebus, Gk. ἔρεβος, darkness; a region of utter darkness in the nether world.

805. *Saturn*, the Latin god *Saturnus* identified with Gk. *Cronus*. The legend was that at one time Cronus and the Titans ruled in Olympus, till Zeus (having obtained thunder and lightning from the Cyclops) hurled them into the nether world, and ruled instead. The warfare (*Titano-machia*) of the gods and Titans is often referred to in classical writers, and is to some extent the model followed by Milton in describing in *Paradise Lost* the downfall of Satan and his followers.

I must dissemble. This hackneyed phrase occurs in Marlowe's *Jew of Malta*, IV.; cf. also 2 *Henry VI.* V. I. 13.

808. *the canon laws of our foundation*, the fixed rules and regulations of our establishment (or institution). An allusion to the technical phrase *canon law*="ecclesiastical law as laid down in decrees of the Pope and statutes of Councils"—*Dr Murray.*

Warton notes that Milton in his prose tracts uses *canon* in contemptuous combinations: e.g. "canon iniquity'; "an insulting and only canon-wise prelate." To the Puritan poet anything suggestive of Catholicism was distasteful. Gk. κανών =rule.

The same sarcastic purpose is seen in Milton's applying the terms "consistory" (*Par. Regained*, I. 42) and "conclave" (*Par. Lost*, I. 795) to the assembly of the evil angels: the former word being specially used of the council-chamber of the Pope and the Cardinals, and the latter of the meeting at which the Cardinals elect a Pope. Perhaps a similar sneer underlies "pontifical" in *Par. Lost*, X. 313.

foundation; spoken as though Comus represented some religious institution. "God save the foundation" is Dogberry's petition, *Much Ado About Nothing*, V. I. 327, that being the form of thanks usual among those who received alms at the door of a monastery—*Schmidt.*

809, 810. "Ancient physicians recognised four *Cardinal Humours*, viz. blood, choler, phlegm and melancholy (black bile), regarded by them as determining, by their conditions and proportions, a person's physical and mental qualities and dispositions" (*Century Dictionary*). This old physiology of the 'humours' is often alluded to by Milton; cf. *Samson Agonistes*, 600, and *Par. Lost*, XI. 543—546; in each passage he speaks of depression of spirits as caused by the black bile or humour (= *melancholy* from Gk. μέλας, black + χολή, bile). There is much on the subject in Burton's *Anatomy of Melancholy*.

812, 813. The alliteration is remarkable.

814. If the "false enchanter" had not escaped there would have been no place for Sabrina, whom Milton introduces of course out of compliment to his audience.

815. Cf. 653, "seize his wand."

816, 817. i.e. incantations spoken backwards which are potent in breaking a spell. "As old as the belief in magic itself seems to have been the belief that the effects of enchantment could be undone by reversing the spell, pronouncing the words of charm backward etc...Mesmerists now reverse their 'passes' to restore their patients"—*Masson*. In *The Faerie Queene* Britomart frees Amoret by forcing the enchanter "his charmes back to reverse" (III. 12. 36).

822. *Melibœus*, another pastoral name in classical poetry, e.g. of one of the shepherds in Vergil's first *Eclogue*; the second part of the word seems connected with βοῦς, an ox. There is thought to be a sly allusion here to Geoffrey of Monmouth, the Chronicler whose account of Sabrina Milton followed, but who was not the "soothest," i.e. most trustworthy, of writers. The reference would be parallel to Spenser's mentioning Chaucer under the pastoral pseudonym *Tityrus*. See *The Shepheards Calender*, *Februarie*, 92, 93, with the *Glosse*.

823. *soothest*, truest; see G.

824—842. For the Story of Sabrina see *Appendix*.

825. *sways*, rules; cf. 18, 19. *curb*; cf. "bridle in," 887.

830. *stepdame*; not strictly accurate. But it is a very artistic inaccuracy because it suggests a cause of hostility between Guendolen and Sabrina other than the real cause, and dissociates the "guiltless damsel" from her guilty mother Estrildis, whom the poet purposely omits.

834. *pearled*, adorned with pearl, which is so frequently associated with the deities of river or sea. Thus a stage direction in Ben Jonson's *Masque of Blackness* tells us that the nymphs wore on "the front, ear, necks and wrists, ornament of the most choice and orient pearl." Doubtless Sabrina and her water-nymphs would be adorned thus when they appear later on. Pearls are found in many parts of Great Britain; particularly in some of the Welsh rivers, e.g. the Esk and Conway.—*Streeter*.

835. *Nereus*, the father of the Nereids, dwelling at the bottom of the sea. Leaf remarks that he appears in Homer as πατὴρ γέρων and ἅλιος γέρων ('old man of the sea'), but is never mentioned by name. "The epithets given him by the poets refer to his *old age*, *his kindliness*, and his trustworthy knowledge of the future"—*Classical Dictionary*. Cf. Vergil's *grandævus Nereus* ("*aged* Nereus"), *Georgics*, IV. 392.

836. *reared*, raised; rather a favourite word with Milton. *lank*, drooping; A.-S. *hlanc*, 'bending.'

837. *his daughters;* the 50 sea-nymphs called Nereids.

838. i.e. vessels into which nectar (or liquid fragrant as nectar) had been poured and in which asphodel flowers were floating.

lavers; see Glossary, and cf. *Samson Agonistes*, 1727, 1728:

"With lavers pure, and cleansing herbs, wash off
The clotted gore."

nectared; cf. 479. *asphodil;* a plant of the lily genus, its commonest varieties being the yellow and the white ('King's Spear'). It is one of the favourite flower-names in poetry, from the classical legend that the Elysian fields were covered with 'Asphod*el*' (the modern form of the name).

839. Clearly a reminiscence of *Hamlet*, I. 5. 63, 64:

"And in the porches of mine ears did pour
The leperous distilment."

840. The editors find here echoes of the *Iliad;* e.g. of XIX. 38, where Thetis anoints the dead body of Patroclus; and XXIII. 186, where Aphrodite performs a similar office (and "ambrosial" is said of the olive oil used).

841. i.e. a change that quickly made her immortal; cf. "goddess," 842.

842. This idea of a river having a tutelary deity who dwelt in and ruled over it is essentially classical.

845. *Helping*, remedying. *urchin blasts*. Usually *urchin* signifies a hedgehog, but from the belief that evil spirits sometimes took the form of a hedgehog, *urchin* came to mean a sprite or wicked elf. Cf. *The Merry Wives of Windsor*, IV. 4. 49, "Like urchins, ouphs and fairies." So *urchin blasts*=mildew upon corn, diseases in cattle, etc., sent by evil spirits. From *urchin*='imp' comes the sense 'small boy.' Lat. *ericius*, a hedgehog.

ill-luck signs. For the typical tricks played by fairies see *L' Allegro*, 101—104, and *A Midsummer-Night's Dream*, II. 1. 32—57, where Puck (Robin Goodfellow) is described as a "*shrewd* and knavish sprite." Cf. also Edgar's account in *King Lear*, III. 4. 123, of the "foul fiend."

846. *the;* as if he had some particular elf in view; probably Robin Goodfellow, the influence of *A Midsummer-Night's Dream* on Milton being so strong. *shrewd*, wicked, mischievous; see G.

848. *the shepherds at their festivals;* cf. 171—177.

850. A recognised method in pastoral verse of showing gratitude. Cf. Phineas Fletcher, *Piscatorie Eclogues*, II. 8 (speaking of the river Cam):

"Ungrateful Chame! how oft thy Thyrsis crown'd
With songs and garlands thy obscurer head."

851. Cf. *Lyc.* 144. *daffodil;* see G.

852. *the old swain;* Melibœus (822). What follows was an addition by Milton to the account of the Chronicler.

Song; a solo, sung by Lawes.

862. No doubt, when Sabrina rises later on she wears a chaplet of lilies and other water-flowers.

863. *amber-dropping*, i.e. wet with the amber-coloured water of the river. Compare *Par. Lost*, III. 359, where the River of Bliss "Rolls o'er Elysian flowers her amber stream"; and Gray's *Progress of Poesy*, II. 3, "Mæander's amber waves." Exactly similar is Horace's phrase 'the yellow Tiber,' *vidimus flavum Tiberim* (*Od.* I. 2. 13), and in Matthew Arnold's *Sohrab and Rustum*, "The yellow Oxus." In these cases the adjective certainly adds to the picturesqueness of the narrative; and it may be literally true, because the tint of the river is affected by

the soil of the land through which it flows. Of course, Sabrina herself will have amber hair to symbolise the river-waves.

Some editors take *amber=ambergris* (the perfume), as in *Samson Agonistes*, 720, and compare 105, 106.

dropping. It has been objected that Sabrina is still *beneath* the water, where there could not be "drops"; but the general sense may be simply 'wet, dripping with.'

865. *lake;* a complimentary description of the broad Severn. Cf. *lacus* used of the Tiber in *Æneid*, VIII. 74.

867. Note that, as Sabrina is a river-goddess, the invocation mentions only deities of the waters, and that each is described in terms taken direct from the classics, more especially from Homer. It may seem a little inappropriate that a British river-nymph should be associated so closely with Greek and Latin divinities, but Milton has forestalled the objection by placing "this Isle" (Britain) under the charge of the classical deity Neptune and his "tributary gods" (18—29).

868. *In name of*, i.e. we implore you in the name of. These lines (867—889) are the "adjuring verse" (858).

great Oceanus. The god of the river Oceanus supposed by the ancients to encircle the world; called "the Atlantic *stream*" in 97, the epithet 'Atlantic' being applied in classical writers to this great river or sea of the west. He is addressed first as being "the father of all streams," *Iliad*, XIV. 245. *great*. The epithets applied to him in the *Iliad* emphasise his power; cf. XXI. 195: "the great strength of deep-flowing Ocean, from whom all rivers flow."

869. *earth-shaking*. In Homer, the Greek god of the sea, Poseidon, is 'the earth-shaker' (*κινητὴρ γᾶς, ἐννοσίγαιος, ἐνοσίχθων*), "either because he is the lord of earthquakes or simply because the waves of the sea are for ever beating the land"—*Leaf*. Neptune being identified in the Roman poets with the Greek deity, "all the attributes of the latter are transferred to the former"—*Classical Dictionary*.

mace, i.e. the trident (27) which he used as sceptre. For *mace*= 'sceptre' cf. *Henry V*. IV. 1. 278, "the mace, the crown imperial."

870. "*Tethys*, the wife of Oceanus, and mother of the gods (see *Iliad*, XIV. 201), may well be supposed to have *a grave, majestic pace*, and Hesiod calls her *the venerable Tethys;* Theogony, 368"—*Newton*.

871. *hoary...wrinkled;* cf. "*aged* Nereus," 835.

872. Referring to Proteus. *Carpathian;* he dwelt in the isle of *Carpathos*, between Rhodes and Crete. *wizard;* he had the power of foreseeing events and of changing his shape (hence *Protean*=shifting, changeable). Homer calls him "infallible" (νημερτής) and "that ancient one of the magic arts" (*Odyssey*, IV. 349, 460). *hook*, i.e. shepherd's hook (cf. *Lyc.* 120), because Proteus was shepherd of the flocks (seals) of Poseidon.

873. *Triton;* he acted as the trumpeter or herald of the marine deities, summoning or dismissing their assemblies with his "winding shell" (*concha*) or trumpet. In the lower part of his body he resembled a fish: hence "scaly." *winding*= 'crooked,' 'curling;' cf. Wordsworth's line, "Or hear old Triton blow his wreathèd horn," from the sonnet "The world is too much with us." But 'sounding' is a possible sense; we speak of 'winding a horn.' So Keats calls him "shell-winding Triton," *Endymion*, II. See *Lyc.* 89.

874. *Glaucus;* the Bœotian fisherman who eating of a certain herb became metamorphosed into a sea-god. He, too, like many sea-deities, possessed the gift of prophesying; hence "soothsaying" and "spell." He was associated with the expedition of the Argonauts, having built the ship Argo.

875. Milton alludes to Ino, daughter of Cadmus (*Odyssey*, V. 333—335), wife of Athamas, by whom she had two sons. Athamas in a fit of madness killed one son; she with the other plunged into the sea, and became a sea-goddess, under the name *Leucothea* (λευκός, white+θεά, a goddess).

"She, being *Leucothea* or the *white goddess*, may well be supposed to have *lovely hands*, which I presume the poet mentioned in opposition to Thetis' *feet* afterwards"—*Newton*. There is, indeed, a direct allusion to her hands in *Odyssey*, V. 462.

876. *her son;* Melicertes; after his deification he was called Palæmon, whom the Romans identified with Portumnus, the god of harbours (Lat. *portus*, a harbour).

877. *Thetis;* one of the Nereids, wife of Peleus and mother of Achilles.

tinsel-slippered, with flashing feet; a variation of Homer's epithet for Thetis, viz. ἀργυρόπεζα, 'silver-footed,' which Milton perhaps avoided using because it had become hackneyed.

Browne had already written in *Britannia's Pastorals*, book II:

"When Triton's trumpet (with a shrill command)
Told silver-footed Thetis was at hand";

and Ben Jonson had used *silver-footed* more than once in his Masques (e.g. in *Neptune's Triumph* and *Pan's Anniversary*). *Tinsel* suggests a silvery, flashing surface, such as that of the shining cloth called *tinsel*, to which the Elizabethans often refer. Hero's wedding-dress in *Much Ado About Nothing*, III. 4. 22, was trimmed with tinsel. F. *étincelle*, a spark.

879. *Parthenope;* one of the Sirens (cf. 253); said to have been buried at Naples. Her name occurs as a synonym of Naples. Thus Wordsworth, in the fine sonnet composed on the eve of Scott's voyage to Italy, writes

"Be true,
Ye winds of ocean, and the midland sea,
Wafting your charge to soft Parthenope."

So in Landor's *Thoughts of Fiesole*:

"Sorrento softer tale may tell,
Parthenopè sound louder shell."

880. *Ligea;* another of the Sirens; appropriately named λιγεία = 'shrill-voiced.' The reference to her "soft alluring locks" may have been suggested by Vergil, who describes Ligea and several sea-nymphs "with their bright locks flowing over their white necks" (*Georgics*, IV. 337). Otherwise, as Masson notes, it is rather the mermaids of northern mythology who comb their tresses, like the faithless wife in Matthew Arnold's *Forsaken Merman*, and Tennyson's *Mermaid*.

881. *diamond rocks;* see 732, note.

882. *sleeking*. Cf. Tennyson's description of the shepherds tending the dead Paris, "One raised the Prince, one sleek'd the squalid hair" (*The Death of Œnone*).

883, 884. Cf. *Arcades*, 96, 97.

885. How exquisitely the double alliteration suggests the effort of rising.

heave, lift. Cf. *L'Allegro*, 145, "That Orpheus' self may heave his head." So in *Par. Lost*, I. 211; *Samson Agonistes*, 197.

886. *coral-paven*. *Paven* did not necessarily imply artificial work. The "paved fountain" in *A Midsummer-Night's Dream* II. 1. 84 was "a fountain with pebbly bottom" (Clarendon Press

ed. of that play). Here the floor of the river-bed is supposed to be of coral.

Sabrina rises. From the stage-directions in other Masques it may be inferred that the appearance of the river-goddess would be effected as in a modern theatre. Part of the centre of the stage would be displaced, and through the aperture the goddess would rise, seated in her car and surrounded by a group of nymphs in picturesque dresses. The introduction in this way of deities—especially deities of the sea or rivers—was a favourite device with Masque-writers, as it gave scope for the skill of Inigo Jones, the great architect, who often designed the scenery and stage-mechanism of Masques.

890. *rushy-fringed.* A specimen of what Earle calls the 'literary' compound; that is to say, the composite word created purely for picturesque effect and confined to literature. He notes that Milton, Keats and Tennyson are conspicuous for their use of this artifice of language. Cf. "flowery-kirtled," 254; in each the simpler compound would be with a noun, not adjective—e.g. '*rush*-fringed.'

893. *agate.* Derived from the name of the river Achates in Sicily, where it is said the agate was first found.

azurn, sky-blue; see G.

894. *turkis*, turquoise; see G.

895. The line illustrates Milton's way of always correcting his work for the better. In the *Cambridge MS.* the verse runs: "That my rich wheel inlays." This is practically a repetition of the previous couplet, and we miss the pretty idea in "strays." With the cancelled line cf. *Par. Lost*, IV. 701.

897. *printless*, that leave no mark. From *The Tempest*, V. 34:

> "And ye that on the sands with printless feet
> Do chase the ebbing Neptune."

898. *velvet;* soft as velvet; one of the stock epithets of "poetic diction." Criticising the phrase "Idalia's velvet-green" (i.e. smooth lawn) in Gray's *Progress of Poesy*, Johnson said: "an epithet or metaphor drawn from Nature ennobles Art; an epithet or metaphor drawn from Art degrades Nature."

899. Vergil had said much the same thing of Camilla, and others have said it since.

903. The metre employed from this point to the end is

much used in the Masques of Ben Jonson and other Masque-writers; perhaps because it lent itself easily to musical recitative. Cf. many of the fairy-speeches in *A Midsummer-Night's Dream.*

904. Cf. 852, 853.

907. *unblessed,* cursed; cf. 571.

908—921. The editors have noticed here, and indeed throughout the last part of *Comus,* echoes of *The Faithful Shepherdess.* Doubtless, Milton had read Fletcher's Pastoral.

912. *fountain,* i.e. the river's source, where its water is purest.

914. *Thrice;* always a significant number.

916. Cf. "enchanted chair" in the stage direction at 658.

918. *moist,* i.e. with the "drops from her fountain pure" (912). *cold;* in antithesis to the last line ("heat"), and implying 'chaste.'

919. *his,* its. We must suppose that during lines 911—918 the Lady gradually indicates her recovery of freedom.

921. *Amphitrite;* wife of Poseidon (Neptune) and goddess of the sea. The name often stands for 'the sea.' Compare Shelley's *Lines written among the Euganean Hills:*

> "Underneath day's azure eyes
> Ocean's nursling, Venice, lies,
> Amphitrite's destined halls."

923. *Anchises' line.* The legendary genealogy being: Anchises father of Æneas; Æneas father of Ascanius; Ascanius of Silvius; Silvius of Brutus; Brutus of Locrine. Cf. 827, 828.

924—937. This invocation is in the manner of pastoral verse. In Browne's *Britannia's Pastorals,* I. 2, the friendly nymph of a stream receives the same kind of blessings. But if a river proved unkind—e.g. drowned the poet's friend—it was covered with curses. Thus we find an imprecation upon the Cam in Phineas Fletcher's *Piscatorie Eclogues,* II. 23:

> "Let never myrtle on thy banks delight—
> Let dirt and mud thy lazie waters seize,
> Thy weeds still grow, thy waters still decrease."

924. *brimmed,* full to the river's brim. Tennyson's "Brook" flows along "To join the brimming river."

927. *hills.* The Welsh mountains where the Severn rises.

928. *singed air,* i.e. the torrid air of Midsummer when the dog-star prevails. Cf. *Lyc.* 138, note. The participle has an active force='singeing, i.e. scorching.'

929. *tresses;* "the foliage of the trees and shrubs along the banks"—*Dr Bradshaw.*

931. The water of the river is likened to liquefied crystal.

932. *billows.* By this time Milton has traced the Severn down to Gloucester, where it becomes an arm of the sea, and as such may be said to have 'billows.' "Severn *Sea*" is a common local name for the upper part of the Bristol Channel.

933. *beryl;* a yellow crystal. L. *beryllus* (Gk. βήρυλλος), whence F. *briller*=to sparkle like a beryl.

934. I think now that *lofty head* must be taken literally of the river's *source* contrasted with its *banks* (936)—the general sense being, 'May many a tower and terrace (i.e. some great city) encircle, like a crown, your source in the Welsh hills, and may groves adorn your banks at intervals along your course to the sea.'

Some interpret *head* of the river itself, not merely its source; compare Dr Bradshaw's paraphrase: "May you be crowned with many a tower and terrace on your lofty sides, and here and there with groves of myrrh on the banks." But surely "on your lofty sides" is the same as "on the banks," whereas some contrast between *head* and *banks* seems to be intended.

The metaphor in 934, 935 suggests, possibly was suggested by, the phrase στεφάνωμα πύργων, 'the encircling towers,' literally 'the crown of towers' (round Thebes), in the *Antigone*, 121, of Sophocles. Here the metaphor gains appropriateness from the fact that the river is personified as a maiden.

936, 937. Strictly dependent on the construction in 934, 935, i.e. 'and may thy head be crowned with groves upon thy banks.' But from *thy head* we can easily supply *thou*='mayst *thou* be crowned with groves upon thy banks.'

937. The landscape is obviously ideal, "groves of myrrh and cinnamon" being common enough in the land of poetic fancy, but not found in the West of England.

942. *waste,* unnecessary; cf. "waste fertility," 729.

945. *this gloomy covert,* i.e. the wood in which the "stately palace" of Comus lay. Either the scene is still in this palace, but the stage is so arranged that the wood can be seen outside; or there has been some change of scenery so as to represent the original wood again instead of the interior of the palace.

949. *gratulate,* welcome; cf. "And gratulate his safe return to Rome," *Titus Andronicus,* I. 221.

then come in Country Dancers. Technically this is the second *Anti-masque;* the first being the "monstrous rout" at line 92.

958, 959. A variation on *L'Allegro,* 97, 98.

960. i.e. not in the rude style of a peasants' dance.

962. *court guise,* i.e. an elegant bearing such as befits a dance like the *pavane* or *minuet.*

964. *mincing,* moving with dainty steps; F. *mince,* 'dainty, neat.' Editors refer to *Isaiah* iii. 16. *Dryades*=wood-nymphs; from δρῦς, an oak. With the rhyme, cf. *Lyc.* 154—156.

965. *lawns;* see 568.

Song. No doubt there were dances ("other trippings") before and after it. Characters not named would take part in them, as well as the Lady, the two Brothers and the Spirit.

966. For the actors to come forward and address some member, or members, of the audience was not unusual in Masques. Thus in Shirley's *Triumph of Peace* the chorus twice advance to the front of the stage and salute the king and queen.

970. *timely,* early; as always in Shakespeare; cf. *The Comedy of Errors,* I. I. 139, "happy were I in my timely death."

972. *assays,* trials, tests; see G.

976—980. The metrical and general resemblance of these verses to *The Tempest,* V. I ("Where the bee sucks"), has often been noticed. It is to me clear that from line 976 to the close Milton's conception of the Attendant Spirit owed much to Shakespeare's Ariel, and to Puck in *A Midsummer-Night's Dream.* As already explained, the Epilogue spoken at the actual performance of *Comus* began at line 1012. Lines 976—1011 had been used at the outset.

976. *the ocean;* the regular classical term for the great sea of the west (the Atlantic) in which tradition placed the "happy isles...thrice happy isles" (*Par. Lost* III. 567) containing the Gardens of the Hesperides.

977—979. i.e. those happy regions where the sun ever shines in the broad heaven.

clime; see G. 'Eye of day, or heaven' is a favourite phrase for the sun in Elizabethan poetry. Cf. Milton's Sonnet to the nightingale, "Thy liquid notes that close the eye of day." Line 979 is practically from Vergil, *Æneid,* VI. 887.

980. *There;* in those "happy climes." *liquid*, clear, brilliant (Lat. *liquidus*).

982. *Hesperus;* see 393—396, note.

983. *golden;* transferred from the apples to the tree itself.

984. *crisped*, i.e. by the wind ruffling the leaves; more often applied to a breeze stirring the surface of water, as in *Childe Harold* IV. 211, "I would not their vile breath should crisp the stream."

985. *spruce*, dainty, prettily adorned, i.e. with flowers etc.

986. *Graces*, Lat. *Gratiæ*, Gk. χάριτες; three goddesses (Euphrosyne, Aglaia, Thalia) who personified the refinements and elevated joys of life.

Hours, Lat. *Horæ*, Gk. ὧραι; goddesses personifying the seasons of the year; the course of the seasons was symbolically described as "the dance of the *Horæ*" (cf. *Par. Lost*, V. 394, 395). Classical writers often mention them along with the Graces. The Graces and Hours were favourite allegorical *dràmatis personæ* in Masques.

rosy-bosomed; Gk. ῥοδόκολπος. Cf. Gray, *Ode on the Spring*,

"Lo! where the rosy-bosom'd Hours,
Fair Venus' train, appear";

and Thomson, "the rose-bosomed Spring" (*Spring*, 1010).

A very notable feature of English poetry from the Restoration to (about) the French Revolution, i.e. during the period beginning with Dryden and ending with Johnson (died 1784), is the great influence of the diction of Milton's poems, *especially* the minor poems. In Dryden and Pope, Collins and Gray and Thomson, and the minor writers, we are struck by constant echoes of *L'Allegro and Il Penseroso*, *Lycidas* and *Comus*—thanks, no doubt, to their extreme verbal felicity, their fulfilment of Coleridge's definition of poetry as the right words in the right places.

989. *west winds*, the 'Zephyrs' of classical poetry; traditionally the fragrance-laden winds; cf. again Gray's *Ode on the Spring:*

"While, whisp'ring pleasure as they fly,
Cool Zephyrs thro' the clear blue sky
Their gather'd fragrance fling."

990. *cedarn alleys*, paths bordered by cedar trees. *cedarn;* formed from the noun, i.e. *cedar-n*, like *silver-n*, *leather-n*.

Now purely poetic; cf. Matthew Arnold, *The New Sirens*, "The slumb'rous cedarn shade."

991. Cf. "All thy garments smell of myrrh, and aloes, and cassia," *Psalm* xlv. 8.

nard, spikenard (i.e. spiked nard, *nardus spicatus*), a fragrant Indian root. The word comes from Sanskrit *nal*, to smell. Probably the Jews got the perfume and its name through the Persians. *cassia*, a spice of the nature of cinnamon, as in the Bible. *Cassia* is now used of an extract of laurel-bark.

992. *Iris;* the goddess of the rainbow (cf. "bow") and messenger of the gods, especially of Juno. Cf. the 'Masque' in *The Tempest*.

993. *blow*, make to bloom; rarely transitive. See *Lyc*. 48.

994—997. On the rhymes see 511, 512, note.

purpled, embroidered; see G. *Elysian*, heavenly; see 257.

997. *if your ears be true*, "i.e. if you have minds fine enough to perceive the real meaning of the legends I am about to cite"—*Masson*.

These legends of Venus and Adonis, Cupid and Psyche, have often been treated from a mundane, indeed sensual point of view; whereas we ought to see in them an elevated, spiritual significance which is hidden from those whose vision is dimmed by sin. Such seems the general bearing of the passage.

999—1002. The legend of Adonis, the youth beloved by the Greek goddess Aphrodite (=the Roman goddess Venus), was that he was killed in the chase by a wild boar, mourned for by Aphrodite, and at last, in consideration of her sorrow, suffered by the gods of the lower world to spend six months in every year upon earth with her. His yearly return to earth was celebrated by religious rites such as Theocritus describes in the xvth *Idyl*. Usually the legend is explained as being a symbolisation of the annual return of spring: "in the Asiatic religions Aphrodite was the fructifying principle of nature, and Adonis appears to have reference to the death of nature in winter and its revival in spring—hence he spends six months in the lower and six in the upper world"—*Classical Dictionary*. In fact Adonis was regarded as the god of the Solar year.

The story is of Phœnician origin, Adonis being the same as Tammuz ('Sun of Life') mentioned in *Ezekiel* viii. 14, "behold, there sat women weeping for Tammuz." See the fuller reference in *Par. Lost*, I. 446—452, and *Nativity Ode*, 204, "In vain the *Tyrian* [Phœnician] maids their *wounded Thammuz* mourn."

His yearly six months on earth were supposed to be spent in the 'Garden of Adonis,' which became a synonym of an exquisitely lovely spot like the Garden of Eden. The chief reference to it in the classics is in Pliny's *Natural History*, XIX. 4. The allusion is a favourite with poets. See *Par. Lost*, IX. 439, 440; 1 *Henry VI*. I. 6. 7; Spenser's *Hymne in Honour of Love*, 22—28; Keats's *Endymion*, II.; and above all, *The Faerie Queene*, III. 6. 29—49, which Milton had undoubtedly in his thoughts here. For like Milton Spenser treats the story as an allegory of the immortality of love and says (III. 6. 46—48) that after his restoration to life Aphrodite would not let Adonis descend to the nether world but kept him in the 'Garden.'

Milton has not, I believe, any classical authority for associating the Gardens of Adonis and of the *Hesperides*, but his purpose here is to bring together all the most beautiful things in nature of which classical legend tells, and thus form an ideal region, a paradise of perfect loveliness. And he exercises the privilege of making the classics serve his poetic purpose.

Lines 999—1002 remind us of Tennyson's picture in the *Palace of Art* of King Arthur after his "passing" to the island-valley:

"Or mythic Uther's deeply-wounded son
  In some fair space of sloping greens
Lay, dozing in the vale of Avalon,
  And watch'd by weeping queens."

1000. *Waxing*, growing. Cf. Germ. *wachsen*, to grow.

1002. *the Assyrian queen*, i.e. Aphrodite, whose "worship was of Eastern origin, and probably introduced by the Phœnicians to the islands of Cyprus, Cythera and others, from whence it spread all over Greece. She appears to have been originally identical with Astarte, called by the Hebrews Ashtoreth, and her connection with Adonis clearly points to Syria"—*Classical Dictionary*. Identical with the *Assyrian* goddess *Istar*.

1003—1011. He passes to a yet more spiritual love: not on earth, as that of Adonis and Aphrodite, but in heaven itself.

The myth of Psyche is an allegory of the human soul (ψυχή) which, after undergoing trials and tortures, is purified by pain and eventually reaches happiness and rest. Milton wished to emphasize the sanctity of love still more, by showing that there is a place for it among the gods. "Comus," says Masson, "had misapprehended Love, knew nothing of it except its vile counterfeit...had been outwitted and defeated. But there *is* true Love, and it is to be found in Heaven." The idea is well illustrated by *Par. Lost*, VIII. 615—629, where Adam questions the archangel Raphael—"Love not the Heavenly Spirits?"—and receives the reply—"without Love no happiness."

No doubt Milton was influenced by that conception of Divine Love of which Plato treats in the *Phædrus* and elsewhere. The story of Cupid and Psyche is applied in much the same way by Spenser, *The Faerie Queene*, III. 6. 49, 50. See also Keats's *Ode to Psyche*.

1003. Cf. *Midsummer-Night's Dream*, II. 1. 29, "By fountain clear or spangled starlight sheen." *sheen;* akin to Germ. *schön*, beautiful.

1004. *advanced*, raised aloft.

1011. *Youth and Joy*. Later in life Milton made Virtue and Knowledge the offspring of pure Love; see note on 784—787. "Editors find a reason for this in the greater gravity of spirit which eight years had brought upon Milton"—*Masson*.

1012. A series of reminiscences of Shakespeare; cf. *A Midsummer-Night's Dream*, IV. 1. 102, 103, where Oberon says: "We the globe can compass soon;" and II. 1. 175, Puck's words, "I'll put a girdle round about the earth," i.e. make the circuit of the universe; and *Macbeth*, III. 5. 23, 24:

"Upon the corner of the moon
There hangs a vaporous drop profound."

There and here (1017) *corner*='horn' (Lat. *cornu*), as in *cornua lunæ*; cf. Vergil's third *Georgic*, 433.

1014. *the green earth's end;* meaning probably the Cape Verd Islands—*Sympson*. Cf. *Par. Lost*, VIII. 631, "Beyond the Earth's green Cape and verdant Isles." They or the Canaries were commonly identified by the Elizabethans with the classical *Hesperidum Insulæ*.

1015. *bowed*, because in any landscape the horizon appears to come down to the earth. *welkin;* see G. *slow*, i.e. gradually.

1018—1023. These lines are particularly notable as summing up the whole teaching of the poem. The special aspect of virtue which it has depicted is, of course, "saintly chastity" (453).

And chastity (the Lady) has triumphed over the temptations of intemperance (Comus), through its own "hidden strength" (418), and through supernatural aid (the Attendant Spirit and Sabrina) such as the Elder Brother spoke of (455, 456) and the last line of the Masque promises.

1019. Ben Jonson's *Pleasure Reconciled to Virtue* (the Masque in which Comus appears) ends with a similar song in praise of Virtue.

1021. *sphery clime.* An allusion to the notion, said to have originated with Pythagoras and described by Plato in the *Republic* (x. 616, 617), of the "music of the spheres." As *popularly* understood and referred to, it was that the rapid revolution of each planet in its "sphere" or orbit (i.e. a circular space round the central earth) produced a sound, and the combination of the sounds a harmony. Poetry is full of allusions to "the great sphere-music of stars and constellations" (Tennyson, *Parnassus*). It was a favourite idea with Milton, who studied the Ptolemaic theory of the "spheres" deeply, and adopted it for the astronomical system of *Par. Lost.* Cf. *The Nativity Ode*, 125—132, Ode *At a Solemn Music*, and *Arcades*, 62—73. Perhaps Echo was called "Daughter of the sphere" (241) in allusion to the music of the spheres, i.e. as though she had her origin in it and were part of it.

sphery, belonging to the spheres.

1023, 1024. Masson notes that an interesting personal anecdote is associated with these lines, viz. that Milton wrote them, and his name, in the autograph-book (still preserved) of a foreigner whom he visited in June 1639 at Geneva, on the way home from his travels in Italy.

LYCIDAS.

The explanatory sub-title ("In this Monody" etc.) first appeared when *Lycidas* was reprinted in 1645. No doubt, Milton added it then for two reasons: first, because to the general public, who had never heard of Edward King, the point of the poem would not be very clear without some explanation of the peculiar circumstances which led to its composition; secondly, because in 1645 Milton would not fear to announce openly that the elegy contained an attack on the Church and a prophecy of its downfall, a prediction which might then have been considered partially fulfilled.

Lycidas; a common name in pastoral poetry, e.g. of the shepherd who shows himself so skilled a singer in Theocritus, *Idyl* VII., and of one of the speakers in Vergil's ninth *Eclogue*. Note the appropriateness of the names introduced throughout *Lycidas*; many are specially associated with the pastoral type of verse to which this elegy belongs.

Monody. "A species of poem of a mournful character, in which a single mourner expresses lamentation"—*Webster*. Gk. μονῳδία, from μόνος, alone + ᾠδή, a song.

Among Sylvester's *Remains* is an elegy *On Dame Hellen Branch* which he entitles a *Monodia*; see Grosart's ed. II. 329. West's poem on the death of Queen Caroline 1737, and Mason's *Musæus*, each an imitation of *Lycidas*, were described in the same way; and Matthew Arnold's *Thyrsis*.

by occasion, i.e. incidentally, taking advantage of the opportunity.

1, 2. The *laurel* or bay (Lat. *laurus*) is mentioned first because it symbolises poetry in general, being the sacred tree of Apollo, the God of song. Horace says that Pindar is 'all-deserving of Apollo's bay,' *laurea donandus Apollinari* (*Odes*, IV. 2. 9). Hence *laureate*=crowned with laurel; see 151. The publisher's preface to the 1645 edition of Milton's poems speaks of them as "evergreen and not to be blasted laurels."

The *myrtle* and *ivy* symbolise particular aspects of poetry. Myrtle is specially associated with the laurel by classical poets (e.g. Vergil, *Eclogue* II. 54); therefore Milton puts it next to the laurel. As the flower of Venus, myrtle may typify love-poetry (cf. Horace, *Odes*, III. 4. 18, 19); here it harmonises with the affection which *Lycidas* expresses for Milton's lost friend. *Ivy* symbolises poetry on the side of learning; here it typifies the wealth of classical learning in which *Lycidas* is preeminent. By plucking these three flowers, as if to weave of them a poet's garland or crown, Milton figures his return to verse-writing, and glances at the character of the poem he is about to compose.

Another explanation may be mentioned—that Milton gathers the laurels, etc. (as in the *Epitaph on the Marchioness of Winchester*, 57, 58) to lay them on the tomb of Lycidas, in fact to strew "the laureate hearse"; and that the premature plucking of them figures the premature death of his friend. But the drift of the passage (1—7) shows that Milton is thinking less of Edward King than of himself. He had not published any poetry for some years; he had intended to keep silence: the period of preparation for the poet's office of which he often speaks was not completed: but the death of his fellow-student forces him to break through this reserve, and here is his reason for doing so. Note that in this same year he had indicated, by the quotation on the title-page, some lothness to publish *Comus*.

1. *Yet once more.* Some critics would limit the reference to elegiac compositions such as Milton had written in the *Death of a fair Infant* and the *Epitaph on the Marchioness of Winchester*. But he probably means that he is here taking up again his poet's pen which had not been at work on any kind of poetry since 1634, when *Comus* was written.

Professor Hales well remarks that the plants mentioned in 1—2 are not funereal emblems, and that if Milton had wanted such, he would have chosen cypresses or flowers "that sad embroidery wear" (148).

2. *brown*=dark, as the leaves of the myrtle are. 'Dusky' (*pulla*) is Horace's epithet for the plant. *brown*; see G.

never sere, i.e. 'evergreen,' and so typical of "high *immortal* verse," *Comus*, 516. *sere;* see G. Cf. Tennyson's *Ode to Memory:*

"Those peerless flowers which in the rudest wind
Never grow sere."

3. *crude*, unripe; cf. *Comus*, 480.

4. *forced*, unwilling; it represents the poet's feeling, while *rude* represents the feeling of the plants. On the word-order see *Comus*, 207, note, and cf. 6, 42.

Shatter=disturb; cf. *Par. Lost*, x. 1066, 67.

mellowing; said of the berries rather than of the leaves. What Milton really means is the want of "inward ripeness" (cf. his second Sonnet) in himself and his poetry.

6. Cf. Keats's *Ode to Psyche:*

"O Goddess! hear these tuneless numbers, wrung
By sweet enforcement and remembrance dear."

Spenser was moved by "hard constraint" to compose his *Pastorall Œglogue* on Sir Philip Sidney. Cf. *Par. Lost*, x. 131, 132.

dear. In the English of this period *dear* "is used of whatever touches us nearly either in love or hate, joy or sorrow," Clarendon Press note on *Hamlet*, I. 2. 182 ("my dearest foe in heaven"). Shakespeare often applies it to that which is strongly disagreeable; e.g. in *Henry V*. II. 2. 181, "all your dear offences," i.e. grievous. The sense is thought to have been influenced by confusion with A.S. *déor*, grievous.

7. *Compels*. The singular sounds natural since *constraint* and *occasion* form one idea. It is a very common Elizabethan idiom. Cf. Milton's Sonnet to Lawes, 5, "Thy worth and skill exempts thee from the throng," i.e. your merit as man and musician. So in *Troilus and Cressida*, IV. 5. 168, 170, "faith and troth...bids thee." See Abbott's *Shakespearian Grammar*, p. 239.

ere his prime; in his 25th year. Cf. the account of Edward King given in the Cambridge volume in which *Lycidas* is printed: *animam deo reddidit...anno ætatis* XXV. "Complete in all things, but in yeares," says another contributor (Beaumont) to the same collection.

9. The repetition of a name was a recognised device whereby to heighten the pathetic effect; cf. Spenser's *Astrophel*, 7, 8:

"Young Astrophel, the pride of shepheards praise,
Young Astrophel, the rusticke lasses love."

peer, i.e. equal, Lat. *par*, F. *pair*. "Peers are properly the chief vassals of a lord, having *equal* rights one with another"—*Brachet*.

10. The line is from Vergil, *Eclogue* X. 3.

10, 11. *he knew Himself to sing.* Perhaps a poetic exaggeration, to increase the pathos of his friend's death. Masson has been able to trace only a few pieces of Latin verse by Edward King contributed to different collections of Cambridge poetry. It was an age, however, when poets circulated their writings in MS among their friends, and Milton may have seen verses by King which did not find their way into print. Another writer in the volume says that he "drest the Muses in the brav'st attire that ere they wore"; so that, very likely, Milton had some ground for his praise. In any case, tradition required that a shepherd should 'pipe' and sing.

build; an imitation of the figurative use of Lat. *condere*, which means (1) to put together, (2) hence to construct, build (the ordinary sense), and so (3) figuratively to compose, e.g. *condere carmen*, to compose a song, poem (Horace, *Epistles*, I. 3. 24). Editors also compare the figurative use of Gk. *πυργῶσαι* (from *πυργόω*) = to raise up to a *towering* height; cf. *πύργος*, a tower. Aristophanes in the *Frogs*, 1004, speaks of Æschylus having used majestic, towering phrases (*πυργώσας ῥήματα σεμνά*). The Greek phrase implies more than mere composition (Lat. *condere*); it connotes elevated "lofty" diction. No doubt, Milton had both *condere* and *πυργῶσαι* in mind when he wrote "build" and "lofty."

So Coleridge (in the *Nightingale*) imitating Milton:

"And many a poet echoes the conceit,
Poet who hath been building up the rhyme."

The metaphor is put even more boldly in Tennyson's *Œnone*:

"Hear me, for I will speak, and build up all
My sorrow with my song."

For the idiom *knew to* see *Comus*, 87, note.

12. *He must not*, it is not right that..., I cannot let him.

bier; because the waters *bear* the body; cf. "float." Shelley borrows Milton's phrase and applies it to Venice as resting on the waves that surround it; cf. *Lines written among the Euganean Hills*:

"If the power that raised thee here,
Hallow so thy watery bier."

A.S. *bǽr*, a bier, and *beran*, to carry, are akin to Lat. *feretrum*, a bier and *φέρετρον*.

13. *welter to*, i.e. be tossed about at the will of (*to*) the wind; akin to *wallow*, to roll about. Note Milton's favourite alliteration (*w...w*); cf. *Comus*, 87, 88, note.

14. Cf. Coleridge's lines *To A Friend:*

"Is thy Burns dead?
And shall he die unwept and sink to earth
Without the meed of *one* melodious tear?"

meed, tribute (implying 'well-deserved, well-earned,' i.e. by his merits and friendship); cf. 84.

some; in reality, he had a whole volume of laments.

tear; often used of elegiac compositions (hence "melodious"); probably in imitation of the post-classical use of *lacrima*.

Cf. Sylvester's Monody (Grosart, II. 339):

"You springs of Arts, eyes of this noble Realme,
Cambridge and Oxford, lend your learned teares."

The same writer's poem *Lacrymæ* is called on the title-page "The Spirit of Teares." Many of the collections of elegiac verse issued by the Universities bore the title *Lacrymæ*.

15. *Begin.* The invocation is cast in the pastoral style. Cf. Theocritus, *Idyl* I. 64, ἄρχετε βωκολικᾶς, Μῶσαι φίλαι, ἄρχετ' ἀοιδᾶς, "begin, ye Muses dear, begin the pastoral song!" And the refrain of Moschus's *Lament for Bion* is "Begin, ye Sicilian Muses, begin the dirge."

15, 16. The "Sisters" are the Nine Muses: the "sacred well" is the fountain Aganippe on Mt Helicon: the "seat of Jove" is the altar on the hill dedicated to Jove. It has been shown that Milton modelled these lines upon the commencement of the *Theogony* of Hesiod, who mentions the κρήνην ἰοειδέα...καὶ βωμὸν ἐρισθενέος Κρονίωνος ('violet-coloured spring and altar of mighty Zeus'). Milton invented the detail that the waters of Aganippe had their source beneath the altar, perhaps to emphasise the sanctity of the poet's inspiration. See *Il Penseroso*, 48. Note the delicacy of the dominant vowel-sound (*i*) in lines 15—17, and cf. the opening lines of *Paradise Lost*, 1—6, where the paucity of *a* sounds is as remarkable as their prevalence in the first two stanzas of Dante's *Inferno*. Milton seems to have designed to create a sense of the mysterious.

17. *sweep;* a favourite 18th century word.

19. *So*=on condition that I mourn for Lycidas; cf. *Comus*, 242. Some think there is a similarity to the Latin use of *sic* with

an imperative clause, as a "formula of invocation;" cf. *Comus*, 242, *P. L.* III. 34. See Horace *Odes* I. 3. 1—4 (*Sic te diva potens* etc.). *Muse*=one who is inspired by the Muses, a poet. Prof. Hales (in illustration of Spenser, *Prothalamion*, 152) quotes Dryden's *Absalom and Achitophel*, I:

"Sharp-judging Ariel, the muses' friend,
Himself a muse."

20. *lucky;* that wish me good fortune, e.g. *vale, vale* ('fare thee well'), and *requiescas in pace* ('mayst thou rest in *peace*,' cf. 22). *my destined urn*, the grave that is destined for me.

For *urn*=tomb, cf. Herrick (Grosart, II. 219):

"We hence must go,
Both to be blended in the urn,
From whence there's never a return."

favour, salute, invoke a blessing on. Fifty years later (1688) Dryden wrote the famous lines on Milton ("Three poets, in three distant ages born"). But perhaps the noblest poetic tributes to his memory are Wordsworth's great Sonnet, "Milton! thou shouldst be living at this hour," and Tennyson's alcaic verses.

21. Cf. Gray's "passing tribute of a sigh," *Elegy*, st. XX.; and Macaulay's beautiful poem, *A Jacobite's Epitaph:*

"Oh thou, whom chance leads to this nameless stone,
From that proud country which was once mine own,
By those white cliffs I never more must see,
By that dear language which I speak like thee,
Forget all feuds, and shed one English tear
O'er English dust. A broken heart lies here."

22. *shroud*, probably in its usual sense 'winding-sheet'; cf. "sable." Some editors interpret it 'grave.'

23—36. "Here the language of the pastoral is used, as was the rule in all such poems, to veil and at the same time express real facts. Milton and King had been fellow-students at Christ's College, Cambridge, visiting each other's rooms, taking walks together, performing academic exercises in common, exchanging literary confidences; all which, translated into the language of the pastoral, makes them fellow-shepherds, who had driven their flock a-field together in the morning, and fed it all day by the same shades and rills, not without mutual ditties on their oaten flutes, when sometimes other shepherds, or even Fauns and Satyrs, would be listening"—*Masson.*

In fact, a writer of pastoral verse is required by usage to say certain things, and Milton says them. He introduces "Fauns" because Vergil had supplied a precedent, *Eclogue* VI. 27. There are "ditties" because a shepherd without his "oaten flute" would be an anomaly. Damœtas looks on because Melibœus does so in Vergil's seventh *Eclogue.* No type of poetry is more conventional and bound by literary tradition than the pastoral.

23. *nursed*: cf. the common way of describing a university as the *alma mater* of a student.

25. *Together both*; artfully varied in 27. *high lawns*, pastures on the "hill" (23). *lawns;* see G. Of course the landscape is ideal, suggested by the constant and appropriate mention of "hills" in Theocritus's pictures of Sicilian shepherd-life. Vergil treats Italian scenery in the same imitative manner in his pastoral poems; see note on 40. When Milton refers directly to Cambridge and the peculiarly flat country round, he uses no complimentary language; cf. his first Latin *Elegy*, 11—14, where he specially complains of the lack of "woods" (39) in the neighbourhood. Tennyson as an undergraduate at Trinity wrote in a similar strain (*Life*, I. 34).

26. A glance at Milton's own habits. Cf. the *Apology for Smectymnuus*, where he speaks of himself as "up and stirring, in winter often ere the sound of any bell awake men to labour, or to devotion; in summer as oft with the bird that first rouses, or not much tardier, to read good authors," *P.W.* III. 112. Among the Milton MSS found at Netherby Hall in Cumberland and printed by the Camden Society were two scraps of Latin verse, one of which is in praise of early rising. See again 186.

eyelids of the Morn. Cf. *Job* iii. 9 (where the marginal reading is the correct rendering of the Hebrew translated in the Authorised Version "the dawning of the day"), and xli. 18, "his eyes are like the eyelids of the morning." This beautiful phrase has been borrowed by many poets; e.g. by Marlowe, "Now, Phœbus, ope the eyelids of the day" (*Jew of Malta*, II. 1. 59). Cf. also one of the *Juvenilia* of Tennyson (in whose early poems there are many Miltonic echoes), "ray-fringed eyelids of the morn."

27. *drove*, i.e. their flocks. Cf. Gray's *Elegy*, st. VII.

28. *gray-fly*. Some kind of gnat may be meant, but it is hard to say what. Sir Thomas Browne discusses in his *Vulgar Errors* (bk. III. chap. xxvii. sect. 10) the means by which flies make "that noise or humming sound," and his remarks are equally vague. Cf. Collins's *Ode to Evening*, reminiscent of Milton in every stanza:

"Or where the beetle winds
His small but sullen horn."

Some have thought that Milton means the cockchafer, "the shard-borne beetle" of *Macbeth*, III. 2. 42, which begins to stir at nightfall. But "sultry" would not be so true a description, and probably he indicates *three* periods of the day, not merely morning and eve. *winds*, sounds; cf. *Comus*, 873.

sultry serves to fix the time of the day, three periods being indicated—morning, 25—27; noon, 28; and evening, 29—31.

29. *Batten* (see G.) is more usual as an intransitive verb, 'to grow fat'; cf. Herrick, *Content in the Country:*

"We eate our own, and batten more,
Because we feed on no man's score."

with; "along with, in point of time"—*Bradshaw*. Cf. 101.

30, 31. Referring to the evening star Hesperus, whose appearance is a signal to the shepherd to fold his flocks, as in *Comus*, 93. Strictly it does not *rise*. For the original form of the lines see p. 159, and cf. Tennyson's "great Orion sloping slowly to the West," *Locksley Hall*.

32—36. See 23—36, note. We may remember that at that time Cambridge was remarkable for the number of its poets. Many collections of verse, such as the *Lycidas* volume, were issued from the University Press. *ditties*, songs; see G.

32. *were not mute*, were heard; sounded; a *meiosis*.

33. *Tempered*, attuned. Cf. *Par. Lost*, VII. 597, 598:

"All sounds on fret by string or golden wire
Tempered soft tunings."

A favourite word with Milton and Shakespeare, the underlying metaphor usually being to mix either metals or liquids until they have become fused and harmonious: hence the general idea 'agreement,' 'harmony.'

oaten; cf. 88, and see *Comus*, 345. *flute*, pipe.

34. The line is adapted from Vergil, *Eclogue* VI. 27. The

Satyri belonged to Greek, the Fauni to Latin mythology: practically they were identified by Roman writers, and regarded as divinities of the fields and country life. *with cloven heel*, because they were supposed to be half men, half goats.

36. *Damœtas;* a common name in pastoral writers; cf. Vergil, *Eclogue* III. 1. It is thought that Milton had in his mind's eye some well-known Cambridge don, e.g. William Chappell, tutor of Christ's College during part of Milton's and Edward King's residence there, but Provost of Trinity College, Dublin, at the time when *Lycidas* was written.

Masson notes that *old* is a favourite word with Milton, implying compliment; cf. 160.

37—49. The most direct expression of personal grief which *Lycidas* contains. How beautifully the simple diction of 37, 38, contrasting with what immediately precedes and follows, expresses the simplicity of sorrow. Lycidas is gone for ever, and that simple fact is more eloquent than words. The paucity of rhyme in 37—41 is perhaps intended to increase the effect of simplicity.

37. Partially quoted in Wordsworth's *Simon Lee:*

"But, oh the heavy change! bereft
Of health, strength, friends and kindred!"

38. *never must*, i.e. art destined never to.

39. *Thee...thee.* For the repetition (which emphasises the pathos) cf. Vergil's *Te veniente die, te decedente canebat*, *Georgic* IV. 466 ('of thee he sang at daybreak, of thee at eve'—referring to Eurydice, wife of Orpheus).

40. *gadding* points to the straggling growth of the vine; cf. the epithets applied to it elsewhere—'mantling,' *Par. Lost*, IV. 258, and *Comus*, 294, 'clustering,' *Par. Lost*, VII. 320.

It has often been remarked that the landscape in Vergil's pastoral verse is in many points Sicilian rather than Italian, i.e. that Vergil follows Theocritus so closely as to introduce in his descriptions features which belong to Sicily but not to Italy: thus he transfers to his native soil plants for which an Italian shepherd would have searched in vain, and assigns "hills" to the flat country about his native Mantua. Similarly, Milton, one might safely wager, never set eyes on wild "vines" near Cambridge; but they are a familiar and appropriate feature of the pastoral landscape of the classical poets, and so, appropriate or not, they are introduced in the scenery of *Lycidas*. And artistic fitness justifies the sacrifice of literal accuracy.

41. Remembering the classical story of Echo (one of the Oreads or mountain nymphs), Milton here personifies the echoes (cf. *Comus*, 243) and represents them as dwelling in woods and caves. The device of making them lament for Lycidas was borrowed from his Greek models. Cf. the *Lament for Bion*, "the Panes sorrow for thy song and the fountain-fairies in the wood made moan...and Echo in the rocks laments that thou art silent, and no more she mimics thy voice," Lang's translation of Moschus. Cf. too Shelley's *Adonais*, st. XV. In the earlier portions of that poem Shelley followed closely the classical writers of pastoral elegy; as the *Adonais* advanced, the treatment became much freer and the Greek influence declined.

44. i.e. moving their leaves like fans. *joyous;* as though the music of Lycidas, like that of Orpheus, charmed inanimate nature.

45. *canker*, i.e. the worm that preys on blossoms, especially roses. Cf. *Arcades*, 53, "Or hurtful worm with cankered venom bites." The wild or 'dog' rose is especially subject to this disease: hence in Shakespeare *canker* (or *canker-bloom*, as in Sonnet 54) sometimes means a wild-rose; cf. *Much Ado About Nothing*, I. 3. 28. From Lat. *cancer*, 'a crab'—also an 'eating tumour.' Note the emphatic, remorseless effect of the alliteration.

46. *taint-worm*, i.e. some worm that causes disease in sheep and cattle. It has been thought that Milton may be referring to the insect mentioned in the *Vulgar Errors* (bk. III. chap. xvii. sect. 11) of Sir Thomas Browne, who says, "There is found in the summer a kind of spider, called a tainct, of a red colour, and so little of body that ten of the largest will hardly outweigh a grain; this by country people is accounted a deadly poison unto cows and horses; who, if they suddenlie die, and swell thereon, ascribe their death hereto, and will commonly say, they have licked a tainct."

weanling, i.e. young; a diminutive formed from the verb *wean*, like *yeanling* from *yean*.

47. *wardrobe*. Properly used of the chest or place in which dresses are kept; then applied to the dresses themselves. Cf. *The Tempest*, IV. 222, "look what a wardrobe here is for thee!"

Perhaps we have the same metaphor of the flowers putting on their spring garb in "*well-attired* woodbine," 146.

48. *white-thorn*=the hawthorn of *L'Allegro*, 68. Shakespeare uses the same obvious way of pointing to the spring-time, *A Midsummer-Night's Dream*, I. I. 185. *blows*, i.e. flowers. See *Comus*, 993.

50. This appeal to the Nymphs, the powers of mountain (52—54) and river (55), asking why they had not been present in their usual haunts to help their favourite, is modelled partly on Theocritus, *Idyl* I. 66—69, partly on Vergil, *Eclogue* X. 9—12. The places chosen by Milton, viz. the mountains of Denbigh, the isle of Anglesey, and the banks of the Dee, were associated directly with Lycidas, *each being near to the scene of his shipwreck*. In this respect Milton has followed Theocritus, who addressed the Nymphs of those special localities with which the subject of his poem—the shepherd Daphnis—was familiar. Vergil is less definite, mentioning only the usual resorts of the Muses, Parnassus and Mt Helicon. See Warton's note on this passage. Some, however, think that by "Nymphs" Milton means the Nine Muses.

Shelley, borrowing from *Par. Lost*, VII. 1—12, Milton's conception of Urania (Gk. *οὐρανία*, the Heavenly one) as the Muse of divine poetry, makes her the mother of Adonais (just as Calliope was the mother of Orpheus), and blames her (II.) for not preventing the death of *her* "enchanting son":

"Where wert thou, mighty Mother, when he lay,
When thy son lay, pierced by the shaft which flies
In darkness? where was lorn Urania
When Adonais died?"

52. *the steep;* either Penmænmawr, or (as Warton thought) the Druid sepulchres at *Kerig-y-Druidion* in Denbigh, mentioned by Camden as a burial-place of the Druids.

53. *bards;* specially applied to Celtic poets; cf. Sidney's *Apologie for Poetrie*, "In Wales...there are good authorities to shewe the long time they had Poets which they called *Bardes*" (Pitt Press ed. p. 5).

Druids; also Celtic; cf. Irish *druidh*, an augur. In their priestly character they were "Druids," in their poetic "bards" (Newton). In primitive times the two characters are closely associated.

54. *Mona*=the isle of Anglesey. Cf. Milton's *History of Britain*: "At last over-confident of his present actions...he marches up as far as Mona, the isle of Anglesey, a populous place," *P. W.* v. 207. That the island was formerly well-wooded (cf. "*shaggy* top"), though now bare, we know from Tacitus. Warton identified Mona with the Isle of Man, on the authority of Cæsar, *Bellum Gallicum*, v. 13.

shaggy=Lat. *horrens*, *horridus* applied to woodland scenery. The picture suggested is that of a wood-clad hill-side seen in profile. Cf. Gray, *The Bard*, I. 1, "the steep of Snowdon's shaggy side."

55. *Deva*, the river Dee, which flows into the Irish Channel where King was drowned. Called *wizard* ('prophetic') because it was supposed to foretell, by changing its course, good or ill events for England and Wales, of which it forms the boundary: hence the reverence with which poets mention it. Cf. Milton's *Vacation Exercise*, 98, "ancient hallowed Dee," and "sacred Dee" in Tennyson's *Geraint and Enid*. Also, legend said that the "wizard" Merlin had dwelt by it.

56. *fondly*, foolishly.

57. *for* explains *fondly*: "it is foolish of me to dream (i.e. say to myself) 'if only the Nymphs had been there,' *for* after all what could they have done?"

58. *the Muse herself*, i.e. Calliope, the muse of epic poetry, whose name Milton introduced in the original draft of these lines. See p. 160.

59. *enchanting*, i.e. who worked by enchantment, viz. of music. *Enchant* in Shakespeare has the two meanings, to bewitch, and to delight (as in mod. E.). *Enchant* and *charm* are very similar in derivation—one from *cantus*, the other from *carmen*—and in the weakening of their respective meanings.

61—63. Referring to the death of Orpheus as told by Vergil, *Georgic* IV. 517—527, and more fully by Ovid, *Metamorphoses*, XI. 1—55: that Orpheus in his grief for Eurydice treated with disdain the Thracian women and was torn to pieces by them; his head (also his lyre, according to Ovid) being thrown into the Hebrus and carried across to Lesbos, an island off the coast of Asia Minor, where its supposed place of burial was pointed out at Antissa. Milton rewrote these lines in *Par. Lost*, VII. 32—38.

62. *the stream*, i.e. the Hebrus, the principal river of Thrace, which rising in the mountain range of Rhodope runs into the Ægean near Œnos. It is generally mentioned in connection with Orpheus; cf. Pope, *Cecilia's Day*, VI. The epithet *swift* repeats Vergil's *volucrem Hebrum* in *Æneid* I. 317, where however some editors read *Eurum* ('east wind'), on the ground that the Hebrus is not a swift-flowing river.

63. Note the effect of 'swiftness' which the initial trochee (*dówn the*) gives.

64—84. This passage interrupts the narrative. It is one of two long digressions in *Lycidas*, the other being 113—131. The interest centres in Milton himself. He proclaims his convictions, which find frequent vent in his prose writings, concerning the high office of the poet (which his contemporaries regarded so lightly), the dignity of learning and study, and the worth of true fame.

64. *what boots*, i.e. of what advantage is it? See G.

66. i.e. devote oneself to poetry. He means more than the mere composition of verse: "uncessant care" (64) and "strictly" imply rigorous self-devotion to learning and preparation for the poet's calling; cf. his *Reason of Church Government*, "labour and intense study...I take to be my portion in this life," *P. W.* II. 478.

meditate the Muse; a literal translation of a phrase in Vergil, viz. *meditari Musam* (*Eclogue* I. 2), 'to compose.' See *Comus*, 547, where it is used of composing music rather than verse. Cf. Gk. *μελετᾶν*.

thankless=profitless, because the Muse can do nothing to ward off death from the poet. Also, Milton may have been moved by the feeling that poetry had done little for him materially. Newton explains "that earns no thanks, is not thanked by the ungrateful world."

67—69. A way of saying, would it not be better to use one's poetic gifts in that light vein of love-poetry which pleases the taste of a pleasure-loving age and wins popularity for a writer?

67. *others*=contemporary poets, e.g. Herrick and Suckling (whom Milton may have known at Cambridge). There were too the followers of Ben Jonson such as Randolph, whose Muse was often erotic; and Lovelace, instanced by Mr Jerram.

use, i.e. are wont. Cf. *Psalm* cxix. 132, "be merciful unto me, as thou usest to do unto those that love thy Name."

68, 69. *Amaryllis*, *Neæra;* common names of shepherdesses in pastoral verse; therefore appropriate here. See Vergil, *Eclogue* I. 5, III. 3. These particular names are mentioned together in *Colin Clouts Come Home Againe*. Warton found here an allusion to two Latin poems by the Scotch writer George Buchanan, addressed respectively to Neæra and Amaryllis.

69. Professor Hales compares Lovelace's *To Althea*, "When I lie tangled in her hair."

70. A common sentiment similarly expressed by Spenser, *Teares of the Muses*, 454, "Due praise, that is the spur of dooing well."

clear, i.e. pure, here perhaps with the idea 'free from the taint of worldliness.' Cf. the *Remonstrant's Defence*, where Milton asks whether learning is to be sought in "the den of Plutus, or the cave of Mammon. Certainly never any clear spirit nursed up from bright influences, with a soul enlarged to the dimensions of spacious art and high knowledge, ever entered there but with scorn," *P. W.* III. 81. In the *Adonais*, st. IV. Shelley felicitously applied Milton's words to Milton himself:

"his clear Sprite
Yet reigns o'er earth, the third among the sons of light."

71. An allusion to the famous (cf. "that" = Lat. *ille*) saying in Tacitus' *Histories*, IV. 6, that ambition, literally desire of glory, is the last weakness which a wise man throws off, and even he is slow to do so (*etiam sapientibus cupido gloriæ novissima exuitur*).

72. Descriptive of Milton's life at this period. It was his instinct and habit "to study and love learning for itself, not for lucre, or any other end, but the service of God and of truth, and perhaps that lasting fame and perpetuity of praise, which God and good men have consented shall be the reward of those whose published labours advance the good of mankind," *Areopagitica*, *P. W.* II. 78.

73. *guerdon* = recompense, whether good or bad; see G.

74. *blaze*, flash of glory. Perhaps the word was influenced by the verb *blaze* = to make public, as in *Mark* i. 45, "to blaze abroad the matter"; from A.S. *blǽsan*, to blow a *blast* on a trumpet.

75. *the blind Fury;* meaning Atropos ('the inevitable'),

who, however, was one of the Fates (Gk. Μοῖραι, Lat. *Parcæ*) not one of the Furies (Erinyes). There were three Fates: Clotho who held the distaff and span the threads of each man's life; Lachesis who decided when enough had been spun, i.e. assigned the length of a man's life; and Atropos who cut the web with her shears, i.e. ended the life. The identification of one of the Fates with a Fury, though very unusual, is said to have some slight classical authority, and Milton means to imply that the cutting short of such a life as Edward King's was an act worthy only of a Fury (Bradshaw).

blind; implying 'reckless and indifferent' as to whom she strikes; that she treats genius as carelessly as the common herd. Possibly Milton was thinking of the representation in art of Fortune as a woman whose eyes are covered. Cf. *Henry V.* III. 6. 30—40. *abhorred;* see *Comus*, 535.

76. *slits*, cuts, not necessarily (as now) lengthwise.

But not the praise. Supply some verb from *slits* in the previous clause: Fate may cut the threads of life, but she cannot *touch* or *prevent* the praise that is a man's due. The omission marks the swiftness with which Phœbus meets the poet's complaint.

77. *Phœbus*=Apollo, the Greek god of song.

touched my trembling ears; as a warning to stop and a reminder of something which the poet had forgotten. Taken from Vergil, *Eclogue* VI. 3, 4. The action, says Conington, was a symbolical way of recalling a matter to a person's memory, the ear being regarded as the seat of memory.

78. i.e. fame is not of this world: it belongs to the life after death. The thought is put more fully in 81—84.

79. Understand *is*: 'nor is fame in,' etc. True fame, he means, does not consist in the dazzling appearance of success which a man presents to society; nor has it aught to do with popular applause and report. Rather, it is a thing spiritual and unworldly in its essence. Some editors connect the clause with *lies* in the next verse.

glistering; a variant form of *glitter*; cf. the older form of the proverb "all that glisters is not gold." See *Comus*, 219.

foil, the brilliant setting of a jewel; see G.

80. *nor in broad rumour lies.* Cf. Pope, *Essay on Man*, IV. 237, "What's fame? A fancied life in others' breath!"

81. *spreads;* continuing the metaphor of *plant*, 78.

by, by means of, through his influence. True fame has no reality, no existence, except through the approval of Jove.

those, the glorious, the immortal; cf. *Comus*, 2.

83. *lastly*, with the final decision; or at the last.

84. *meed*, reward. Cf. 14 and see G.

85. Here he returns to the main theme, taking up the pastoral style which had been in abeyance from 69; and as at 132 apologising to the pastoral Muse for his digression. "We find Milton twice [85, 132] checking himself for having gone beyond the limits of the pastoral"—*Stopford Brooke*.

In this section (85—102) he touches on the circumstances of Lycidas's drowning: how and when did it happen?

The fountain Arethusa, at Syracuse, was "conventionally the pastoral fountain" (Conington). It is to her that Daphnis in the first *Idyl* of Theocritus (117) addresses part of his farewell. Being in Sicily, the spring was taken to symbolise the stream of inspiration that flowed in the pastoral poetry of the Greek writers, Theocritus (see p. 128) and Moschus, natives of Greek colonies in Sicily, and Bion, who settled in Sicily and wrote in the style of Theocritus. Thus Moschus says that Bion "would ever drain a draught of Arethuse," *Idyl* III. 77, 78.

85, 86. As the spring Arethusa typified Greek pastoral verse, the river Mincius is made to represent Latin pastoral verse, i.e. the *Eclogues* or pastoral poems of Vergil (to whom "honoured" is a passing compliment). His native place Mantua was not far from the junction of the Mincius with the Po, and he "honoured" the river not only by mentioning it in his poems but by dwelling in his childhood on its banks. Cf. Crabbe's *Village*, canto I, where he condemns false pictures of rural life drawn in imitation of Vergil:

"On *Mincio's banks*, in Cæsar's bounteous reign,
If Tityrus found the Golden Age again,
Must sleepy bards the flattering dream prolong,
Mechanic echoes of the *Mantuan song*?"

(Tityrus=the shepherd in Vergil's *Eclogue* I.) Milton's description of the Mincius echoes *Georgic* III. 14, 15; cf. in particular "crowned with vocal reeds." *vocal*, because used for the shepherd's pipe; or perhaps 'whispering' with the wind.

87. *That strain*, the voice of Apollo. *higher*, i.e. than the pastoral strain which he dropped at 70. *mood*, style or tone;

from its use as a musical term, as in *Par. Lost*, I. 550, "the Dorian mood of flutes." Sometimes spelt *mode*. From Lat. *modus*; distinct from *mood*=disposition, Germ. *muth*.

88. *my oat proceeds*, i.e. now I resume my pastoral story; the instrument stands for the poet, and thus can be said to "listen." *oat;* cf. 33.

89. *the herald;* Triton. See *Comus*, 873, note.

90. *in Neptune's plea*, in the sea-god's defence, to clear him of the charge of having been "remorseless" (50) and drowned the poet's friend. *plea;* see G.

91. *felon*, because presumed to be guilty of the death of Lycidas.

93, 94. i.e. every rough-winged blast of wind. *Rugged*, *rough* and *ragged* are akin. *every...each;* see *Comus*, 19, note.

95. i.e. they knew nothing about what had happened to him.

96. *Hippotades*, son of Hippotes, i.e. Æolus. He was the god of the winds, which he kept enclosed in a mountain-cavern, and let out when he chose. The prison of the winds is described by Vergil in *Æneid* I. 52—63.

97—102. Curiously enough, the poem in the Cambridge collection by Edward King's brother implies that the vessel struck on a rock during a gale. Cf. the lines

"He, the fairest arm,
Is torn away by an unluckie storm."

Probably Henry King was better informed as to the details of the shipwreck than Milton could be. Nowhere else is there a hint that the ship was simply unseaworthy.

98. *level;* implying that the water was smooth. But the epithet also conveys an impression of the broad expanse of sea; cf. Tennyson's *Morte d'Arthur:* "And on a sudden lo! the level lake." Cf. "the flat sea," *Comus*, 375.

99. *Panope*. One of the fifty daughters (cf. "all her sisters") of Nereus; cf. *Comus*, 837.

101. An eclipse was proverbially of evil omen, the precursor of troubles; cf. *Par. Lost*, I. 596—599. Being an unlucky moment for beginning any lawful design, it was proportionately favourable to wicked schemes. The witches' caldron in *Macbeth* (IV. I. 28) has slips of yew broken off "in the moon's eclipse." Horace (*Odes* II. 13. 1—4) says that the tree which fell and nearly killed him must have been planted on a most unlucky day (*nefasto die*).

with curses, i.e. amid curses. For *with*, cf. 29.

103. Here the mourners for Lycidas are introduced. The river-deity Camus—representing, of course, Edward King's University in its grief at the loss of so admirable a scholar—is a familiar character in the academic verse of the period, especially pastoral verse like Phineas Fletcher's *Piscatorie Eclogues*. Fletcher makes him speak the prologue of the *Sicelides*, a pastoral drama acted at King's College. *Camus;* the Latinised form of *Cam*. Mr Jerram notes that *sire* is the common title of a river treated as a protecting power. He cites Livy, II. 10, *Tiberine pater;* so "father Thames" in Gray's *Ode on Eton College*, III.

went footing. Giles Fletcher (a writer whom Milton studied closely) had previously written (*Christ's Victorie on Earth*, 15):

"At length an aged syre farre off He sawe
Come slowely footing."

slow. Gray alludes more delicately to the *very* sluggish current of the Cam; cf. his Cambridge *Ode for Music* in which he celebrates the scenes "Where willowy *Camus lingers* with delight."

104. For *bonnet*=a covering for the head worn by men, cf. Bacon, *Essay* XLI., "Many say that...*Usurers* should have Orange-tawney Bonnets." *hairy*, shaggy; referring to the reeds along the Cam.

sedge; the usual adornment of river-deities, a piece of symbolism similar to the olive-branch borne by Peace. In the *Entertainments at the Coronation of James I.* Ben Jonson introduces the river-god Tamesis, with "bracelets about his wrists of willow and sedge, a crown of sedge and reed upon his head." Similar descriptions are common in the stage-directions of Masques.

105. *figures dim;* probably=symbolical devices and representations worked in embroidery; they may have had reference to the history of Cambridge University. For *figure* used of embroidery, cf. Shakespeare, *A Lover's Complaint*, 17. This agrees well with "inwrought." *dim*, because faded with age. The line heightens the dignity of the representative of the University, and to increase the majesty of those who mourn for Lycidas is to pay him a compliment. So the next comer, St Peter, is invested with all the ceremony of his high office.

Some interpret the "figures" of the dusky streaks which appear on withered sedge-leaves. This adds little to the suggestiveness of the picture. Most prefer the other view.

106. The *sanguine flower* is the hyacinth. According to the story told by Ovid, *Metamorphoses*, X. 162—219, Hyacinthus, son of the Spartan king Amyclas, was killed by Zephyrus, and from his blood sprang the flower named after him, on the petals of which could be traced *al, al*, 'alas! alas!'. Cf. "inscribed with *woe*."

sanguine; literally 'blood-coloured' (*sanguineus*), but blood is often called 'purple' by the poets, and purple is the sense here.

107. *pledge*, i.e. child; cf. *pignus*. So in *Par. Lost*, II. 818.

108. *Last came*. The solemnity with which the entrance of St Peter is heralded has something of the dramatic vividness of the stage, raising in the reader "a thrill of awestruck expectation" (Mark Pattison). The introduction of the Apostle among the Pagan deities and associations of the poem has been much censured.

109. i.e. St Peter, regarded as the founder of the Catholic Church, and here its spokesman. He is introduced because Edward King had intended to take orders in the English Church. In calling the apostle the "Pilot of the Galilean *Lake*" (i.e. inland sea, cf. *Luke*, viii. 22—23) Milton may have used some medieval belief. The title is not in the Gospels.

110. Cf. *Matthew*, xvi. 19, "And I will give unto thee the keys of the kingdom of heaven." That there were two keys was a tradition of the Church; and Milton has varied it very effectively, distinguishing between the metals, and attributing to one the power of exclusion. Mr Ruskin notes that Dante in the *Purgatorio* IX makes both keys (one of gold, the other of silver) admit to heaven, and that Milton's variation is an artistic gain, since the right positively to exclude (i.e. not merely to decline to admit) adds to the authority of St Peter (*Sesame and Lilies*, p. 45).

111. *The golden opes*. Cf. *Comus*, 13, 14.

amain, with force. In Shakespeare it almost always signifies 'with speed,' e.g. in *The Comedy of Errors*, I. I. 93, "Two ships from far making amain to us." *A* = preposition *on* + *main* = A. S. *mægen*, strength.

112. *mitred*, wearing a mitre (bishop's headdress); a

reference to the tradition that St Peter was the first Bishop of Rome. *bespake*; the word was often used, as here, with some idea of reproof, remonstrance.

113—131. As the academic life was figured in pastoral imagery in 23—36, so here is the ministerial; and in this case the imagery appears more natural to us because we are so familiar with the conception of the Good Shepherd (*John* x. 1—16), and with the figurative use of 'pastor,' 'fold,' 'sheep.' Note how pregnant the symbolism of the passage is—that almost each detail has some inner significance, each fault of the unworthy bucolic pastors its analogue among the spiritual pastors. Indeed we can, and must, press the comparison more closely than in 23—36, where there was more of *literary* conventionalism. Here Milton is too much in earnest to be merely conventional: he means every word of his indictment.

This indictment is not directed against all the Clergy, but only a certain section ("enow of *such as*"), whom Milton charges with taking holy orders from unworthy motives and seeking preferment by unworthy means (114—118); with spiritual blindness and ignorance (119—121); with indifference about their duties, and failure to give the people proper spiritual sustenance (122—125); with spreading false doctrine, (126, 127), and doing nothing to counteract the active exertions of the Roman Catholics in proselytising (128, 129). These charges are put far more strongly in his prose-tracts; and the imagery of the lines, even the language, might be illustrated by endless quotations.

114, 115. This censure of those who are induced to take orders by desire of money comes with special significance from the lips of St Peter; cf. 1 *Peter* v. 2.

115. *creep...intrude...climb.* Milton chooses words that distinguish the three types of men he has in view—those who enter the Church in a stealthy, underhand way, those who thrust themselves in with self-assertion, and those who are full of ambition to rise to high places. See an interesting criticism of the whole passage in *Sesame and Lilies*, pp. 38, 39. It must be remembered that Milton writes as a bitter enemy of the Church, that he was afterwards even more bitter against the Presbyterians, and during the latter part of his life did not identify himself with any religious body.

116. i.e. make little account of any other duty. Cf. *Comus*, 642.

117. When Milton wrote, the shearing feast was an institution regularly observed. Cf. Spenser's *Astrophel*, 32, and Herrick's *The Country Life*. See *Comus*, 173—177, note.

118. Referring to the parable of the marriage of the king's son, *Matthew* xxii. 1—9; cf. verse 8, "they which were bidden were not worthy."

119. *blind*, i.e. spiritually. *mouths*, gluttons; carrying on the idea in "feast" (117) but implying gluttonous desire of money and preferment. How vivid a use it is of 'the part for the whole' —"as if the men were *mouths* and nothing else"—*Masson*. Exactly similar is the description of a people as "slow bellies" (γαστέρες ἀργαί), Epistle to *Titus* I. 12.

119—121. Of course, these lines imply that Edward King was a true student. Several of the other contributors to the Cambridge volume celebrate his learning in varying degrees of extravagant praise. Hitherto, says Cleveland, the sea had lacked

> "Books, arts and tongues...but in thee
> Neptune hath got an Universitie";

a 'conceit' echoed by another writer:

> "Nor did it seem one private man to die,
> But a well-ordered Universitie."

120. The sheep-hook (cf. *The Winter's Tale*, IV. 4. 430, 431), in accordance with the imagery that runs throughout, represents the pastoral staff of the Church in its character of the Good Shepherd. So in Milton's tract *Of Reformation*: "let him advise how he can reject the pastorly rod and sheep-hook of Christ,' *P. W.* II. 412.

the least; put in rather loose apposition to *aught*: 'they have scarcely learnt any other duty, even the smallest, that belongs,' etc.

121. *herdman* = shepherd. For the form cf. *Venus and Adonis*, 456.

122. *What recks it them?* what do they care? For the impersonal use, cf. *Comus*, 404.

sped = provided for. What Milton means is that these well-beneficed clergy have got all *they* want: they "need" nothing. Shakespeare always has *sped* in a bad sense. Cf. *The Merchant of Venice*, II. 9, 72, "So be gone: you are sped," i.e. dispatched.

So in Pope's line "A dire dilemma! either way I'm sped," i.e. (colloquially) 'done for'—*Epistle to Arbuthnot*, 31.

123. *their songs.* The miserable singing and piping of the shepherds represent, very naturally, the miserable preaching and teaching of the ministers. With his Puritan sympathies, Milton would set very great store on preaching.

when they list, i.e. *only* when they choose.

lean, thin, and so, as applied to sermons, = yielding no spiritual nourishment.

flashy, tasteless; see G. What worse can be said of food than that it neither nourishes the body nor pleases the palate? So with the sermons of these clergy: they lack both moral worth and literary grace and polish.

123. The line is imitated from one in Vergil's third Eclogue, 27. *scrannel*; properly 'thin, weakly, wretched.' It carries on the idea in "lean," implying that the *sound* of the pipes is as poor in tone as the *matter* of the songs is "lean." *The Imperial Dictionary* quotes (without reference) from Carlyle, "to twang harps for thee, and blow through scrannel pipes." Cf. also a letter by him in Lord Houghton's *Life*, I. 265: "Like a 'chapped flute,' which you steep in the ditch until it close again and become a whole flute or scrannel." The sound in 123, 124 is intentionally harsh. *straw*; cf. "oat," 88.

125. The sheep neglected by their shepherd are a common feature of pastoral poetry; cf. Matthew Arnold's *The Scholar-Gipsy*, "No longer leave thy wistful flock unfed."

126. The "rank mist" is the false doctrine, or what Milton as a Puritan considered false. *rank* = noisome, pestilential. *draw*, i.e. breathe. Cf. *Samson Agonistes*, 7.

128, 129. Milton refers to the system of secret ("privy") proselytism which was then carried on so actively by the Roman Catholic party in England that the "grim wolf" would be readily identified. The reaction was specially strong at Cambridge; cf. the case of Crashaw the Cambridge poet: hence the significance of the reference here. The last work Milton published, the tract *Of True Religion*, 1673, was directed "against the growth of Popery." Some editors believe that the "wolf" is Laud, who had been archbishop since 1632, and who through the Court of High Commission was then enforcing severe pains and penalties against the Puritans. "Our author," says Warton, "anticipates the execution of Archbishop Laud, by a *two-handed engine*, that is, the axe; insinuating that his death would remove all grievances in religion, and complete the reformation of the Church." But this is to explain by the light of after-events. Milton could scarcely have foreseen in 1637 the death of the primate (which took place in 1645); and even if this had been his meaning, it would not have been clear to others, or if clear, would not have been permitted to appear in a volume published by the University Press. Further, the operations of Laud and the High Church were not "privy." See Masson's *Life of Milton*, I. 638; Birrell's *Life of Marvell*, pp. 12—14.

128. *with privy paw.* Cf. the Sonnet to Cromwell, 13, 14:

"Help us to save free conscience from the paw
Of hireling wolves, whose gospel is their maw."

129. *and nothing said;* an absolute construction. He means, without opposition from the prelates. Masson shows that the charge is not true of Laud. There may also, as Mr Jerram argues, be an imputation on the Court; for the Queen, a Roman Catholic, was known to favour very strongly the cause of her own Church.

130, 131. Many editors believe that what Milton has in mind is "a thorough and effectual reformation" (Newton) of the Church, and that this reformation is figured under the image of a "*two*-handed engine" in allusion to either "the ax laid unto the root of the trees" (*Matthew* iii. 10, *Luke* iii. 9), or the "*two* edged sword" of *The Revelation* i. 16. The "ax" and the "*two* edged sword" are equally symbolical, in their respective Scriptural contexts, of a thorough reformation, and therefore equally appropriate here; though "*two*-handed" rather favours the latter.

Personally I cannot help thinking that the power Milton means is not Reformation but Justice, and that the "two-handed engine" is the sword of Justice. Cf. his pamphlet *The Tenure of Kings*, "be he king, or tyrant, or emperor, the sword of justice is above him"; and the same work, "they plead for him, pity him...protest against those that talk of bringing him to the trial of justice, which is the sword of God, superior to all mortal things," *P. W.* II. pp. 4, 8. Cf. *Othello*, V. 2, 17. True, Milton does not here introduce the word *Justice*, but the drift of the passage seems to be that the power of just retribution will execute vengeance, and the instrument used might well be the sword that hangs over wrong-doers.

The "engine" has also been identified, as we saw, with the axe which was to behead Laud, and with the sword of Michael. Each view is very improbable; the latter is simply due to the fact that the sword of Michael, with which he laid low the rebellious angels in the great battle in Heaven, is called "two-handed" in *Par. Lost*, VI. 250, 251.

130. *that;* he speaks as if he saw it there.

two-handed, wielded with both hands because of its size and weight. Cf. 2 *Henry VI.* II. 1. 46, "Come with thy two-hand sword." It seems to me simply a descriptive epithet, as in *Par. Lost*, VI. 251, emphasising the potency of the sword. Masson, however, thinks there may be a hint at the Two Houses of Parliament. "For eight years prior to 1637 Charles had not called a Parliament;...yet this word was in the hearts of all, and it was to a coming Parliament with its Two Houses that all looked forward for the rectification of the accumulated abuses in Church and State"—*Masson.*

engine; formerly used in the general sense 'instrument'; hence equally applicable to a sword or to an axe. See G.

at the door=ready at hand; from *Matthew* xxiv. 33, "know that it is near, even at the doors." Cf. the *Remonstrant's Defence*, "thy kingdom is now at hand, and thou standing at the door."

131. *and smite no more*, because the blow when it does fall will be final. Cf. 1 *Samuel* xxvi. 8.

132. As after a previous digression (see 85), he recalls the pastoral Muse. Alpheus, the river of Peloponnesus, was the lover of Arethusa, the Syracusan fountain (cf. Shelley's beautiful poem), and like her symbolises the pastoral verse of the Greeks, so that "shrunk thy streams" is a figurative way of saying 'checked the course of my pastoral strain.'

133. *shrunk*, made to shrink, scared.

Sicilian, i.e. the Muse of pastoral poetry, who inspired the pastoral writers Theocritus, Bion, and Moschus. The phrase "Sicilian Muses" (*Sicelides Musæ*) is used by Moschus in his *Lament for Bion*, and by Vergil, *Eclogue*, IV. 1.

133—141. Wordsworth in the poem *Margaret* defends the poetic practice of calling on inanimate nature to join in lament for the dead:

"The Poets, in their elegies and songs
Lamenting the departed, call the groves,
They call upon the hills and streams to mourn,
And senseless rocks; nor idly; for they speak,
In these their invocations, with a voice
Obedient to the strong creative power
Of human passion";

i.e. the passion (or 'pathetic fallacy,' as Ruskin calls it) which leads us to attribute to nature and natural objects our own feelings. Thus it is a "fallacy" to call the sea "remorseless" (50), or to speak of "the *cruel* crawling foam," as Kingsley does.

134. *Hither*, as though he pointed to the "laureate hearse."

135. *bells*, i.e. of flowers. Cf. Ariel's "In a cowslip's bell I lie," *The Tempest*, V. 89.

136. *use*, haunt, dwell. Sylvester speaks of the mountain (Helicon) "Where the Pierian learned ladies use" (=the Muses dwell).

137. *wanton*, i.e. blowing where they please; cf. *Comus*, 49. "Wanton wind" occurs in *A Midsummer-Night's Dream*, II. I. 129, but with a different sense ('lustful').

138. *whose*, of the valleys. Cf. *A Midsummer-Night's Dream*, II. I. 107, 108:

"hoary-headed frosts
Fall in the fresh lap of the crimson rose."

the swart star=the dog-star, Sirius; see *Comus*, 928.

swart; properly 'darkened by heat,' as the flowers, he implies, would be after the star had "looked" on them; more applicable therefore to the star's effect than to the star itself.

looks. Warton is probably right in thinking that *looks* refers to the astrological theory of the 'influence' exercised by the 'aspects' of the stars; cf. *The Winter's Tale*, II. I. 105—107:

"There's some ill planet reigns:
I must be patient till the heavens *look*
With an *aspect* more favourable."

139. *quaint*, pretty, fanciful; see G. *enamelled*, i.e. variegated and glossy as enamel-work. A favourite epithet with Milton, as with other writers of this period, especially Herrick. Cf. *Par. Lost*, IV. 149 (used of fruit and flowers). Mr Ruskin remarks on its frequent misuse, *Modern Painters*, III. 229. It is open to the same criticism as "velvet"; see *Comus*, 898.

eyes; cf. *A Midsummer Night's Dream*, IV. 1. 59, 60:

"orient pearls (i.e. dewdrops)
Stood now within the pretty *flowerets' eyes*."

140. *honied*, sweet to them as honey.

141. *purple=impurple*; cf. *Par. Lost*, III. 364, "Impurpled with celestial roses." The sense is 'to make brilliant,' *purple* with Milton being sometimes equivalent to Lat. *purpureus*, i.e. dazzling or rich of hue.

142—150. This device of enumerating a number of flowers belongs as much to the pastoral style as did the invocation to the Muses, or the rural imagery of lines 25—36. In a well-known passage of *Modern Painters* Mr Ruskin contrasts Milton's lines with those in *The Winter's Tale*, IV. 4. 118—127. The gist of the criticism is, that in Shakespeare the description is imaginative, giving us the essential characteristic of each flower, but in Milton fanciful, or even fantastic. Roughly speaking, the difference is that between the poet who goes straight to nature, and the poet who knows nature mainly through the medium of books. Turn to the passage in *The Winter's Tale*; also to *Cymbeline*, IV. 2. 218—229.

Newton observes that most of the flowers mentioned, being early flowers, are "suited to the age of Lycidas." The objection that the flowers do not all bloom at the same time, though Milton calls them "vernal" (141), seems to me somewhat carping.

142—150. A much corrected passage; see p. 161.

142. Cf. Wordsworth's poem *To May:*

"Such greeting heard, away with sighs
For lilies that must fade,
Or 'the rathe primose as it dies
Forsaken' in the shade!'

rathe, i.e. early, as the name, *prima rosa*, implies. See G.

forsaken. The earlier draft of the passage suggests the sense 'unwedded' (by the sun) i.e. because the primrose grows in shady places. The notion of the sun being in love with certain flowers is often alluded to; cf. the description in *The Winter's Tale*, IV. 4. 105, 106, of the marigold. Apart from the earlier version one would rather interpret 'left alone' in the wood; unadmired, like other wildflowers that "blush unseen."

143. *crow-toe;* identified by most editors with the *crow-flower* (see *Hamlet*, IV. 7. 170), formerly used of the Ragged Robin but now of the buttercup. In Gerarde's *Herbal*, 1597, however, the standard Elizabethan book on botany, the crow-toe is called a hyacinth. So also in Lyte's still earlier *Herbal* (1578), p. 206.

144. *pansy;* especially appropriate here as being the flower of thought (*F. pensée*) or remembrance; cf. *Hamlet*, IV. 5. 178.

freaked, i.e. variegated or spotted; etymologically=*freckled*, which Shakespeare uses in a similar way; cf. "the freckled cowslip," *Henry V.* V. 2. 49. From Icelandic *frekna*, Middle E. *frakne*=a freckle.

145. *glowing*, i.e. of a rich deep purple; truer of the cultivated violet than the wild (which Shakespeare describes so beautifully in *The Winter's Tale*, IV. 4. 120, "violets *dim*").

146. *well-attired.* The metaphor may be that of *attire* in its ordinary sense—cf. Milton's Sonnet "To Mr Laurence," 6, 7; or of *attire*=*tire*, i.e. head-dress, as in *Leviticus* xvi. 4, "with the linen mitre shall he be attired."

woodbine=honeysuckle; as in *Much Ado About Nothing*, III. 1. 8, 30.

147. *wan;* referring to its pale, delicate shade of yellow.

148. Cf. Tennyson, "Rare broidry of the purple clover," *A Dirge*. Elsewhere Milton speaks of the ground being *embroidered* (*Comus*, 233), or *broidered* (*Par. Lost*, IV. 702) with flowers.

149. *amaranthus;* from Gk. ἀμάραντος, 'unfading'—the word used in 1 *Peter* v. 4, of the "crown of glory that fadeth not away." The flower is the favourite poetic symbol of immortality, and so the *most* appropriate of those mentioned here. See the exquisite description in *Par. Lost*, III. 353—359. Tennyson glances at "Milton's Amaranth" in *Romney's Remorse*.

150. *daffadillies;* a rustic form (the imaginary speaker is a shepherd) of *daffodil;* cf. *The Shepheards Calender*, April, which also has *daffadowndillies*.

151. *laureate*, crowned with laurels (as the Poet *Laureate* is, theoretically), symbolising Edward King's poetic faculty; cf. 10, 11. Perhaps the laurels might also represent the memorial poems of Milton and his fellow-contributors, and some editors think that he has in mind the old custom of attaching memorial stanzas to a hearse or grave. Perhaps the

most celebrated piece of poetic eulogy of this type ever composed was Ben Jonson's epitaph on the Countess of Pembroke, "Underneath this marble hearse"; see Mr Aldis Wright's note on *Henry V.* I. 2. 233.

hearse; probably = bier. Derived from Lat. *hirpex*, 'a harrow,' *hearse* originally meant a triangular frame shaped like a harrow, for holding lights at a church service, especially the services in Holy Week. Later, it was applied to the illumination at a funeral, and then to almost everything connected with a funeral. Thus it could signify the dead body, the coffin, the pall covering it, the framework of wood on which a coffin was placed in the church before the altar, the bier, the funeral car (as always now), the service (cf. the Glosse to *The Shepheards Calender*, November), and the grave. See Way's *Promptorium*, p. 236.

Lycid. Spenser has this shortened form, *Colin Clout*, 907. The alliteration seems to me to give a peculiar effect of pathos.

152—162. The main verb is *let* in 153—'let our thoughts dally whilst' etc.; then come a series of clauses dependent on their respective conjunctions, *whilst*, *whether*, *where;* and afterwards (163, 164) two imperatives are introduced somewhat abruptly. The train of thought connected with that of the previous passage, 142—151, is: 'let us strew the hearse with flowers: let us, to ease our grief, play with the false notion (*surmise*) that the body of Lycidas is covered by those flowers: though in reality alas! it is being borne in its "wandering grave," perhaps northwards to the Hebrides, perhaps south to the Land's End.' See Warton's note.

154, 155. Strictly "shores" does not fit well with "wash"; but taken closely with "sounding seas" it gives us a vivid picture of the body dashed from coast to coast, as though land and sea were leagued against it.

157. For the reading in the 1638 ed. (see p. 161), cf. *Pericles*, III. I. 64, "humming water must *o'erwhelm* thy corpse." Perhaps *o'erwhelm* afterwards suggested *whelming*.

158. i.e. the world of monsters. Cf. *Comus*, 533.

154, 156. For the rhyme, cf. Wordsworth's *Solitary Reaper:*

"Breaking the silence of the seas
Among the farthest Hebrides."

159. *moist*, i.e. with tears. *vows*, prayers and funeral rites (Lat. *vota*).

160. *by the fable of Bellerus*=near the grave (or realm) of the legendary Bellerus, i.e. the Land's End. The use of the abstract noun resembles *Par. Lost*, II. 964, 965, "the dreaded name of Demogorgon"=the dreadful Demogorgon himself.

By *Bellerus* is meant one of the giants anciently supposed to have dwelt in Cornwall; Milton seems to have coined the name from *Bellerium*, the Latin name of the Land's End. The *Cambridge MS.* has "*Corineus* old," implying the whole of Cornwall; see *Appendix*, section III. The change to *Bellerus* defined the locality more closely.

Milton had studied the ancient British history with a view to his contemplated poem (see p. xxi) on the Arthurian legend, which is so closely connected with Cornwall. He specially mentions the Cornish giants and relates legends concerning them in his *History of Britain*, v. 172, 173.

161. *the guarded mount;* St Michael's Mount, off Penzance. Though Milton does not mention the name the allusion would be easily understood, for, as Spenser says in *The Shepheards Calender*, Julye,

"St Michels Mount who does not know,
That wardes the Westerne coste?"

Upon the mount was a craggy seat called *St Michael's Chair* (other names for it being "the grey rock" or "the hoare rock in the wood"), in which tradition said that apparitions (i.e. *Visions*) of the archangel had been witnessed. Milton speaks as though the Vision were always there, with gaze directed to the Spanish coast. For other references to the same legend, see Polwhele's *History of Cornwall*, I. 66–67, II. 125–128.

guarded=protected by the presence of the angel; less probably=fortified. There was a fortress on the hill, ruins of which remain; see Bacon's account of Perkin Warbeck and the Cornish rising in 1496, *Hist. of Hen. VII.* p. 167 (Pitt Press ed.).

162. The places mentioned were on the north-west coast of Spain, and Milton made the Vision gaze in that direction because it was a sort of literary tradition that the Land's End "pointed at Spain," as Drayton had said (*Polyolbion*, 23). But a reference to Spain in general terms would not be so effective

as the mention of special places; the artifice of using sonorous names is a favourite with poets. Milton therefore would require the names of some places on the northern coast of Spain, at the point nearest to the Land's End; this was Galicia.

On its coast, a little east of Cape Finisterre, lay Namancos, with Bayona to the south. Todd discovered the names in the map of Galicia in *Mercator's Atlas*. Probably the source consulted by Milton was the first English Edition of that great work, published recently (1636). In that *Atlas* the part of Galicia just west of Namancos is shaded to represent mountains, which gives it prominence as a feature of the coast-line to which the Angel gazes. But Namancos was not a headland (as M. may have thought), nor a town, but a district or county, and the correct form of the name (so attractive for the scansion) was "N*e*mancos." "N*a*mancos" had appeared in an older map and the misprint was copied into later maps. (*Modern Language Review*, Jan. 1907.)

163. *Angel*, i.e. Michael. Warton paraphrases the line thus: "Oh angel, look no longer seaward to Namancos and Bayona's hold: rather turn your eyes to another object: look homeward or landward; look towards your own coast now, and view with pity the corpse of the shipwrecked Lycidas, floating thither."

Some editors think that Lycidas is the Angel; but there is an obvious antithesis between "looks toward Namancos" in 162, and "look homeward" in 163, and the point of this would be spoilt were the clauses made to refer to different subjects. Moreover the reference to the archangel in 161, 162, makes it very awkward that "Angel" in the next line should not refer to him. Nor is it natural to regard Lycidas as an "Angel" in 163 and simply a "hapless youth" in 164.

No doubt, there is some abruptness in the transition from Lycidas, the "thou" of lines 154—160; but it is, I think, intentional. Shakespeare and Milton use abruptness and irregularity of style to reflect strong emotion. Now here the emotion of the speaker rises in a *crescendo* as he pictures the body of his friend washed about the world; and at last it makes him break into a sudden appeal to the great archangel to show the sympathy he yearns for. For a fine instance in Shakespeare of sudden change of construction indicating a sudden intense consciousness, see *King Lear*, II. 4. 267, where any emendation is ruinous.

ruth, pity; see G.

164. *ye dolphins*. An allusion to the classical story (a great favourite with Elizabethan writers—see *A Midsummer-Night's Dream*, II. I. 150) of the Greek musician Arion. On one occasion the sailors of a ship in which he was returning with many treasures from Sicily to his home at Corinth plotted his murder; whereupon he threw himself into the sea, and was carried safely to land by a dolphin which had been touched by the strains of his lute. The notion of dolphins being fond of music is often alluded to in poetry. (See p. xlvii, footnote.)

They might be expected to help Lycidas who "knew himself to sing" (10, 11). Indeed, another poem in the Cambridge collection asks, why did not some dolphin save Edward King from being drowned when the vessel struck on the rock?

waft, carry, i.e. "homeward." The word was specially used of carrying, or journeying, over the sea. Cf. 2 *Henry VI*. IV. I. 114, "I charge thee waft me safely cross the Channel."

165—185. This is the concluding passage of the Monody, since the last eight lines are a kind of Epilogue. We may compare the end of Milton's Latin poem the *Lament for Damon*. In each case sorrow dies away and gives place to consolation—that through death the lost friend has found life. *The Shepheards Calender*, November, and the two elegiac poems on the death of Sir Philip Sidney, *The Doleful Lay of Clorinda* and *The Mourning Muse of Thestylis*, all close on the same note of resignation and comfort.

165. "This line was evidently suggested by 'Sigh nó more, ladies, sigh no móre,' of the Song in *Much Ado About Nothing*, [II. 3. 74]; and they should both be read in the manner here indicated"—*Keightley*. When Shakespeare has the same word twice in a line he generally varies the accent.

166. "He is not dead" is the refrain of the *Adonais*; cf. 84, "Our love, our hope, *our sorrow, is not dead.*"

your sorrow, he about whom you sorrow; the abstract for the concrete. Cf. phrases like 'he is the hope of his family'; so with 'anxiety', 'delight,' etc.

167. *floor*, i.e. the "level (98)" surface.

168. *day-star*; probably the sun; called the "diurnal star"

in *Par. Lost*, x. 1069. Cf. Sylvester, "While the bright day-star rides his glorious round." But commonly *day-star* = the morning-star, Lucifer, and some interpret it so here.

169. So Gray, of the setting sun, "To morrow he repairs his golden flood;" i.e. the flood of his light (*The Bard*, III. 3).

170. *tricks*, i.e. dresses anew; see *Il Penseroso*, 123.

new-spangled, i.e. flashing with renewed brilliancy because washed in the ocean. Cf. *Comus*, 1003.

171. Cf. *Coriolanus*, II. 1. 57, 58, "one that converses... with the forehead of the morning;" doubtless Milton knew the passage. So Tennyson in *Pelleas and Ettarre*.

172. Perhaps Milton remembered the *Purple Island*, VI. 71:

"That he might mount to heav'n, He sunk to Hell;
 That he might live, He di'd; that he might rise, He fell."

173. *Matthew* xiv. 24—31. The appropriateness of this allusion is obvious, seeing that Lycidas had perished at sea. Another contributor to the Cambridge collection of verses expresses the wish that Edward King could have walked the waves like St Peter.

174. *Where*, i.e. mounted (172) to the region where. For the emphatic *other...other*, implying *better*, cf. *Comus*, 612. Perhaps we are to trace here an allusion to the "living fountains of waters," *Revelation* vii. 17, and "the tree of life," *Revelation* xxii. 2. 14. Richardson cites a very similar passage in Ariosto, *Orlando Furioso*, 34, 72.

175. Nectar is put to a similar purpose in *Comus*, 838. *oozy*, i.e. with sea-water.

176. *unexpressive*, inexpressible, not to be described. Cf. *As You Like It*, III. 2. 10, "The fair, the chaste and unexpressive she." As to the use of the termination *ive* = *ible*, see note on *Comus*, 349. *nuptial;* referring, as Mr Jerram says, to the "marriage of the Lamb," *Revelation* xix. 6, 7.

177. See p. 161. Marvell has an obvious echo of this line in his poem on Cromwell, "The First Anniversary" (218).

180. The rhythm and form of the line remind us of Shelley's *To a Skylark*, 10, "And singing still dost soar, and soaring ever singest." See Tovey's note on Gray, *The Bard*, III. 2 ("Bright Rapture calls, and soaring as she sings...").

181. *wipe the tears*. Cf. *Isaiah* xxv. 8, *Rev.* vii. 17, xxi. 4. Milton has transferred the action to the saints. Pope has a

witty but profane application of the allusion in the *Epilogue to the Satires*, in which he sketches the courtier's ideal spot:

"There, where no father's, brother's, friend's disgrace
Once break their rest, or stir them from their place:
But past the sense of human miseries,
All tears are wip'd for ever from all eyes;
No cheek is known to blush, no heart to throb,
Save when they lose a question or a job."

183. *the Genius of the shore*, the spirit who should watch over that Welsh coast near which Edward King was lost. According to the classical belief every place or individual had a guardian spirit (Gk. δαίμων, Lat. *genius*). The chief character in *Arcades* is the 'Genius of the Wood.'

This introduction of a Pagan belief immediately after the reference to the Scriptural idea of the 'communion of saints,' and the Scriptural language, is another instance of that blending of the classics and Christianity which is so marked a feature of *Lycidas*. Cf. especially 108—131.

184. *thy recompense*, i.e. the compensation which Heaven awards to Lycidas for his untimely fate. He does not perish like an ordinary mortal, but becomes a kind of deity ("Genius").

good, kind, propitious (Lat. *bonus*).

186—193. This concluding passage, as Masson remarks, is detached from the Monody itself so as to form a kind of Epilogue in which Milton "looks back on" his work and "characterises" it by the epithets "Doric," "tender," "various."

186. *uncouth;* perhaps 'simple, rude,' this speaker being a shepherd; though such a description of this exquisitely artificial and learned poem would be a piece of humour. Or 'unknown,' the ordinary Miltonic sense; said in reference to Milton himself being at the time an unknown writer.

187. Cf. *Par. Lost*, VII. 373, 374; *Par. Regained*, IV. 426, 427, where the Morning "Came forth with pilgrim steps, in amice gray" (i.e. garb, dress). The effect of slowness produced by the number of monosyllables suggests the *gradual* dawning. Milton himself was an early riser (see *L' Allegro* 41, note).

188. *stops;* see *Comus*, 345, note. *tender*, because affected by the delicate touch of the fingers. Or possibly referring to the affectionate tone of the poem.

various, "in allusion to the varied strains of the elegy (at

76, 88, 113, 132, 165). This almost amounts to a recognition on the part of the poet of the irregularities of style, the mixture of different and even opposing themes, which some have censured as a defect"—*Jerram.*

quills=pipes; specially used, as here, of the shepherd's pipe; cf. *The Shepheards Calender*, June. To 'tune the quill' was a common phrase; cf. the MS. poem ascribed to Milton, "The sacred sisters tune their quills."

Johnson explained *quill* here to mean the *plectrum* or comb with which the strings of some instruments (e.g. the lute or mandolin) are struck; but according to all tradition the shepherd's instrument is the pipe.

189. *thought.* "Care, great anxiety; as in the old expression to 'take *thought.*' '*Take* no *thought* for your life,' *Matt.* vi. 25"—*Dr Bradshaw.* The shepherd's anxiety is to compose a lament worthy of his friend.

Doric; because written in the pastoral style of Theocritus and the other Sicilian poets who wrote in the Doric dialect. Moschus calls Bion "the Dorian Orpheus" and says that with him perished "the Dorian Song" (Δωρὶς ἀοιδά).

Sir Henry Wotton praised most in *Comus* a "certain *Doric* delicacy" in the lyrics; see p. 4. So in Matthew Arnold's *Thyrsis*, "She loved the Dorian pipe, the Dorian strain." With poets of the last century *Doric quill* (as in Collins's *Ode on the Popular Superstitions*, II.) and *Doric oat* were synonyms for 'pastoral poetry.'

190. From Vergil, *Eclogue* I. 84. *stretched out*, i.e. in their shadows; the setting sun had caused long shadows to be cast by the hills. Cf. Pope's imitation, "And the low sun had lengthened ev'ry shade," *Autumn*, 100.

192. *At last*, i.e. having composed his elegy from "morn (187) till dewy eve." *twitched*, i.e. so as to gather it about him.

mantle blue. "Blue," says Professor Hales, "was the colour of a shepherd's dress, and the poet here personates a poetic shepherd." Cf. *The Shepheards Calender*, November. Grey, however, seems to be the colour more often mentioned. Thus Greene more than once describes the shepherd Paris as "all clad in grey" when he wooed Œnone. See Greene's *Friar Bacon and Friar Bungay*, III. 69, where Dr Ward's note gives numerous instances. Browne (*Eclogue* II.) speaks of an extravagant shepherd who had two suits, one of either colour.

193. A reminiscence of Fletcher's *Purple Island*, VI. 77:

"Home then my lambes; the falling drops eschew:
To morrow shall ye feast in pastures new."

Perhaps no line in English poetry is more frequently misquoted than this last verse of *Lycidas*; even Shelley, who gives it correctly in his *Letter to Maria Gisborne* (the end), writes to T. L. Peacock (Nov. 18, 1818), "To morrow to fresh *fields* and pastures new." Possibly some 18th century edition of *Lycidas* may be responsible for the wrong reading.

An accomplished scholar writes to me: "The reason for the shepherd's going to new haunts, is that the old ones are associated with Lycidas, and so he cannot bear to feed his sheep there alone—a very just idea—and an admirable exit." I have not the least doubt that this explanation, which I have never seen in any edition of *Lycidas*, gives correctly the primary purport of the line.

Nor does it seem to me inconsistent with the commonly accepted view that there is an underlying allusion to Milton's tour in Italy. He tells us in the *Second Defence* that on the death of his mother he became anxious to travel. She died in April, 1637: the Cambridge draft of *Lycidas* is dated November, 1637. The Italian scheme, therefore, may have occurred to him before he began this poem.

Another theory with reference to the line is, that it is a covert way of saying that Milton has finally separated himself from the Anglican and Court party, and means to identify himself with the Puritans. This seeems to me very farfetched. The danger of reading 'allusions' into a writer's words is that there can be no definite limit to the process: each may start his own theory.

TEXTUAL VARIATIONS IN LYCIDAS.

We give here the textual variations between the original MS. of *Lycidas*, the Cambridge edition of 1638, and that published in 1645. By 'margin' are meant the marginal corrections in the MS. Some of these are not found in the 1638 ed.: it is fair to assume that they were made after the volume had been printed. 'Milton's copy' is the copy of the first edition (now in the University Library at Cambridge) which has a few corrections in the poet's handwriting. Differences of reading are marked by italic type:

ll. 3—5.

'I come to pluck your berries harsh and crude
before the mellowing yeare and wth forc't fingers rude
and crop yor young shatter your leaves before the mellowing yeare.'

The words in italics are crossed out. Milton may have intended the last line to run—'and crop yor young leaves wth forc't fingers rude.' Having got as far as *young* he stopped, struck out ll. 4—5, and with slight verbal changes transposed the verses so as to alter the sequence of rhymes.

8. MS. 'for *young* Lycidas;' *young* erased.

10. MS. 'he *well* knew.'

22. MS. '*To* bid;' changed to '*and* bid.'

26. MS. '*glimmering* eyelids;' corrected to *opening;* yet the 1638 ed. has *glimmering*.

30. MS. 'Oft till the ev'n-starre bright' (erased); margin, 'starre *that rose in Ev'ning bright;*' 1638 ed. again gives the earlier reading.

31. MS. '*burnisht* weele;' corrected, *westring;* but *burnisht* in 1638 ed.

39. 1638 ed. has 'Thee shepherds, thee;' i.e. the shepherds are made to mourn; perhaps a misprint.

47. MS. 'gay *buttons* weare;' *weare* changed to *beare;* finally *wardrope weare* substituted. For spelling of *wardrobe* see note on this line. *Buttons*=buds, as in *Hamlet*, I. 3. 40, or *The Noble Kinsmen*, III. I. 6, "gold buttons on the boughs." Fr. *bouton* means a button or a bud.

51. MS. repeats *your*, by mistake; 1638 ed. '*lord* Lycidas;' corrected in Milton's copy to '*lov'd* Lycidas.'

53. 1638 ed. '*the* old bards;' corrected in Milton's copy.

58—63. MS. had:

a. 'What could the *golden-hayrd Calliope*

b. For her inchaunting son,

c. *When shee beheld* (*the gods farre sighted bee*)

d. His goarie *scalpe rowle downe the Thracian lee:*'

a, c, d are crossed out: *b* left. After *b* (i.e. l. 59) the margin has:

e. 'Whome universal nature *might* lament

f. *And heaven and hel deplore,*

g. When his *divine head* downe the streame was sent:'

f is crossed out, also *g* as far as *downe*, and *e* left. Then on the opposite page Milton rewrote the whole passage from l. 58 just as we have it, except that, (i) after writing '*might* lament' he substituted *did;* (ii) he wrote '*divine* visage' and changed it to '*goarie* visage,' cf. *goarie* in *d supra;* (iii) after l. 59 (as it now stands) he repeated the words 'for her inchaunting son,' intending them to form a short line. No doubt, he finally rejected them because he had already used the artifice of repetition in 'The Muse herself,' ll. 58, 59.

66. 1638 ed. misprints *stridly* for *strictly.*

67. 1638 ed. 'others *do;*' altered in Milton's copy to *use.*

69. MS. '*hid in* the tangles;' margin '*or with* the tangles;' but 1638 ed. '*hid in.*'

82. 1638 ed. has the spelling *perfect*, the only place (I believe) where it occurs in Milton: *perfet* in 1645 ed.

85. MS. '*smooth* flood,' *smooth* erased; margin *fam'd*, erased; then *honour'd.*

86. MS. '*soft*-sliding;' *soft* crossed out, margin *smooth;* l. 85 was probably changed after l. 86. 103. 1638 ed. *Chamus.*

105. MS. '*scraul'd ore* with figures;' not crossed out, though *inwrought* is written in margin.

110. MS. '*Tow* massy;' cf. l. 130.

114. MS. *Anough;* 1638 ed. *enough;* 1645 ed. *anow.*

129. MS. '*nothing* sed;' changed to *little;* 1638 ed. *little;* but 1645 ed. *nothing.*

130. MS. *tow-handed;* cf. 110.

131. 1638 ed. *smites* instead of *smite.*

138. MS. '*sparely* looks;' *sparely* erased; margin *stintly*, or

the word may be *faintly*, the writing being indistinct; this was erased and *sparely* re-substituted.

139. MS. *Bring*, crossed out; margin *throw*.

142—150. Of this passage the MS. presents two versions; the first, through which Milton ran his pen, reads thus:

'Bring the rathe primrose that *unwedded* dies
Colouring the pale cheeke of uninjoyd love,
And that sad flowre that strove
To write his own woes on the vermeil graine;
Next adde Narcissus yt still weeps in vaine,
The woodbine and ye pancie freakt wth jet,
The glowing violet,
The cowslip wan that *hangs his* pensive head
And every *bud* that *sorrows liverie* weares,
Let Daffadillies fill thire cups with teares,
Bid Amaranthus all his beautie shed
To strew the laureate herse'—

Underneath this follows the second version. The first four lines are identical with those in the printed editions: then the MS. continues:

'The musk-rose and the *garish columbine*
With cowslips wan that hang the pensive head,
And every flower that sad *escutcheon bears;*'

the last couplet is as in the earlier passage.

Garish columbine is struck out, and *well-attir'd woodbine* (cf. the first draft) substituted. 'Escutcheon *bears*' is changed to *wears;* then, in the margin, to 'imbroidrie *bears;*' and finally to 'imbroidrie *wears.*' Against the concluding couplet—'Let Daffadillies'—Milton wrote '2. 1'; showing that the order was to be reversed, while *let* was altered to *and.*

153. MS. '*sad* thoughts; *sad* crossed out and *fraile* written over it.

154. MS. *floods*, erased, margin *shoars*.

157. MS. '*humming* tide;' altered to *whelming* in margin of MS. and in Milton's copy; but the 1638 ed. has *humming.*

160. MS. *Corineus*, erased; margin *Bellerus*.

176. MS. '*Listening the* unexpressive;' *and heares* substituted.

177. Omitted in 1638 ed.; inserted in Milton's copy, as in 1645 ed.

191. There is some change in MS., but it is not legible.

GLOSSARY.

Abbreviations:—

A.S. = Anglo-Saxon, i.e. English down to about the Conquest.

Middle E. = Middle English, i.e. English from about the Conquest to about 1500.

Elizabethan E. = the English of Shakespeare and his contemporaries (down to about 1650).

O.F. = Old French, i.e. till about 1600. F. = modern French.

Germ. = modern German. Gk. = Greek.

Ital. = Italian. Lat. = Latin.

NOTE: In using the Glossary the student should pay very careful attention to the context in which each word occurs.

alabaster, *Com.* 660, sulphate of lime; Gk. ἀλάβαστρος, said to be derived from the name of a town, *Alabastron*, in Egypt. Misspelt *alablaster* in the original editions, as commonly in Elizabethan writers.

alley, 'a path, walk,' especially one with trees overhead (*Com.* 311), as in a garden (990). Cf. *Much Ado About Nothing*, I. 2. 10, "a thick-pleached alley," i.e. thickly interwoven overhead; and Tennyson, *Ode to Memory*, "plaited alleys of the trailing rose." F. *allée*.

anon, *Lyc.* 169, 'soon, presently.' A.S. *on án*, 'in one,' i.e. one moment.

ambrosial; used by Milton of that which delights the sense of smell (*Com.* 16, 840) or taste. Strictly, *ambrosia*=the food of the gods, as *nectar*=their drink.

aspect, *Com.* 694. Shakespeare always accents *aspéct.* Many words now accented on the first syllable were in Elizabethan E. accented on the second syllable, i.e. they retained the French accent, which (roughly speaking) was that of the original Latin words. By "accent" one means, of course, the stress laid by the voice on any syllable in pronouncing it. Thus Milton wrote "By policy and long *procéss* of time" (*Par. Lost*, II. 297); cf. French *procès*, Lat. *procéssus.* So Shakespeare scans *accéss, commérce, edíct*, when it suits him.

asphodil, *Com.* 838; Gk. ἀσφόδελος, a kind of lily supposed to flourish especially in the Elysian fields. **Daffodil** (*Com.* 851) is a corruption of ἀσφόδελος through Low Lat. *affodillus*; now used of a different flower, viz. the *pseudo-narcissus.* Skeat thinks that the *d* may represent F. *de* in *fleur d'affrodille.*

assay, *Com.* 972, 'trial, test.' The form always used by Milton. To *assay* metals is to test them. Cf. O.F. *essai* and the variant form *assai;* Lat. *exagium*, 'a weighing, trial of weight.'

ay me, *Com.* 511, *Lyc.* 56, 'alas.' O.F. *aymi*, 'alas for me!' cf. Gk. οἴμοι.

azurn, *Com.* 893; perhaps formed from the noun *azure*, like *silvern* from *silver*, where -*n* = the suffix -*en*, as in *wooden, woollen.* Some think that Milton, with his fondness for Italian, coined *azurn* from Ital. *azzurrino.* Instances of his leaning towards half Italian forms are *sdein* (Ital. *sdegnare*), *serenate* (Ital. *serenata*), *sovran, harald* (Ital. *araldo*). See *Par. Lost*, I. 752, II. 518, IV. 50. 769.

balm; properly the aromatic oily resin of the *balsam*-tree: then any fragrant oil or ointment for anointing, soothing pain, and so any fragrant or soothing liquid (as in *Com.* 674). Hence **balmy**='fragrant' (*Com.* 991).

batten, *Lyc.* 29, 'to fatten.' From the same root signifying 'excellence, prosperity,' as *better, best*, Germ. *besser.*

be. The root *be* was conjugated in the present tense indicative, singular and plural, up till about the middle of the 17th century. The singular, indeed, was almost limited in Elizabethan E. to the phrase "if thou *beest*," where the indicative *beest* has the force of the subjunctive; cf. *The Tempest*, V. 134, "if thou be'st Prospero." For the plural cf. *Genesis* xlii. 32, "We be twelve brethren," and *Matthew* xv. 14, "they be blind leaders of the blind."

blank, *Com.* 452, 'dismayed.' Cf. the verb *blank* = 'to confound' in *Samson Agonistes*, 471, literally 'to make to *blanch* or *blench*, i.e. become white' (F. *blanc*).

blow, *Lyc.* 48, 'to flower'; cf. Germ. *blühen*. Cognate with *bloom*, *blossom*.

bolt, or **boult**, *Com.* 760, 'to sift, refine.' O.F. *buleter*, a corruption of *bureter*, 'to sift through coarse red cloth' (Low Lat. *burra*, '*red* cloth,' from the root of Gk. πῦρ, 'fire'). For *r* softening into *l* in French cf. 'pé*l*erin,' 'a pilgrim,' Lat. 'pe*r*egrinus.'

boot, A.S. *bót*, 'advantage, good,' from the same root as *better*, *best*. "There is no *boot*" (*Richard II.* I. I. 164) exactly = 'it is no *good*.' Common as an impersonal verb, e.g. "what boots it?" (*Lyc.* 64) = 'what good is it?'

bosky, *Com.* 313, 'covered with bushes, shrubs'; *bosk* (whence *bosk-y*, like *bush-y* from *bush*) meant a bush or clump of bushes. Cognate with *bush*, *bouquet*, F. *bois*, 'wood.'

bourn, *Com.* 313, 'a brook'; the same as north-country *burn*; akin to Germ. *brunnen*, 'a spring.' Cf. *Bourne*-mouth. Distinct from *bourn*, 'a limit' (F. *borne*).

brinded, *Com.* 443; an older form than *brindled*; it means literally '**marked** as with a *brand*,' and generally indicates stripes of dark colour on the tawny coat of an animal. Cf. "the brinded cat," *Macbeth*, IV. I. I.

brown, *Lyc.* 2; a favourite epithet with Milton, and the 18th century poets influenced by his diction, in the sense 'dark' = Ital. *bruno*; especially of shade, twilight. Cf. *Il Penseroso*, 134, "shadows brown"; Pope, *Odyssey*, XVII. 215, "brown evening spreads her shade."

budge, *Com.* 707. Skeat says: "a kind of fur. *Budge* is lamb skin with the wool dressed outwards; orig. simply 'skin'—F. *bouge*, a wallet, great pouch, Lat. *bulga*, a little bag, a word of Gaulish origin." He refers to the same root the word *budget* = 'a leathern bag,' in *The Winter's Tale*, IV. 3. 20. Others connect with O.F. *bouchet*, 'a kid,' because an old writer says that *budge* was the fur of kids.

character, *Com.* 530, 'to stamp.' Gk. χαρακτήρ, 'a stamp on a coin, seal, etc., engraved mark.' For a good instance of its strict use cf. *The Faerie Queene*, v. 6. 2:

"Whose *character* in th' Adamantine *mould*
Of his true heart so firmely was *engraved.*"

clime, *Com.* 977, 'land, country'; cf. 2 *Henry VI.* III. 2. 84, "Drove back again unto my native clime." Gk. κλίμα, 'a slope,' from κλίνειν, 'to slope.' *Clime* and *climate* are 'doublets,' and each meant 'region,' then 'temperature,' the most important quality of a region.

clouted, *Com.* 635, 'patched, mended'; cf. *Joshua* ix. 5, "old shoes and clouted upon their feet." A.S. *clút*, 'a patch.'

cozen, *Com.* 737. According to the common (but not certain) explanation, to *cozen* a man is to pretend to be his *cousin* for the purpose of getting something out of him: whence 'to cheat.'

curfew, *Com.* 435; literally the signal to cover up (i.e. put out) the fire—F. *couvrir+feu.*

discover, 'to lay open to view, reveal,' literally 'uncover,' F. *découvrir*. Often in stage-directions; cf. Ben Jonson's *Masque of Beauty*, "Here a curtain was drawn [aside] and the scene discovered."

ditty, used strictly of the words of a song (*Lyc.* 32), but in *Com.* 86 of the music; cf. **smooth-dittied**='with smooth-flowing air.' From Lat. *dictatum* 'something dictated'; not from *dictum*.

engine, *Lyc.* 130. Properly 'a contrivance,' i.e. something made with *ingenuity* (Lat. *ingenium*); hence 'instrument.' In the early translations of the Bible it is used of implements of war. Mayhew quotes 2 *Chron.* xxvi. 15, in the Douay (1609) version, "He made in Jerusalem engines of diverse kind."

faery, *Com.* 118, 435; originally a collective noun='fairy folk, fairy land, enchantment'; cf. the title of *The Faerie Queene.* Late Lat. *fata*, 'a fairy,' formed from the plural of *fatum*, 'fate.'

flashy, *Lyc.* 123, 'tasteless'; literally 'watery,' being connected with an old word *flasshe*, 'a pool,' F. *flaque.* Bacon in his Essay *Of Studies* describes a certain class of books as "flashy things," where his Latin translation has *insipidus.*

foil, *Lyc.* 79, 'gold or silver leaf.' F. *feuille*, Lat. *folium.*

Cf. Florio's *Dictionary* (1598), "Foglia, a leafe, a sheete, a foile to set vnder precious stones."

fond, *Com.* 67, 'foolish,' its old meaning. Hence **fondly**= 'foolishly' (*Lyc.* 56). Originally *fond* was the p. p. of a Middle E. verb *fonnen*, 'to act like a fool,' from the noun *fon*, 'a fool.' The root is Scandinavian.

founder; properly 'to sink to the bottom,' Lat. *fundus;* cf. F. *s'effondrer*, 'to sink.' Hence **night-foundered**='plunged in night' (*Com.* 483).

fraught, *Com.* 355, 'laden, filled'; the abbreviated p. p. (*fraughted* was rarely used) of the verb *fraught*, 'to load'—see *Cymbeline*, I. I. 126—which is now obsolete except in this p. p. Akin probably to *freight.*

gloze, or **glose**, *Com.* 161, 'to speak falsely, to flatter.' Middle E. *glosen* meant 'to make *glosses*, explain,' from Late Lat. *glossa*, Gk. γλῶσσα, which signified (1) the tongue, (2) a language, (3) a word, (4) an explanation of a word. The verb *glosen* got the idea 'to explain *falsely*,' whence 'to deceive.' So *glozing*='deceptive'; cf. George Herbert, *The Dotage*, "False glozing pleasures." Especially used of flattering, false speech.

goblin, *Com.* 436. Late Lat. *gobelinus*, a diminutive of Lat. *cobalus*, 'a mountain-sprite, demon'=Gk. κόβαλος, 'a rogue,' or 'a goblin supposed to befriend rogues.'

grain, *Com.* 750; O.F. *graine*=Low Lat. *granum*, which, like the classical Lat. *coccum* ('a berry'), was used of the scarlet dye made from the *cochineal* insect found on the scarlet oak, the insect being like a berry or seed. Properly therefore *grain* ='scarlet hue,' but Elizabethan poets seem to use it in the extended sense 'hue, colour.' As *grain* was a very strong dye, so that the colour of cloth dyed *in grain* never washed out but seemed to be part of the texture itself, the word came to signify 'texture, fibre,' of cloth or wood. An *ingrained* fault is one that has become of the very texture of a man's character.

griesly, *Com.* 603, 'horrible'; cognate with *gruesome* and Germ. *grausig*, *grässlich*. Cf. *The Faerie Queene*, III. I. 17, "Lo! where a griesly foster forth did rush" (i.e. forester).

guerdon, *Lyc.* 73, 'recompense, return.' Through O.F. from Lat. *widerdonum*, "a singular compound of the Old High German *widar*, back again, and Lat. *donum*, a gift"—*Skeat.* Literally therefore 'a giving back,' whether good or evil.

his; this was the ordinary *neuter* (as well as masculine) possessive pronoun in Middle E. and remained so in Elizabethan E. Cf. *Genesis* iii. 15, "*it* shall bruise thy head, and thou shalt bruise *his* heel." There was also a use, not common, of *it* (Middle E. *hit*) as a possessive, though uninflected; especially in the phrase *it own*. Cf. *The Tempest*, II. 1. 163, "of it own kind," and the Bible of 1611 in *Leviticus* xxv. 5, "of it owne accord." This possessive use of *it* without *own* to strengthen it seems to have been somewhat familiar in Elizabethan E., applied especially to children; cf. *The Winter's Tale*, III. 2. 101, "The innocent milk in *it* most innocent mouth."

Then from the possessive use of *it* uninflected there arose, about the close of the 16th century, the inflected form *its* in which *-s* is the usual possessive inflection, as in *his*. This new form *its* came into use slowly, the old idiom *his* being generally retained by Elizabethans. There are no instances of *its* in Spenser or the Bible (1611), and only three in Milton's poetical works (*Paradise Lost*, I. 254, IV. 813, *Nativity Ode*, 106). *Its* does not occur in any extant work of Shakespeare printed prior to his death: hence it seems not improbable that the nine instances in the 1st Folio (five in a single play, *The Winter's Tale*) were due to the editors or printers of the Folio.

hutch, *Com.* 719, 'to enclose.' F. *huche*, 'a *hutch*, bin,' Low Lat. *hutica;* probably from same root as Germ. *hüten*, 'to guard.' A *bolting-hutch* is the bin into which flour is sifted.

influence, *Com.* 336; late Lat. *influentia*, literally 'a flowing in upon' (Lat. *in* + *fluere*). An astrological term applied to the power over the earth, men's characters, fortunes etc., which was supposed to descend from the celestial bodies. Cf. "planetary influence," *King Lear*, I. 2. 136; "skyey influences," *Measure for Measure*, III. 1. 9. Other terms due to astrology are 'dis*aster*' (Lat. *astrum*, 'a star'), 'ill-*starred*,' 'jovial,' 'saturnine.'

inherit; then often used = 'to have, possess,' without (as now) the notion of '*heir*ship' (Lat. *heres*, 'an heir'). Cf. in the Prayer-Book, "And bless thine inheritance"—that is, 'thy peculiar possession, thy people.' Hence **disinherit**, 'to make to cease to have, to dispossess' (*Com.* 334).

inure, *Com.* 735, 'to accustom,' literally 'to bring into practice' (= *ure*). For the obsolete noun *ure* (F. *œuvre*, 'work,'

Lat. *opera*) cf. Bacon's Essay *Of Simulation*, "lest his hand should be out of ure," i.e. out of practice. Cf. 'man*ure*.'

laver, *Com.* 838, 'a vessel for washing'; Lat. *lavare*, 'to wash'; cf. **lave**, *Lyc.* 175. The *laver* mentioned in 1 *Kings* vii. 30 was a large basin in the Temple for the ablution of the priests.

lawn; properly (*Com.* 568, 965) an open grass-covered space in a wood, like the glades in the New Forest; hence a poetical word for any 'pasture' (*Lyc.* 25), 'green.' Perhaps cognate with F. *lande*, 'waste land'; cf. the *landes* or waste country south of Bordeaux.

lewd, *Com.* 465; Middle E. *lewed*=A.S. *læwed*. Its successive meanings were: (1) 'enfeebled,' *læwed* (=*gelæwed*) being the past participle of *læwan*, 'to weaken'; (2) then 'ignorant'; then (3) 'bad'; then (4) 'lustful,' i.e. bad in a particular way. From (2) arose also the sense 'lay, belonging to the laity,' because the laity compared with the clergy were ignorant.

lickerish, *Com.* 700, 'dainty'; something pleasant to *lick*. Cf. the cognate F. *lécher*, 'to lick'; Germ. *leckerei*, 'dainties.'

list, 'to wish, please'; commonly a present (*Lyc.* 123), rarely a preterite (*Com.* 49). Shakespeare once has *listed;* cf. *Richard III.* III. 5. 84, "his savage heart...*listed* to make his prey." Akin to *lust*, which often meant 'pleasure,' as does Germ. *lust;* cf. *Psalm* xcii. 10, "Mine eye also shall see his lust of mine enemies" (Prayer-Book).

livery, *Com.* 455; in Elizabethan E.='any kind of dress, garb'; cf. *L'Allegro*, 62, "The clouds in thousand liveries dight." Originally *livery* meant whatever was given (i.e. *delivered*) by a lord to his household, whether food, money or garments. From F. *livrer*.

lull, *Com.* 260; an imitative word formed from *lu lu* hummed by nurses in composing children to sleep. Hence *lullaby*.

madrigal, *Com.* 495; Ital. *madrigale*, 'a pastoral song,' from Gk. *μάνδρα*, 'a fold, stable.' The madrigal was one of the most characteristic forms of old English music.

main, *Com.* 28; Icelandic *megin*, 'mighty,' common in compounds, e.g. *megin-sjör*, 'mighty sea'; from the same root as Gk. *μέγας*, Lat. *magnus*: whence also **mickle** (*Com.* 31) or *micel*, 'great,' Middle E. *michel* or *muchel* (cf. *much*).

meed; properly 'reward' (*Lyc.* 84) rather than 'tribute' (*Lyc.* 14). From the same root as Gk. *μισθός*, 'pay.'

methinks; **methought**, *Com.* 171, 482. These are really *impersonal* constructions such as were much used in pre-Elizabethan E.; their meaning is, 'it *seems*, or seemed, *to* me.' The pronoun is a dative, and the verb is not the ordinary verb 'to *think*' = A.S. *þencan*, but an obsolete impersonal verb 'to *seem*' = A.S. *þyncan*. These cognate verbs got confused through their similarity; the distinction between them as regards usage and sense is shown in Milton's *Paradise Regained*, II. 266, "*Him thought* he by the brook of Cherith stood" = 'to him it seemed that' etc. Cf. their German cognates *denken*, 'to think,' used personally, and the impersonal *es dünkt*, 'it seems'; also the double use of Gk. *δοκεῖν*. For the old impersonal constructions cf. Spenser, *Prothalamion* 60, "*Them seem'd* they never saw a sight so fayre."

nice; Lat. *nescius*, 'ignorant.' It first meant 'foolish,' as in Chaucer; then 'foolishly particular, fastidious, prudish' (*Com.* 139); then 'subtly,' since fastidiousness implies drawing fine, subtle distinctions. The original notion 'foolish' often affects the Elizabethan uses of the word, which is noticeable as having improved in sense.

ore, *Com.* 719, 933, *Lyc.* 170, 'metal'; A.S. *ór*, 'unrefined metal'; cf. Germ. *erz*. Sometimes Elizabethan writers use *ore* = 'gold,' i.e. through confusion of sound with Lat. *aurum*. Thus it means 'precious metal' in *Hamlet*, IV. I. 25.

orient, 'bright, lustrous'; in Elizabethan poetry a constant epithet of gems, especially pearls. Perhaps, used thus, it first meant 'eastern,' gems coming from the Orient or East; then as these were bright it got the notion 'lustrous.' Commonly Milton applies it to liquids (*Com.* 65) or jewels; cf. "orient pearl," *Par. Lost*, V. 2.

pert, *Com.* 118. Shakespeare always uses it in a good sense = 'lively, alert'; cf. *A Midsummer-Night's Dream*, I. I. 13, "Awake the pert and nimble spirit of youth." Middle E. *pert* is another form of *perk*, 'smart'; it got its bad sense 'saucy' through confusion with *malapert*, from Lat. *male* + *expertus*, 'too experienced,' hence 'too sharp,' 'saucy.'

pester, *Com.* 7, 'to shackle, clog.' Short for *impester* = F. *empêtrer*, which "signifies properly to hobble a horse while he feeds afield"—*Brachet;* from Lat. *in*, 'on, upon'+medieval Lat. *pastorium*, 'a clog for horses at *pasture*.' From 'to shackle' follows naturally the sense 'to annoy, bother.'

pinfold, *Com.* 7, 'a pound, i.e. enclosure for strayed cattle.' Short for '*pind*-fold,' from A.S. *pyndan*, 'to *pen* up.' Cognate with *pound*. Cf. "Lipsbury pinfold," *King Lear*, II. 2. 8.

plea, *Lyc.* 90. O.F. *plait*, Late Lat. *placitum*, 'a decision,' i.e. 'the *pleasure* of the Court or Judge' (from *placere*, 'to *please*').

plighted, *Com.* 301, 'folded.' Spenser uses *plight*='fold' both as noun and verb; cf. *The Faerie Queene*, II. 3. 26, "many a folded plight," and VI. 7. 43, "And on his head a roll of linen plight." Cf. the cognate *plait* (or *pleat*) and F. *pli*, *plier;* all from Lat. *plicare*, 'to fold.'

prank, *Com.* 759, "to deck, adorn'; cf. *The Winter's Tale*, IV. 4, 10, "most goddess-like pranked up." A favourite word with Herrick; cf. *The Harvest Home*, "Some prank them up with oaken leaves." Akin to *prance* (properly 'to make a show'), and Germ. *prunk*, 'pomp.'

prevent, *Com.* 285, 'to anticipate'; Lat. *prævenire*, 'to come before.' Cf. *Psalm* cxix. 148, "mine eyes prevent the night watches."

purfled, *Com.* 995, 'embroidered'; cf. *The Faerie Queene*, I. 2. 13, "Purfled with gold and pearle of rich assay." F. *pourfilé* (*fil*, 'a thread,' Lat. *filum*). The word survives in *purl*, a term used in lace-making.

purchase, *Com.* 607, 'booty, prey.' The verb meant first to hunt after (F. *pour*+*chasser*); "then to take in hunting; then to acquire; and then, as the commonest way of acquiring is by giving money in exchange, to buy"—*Trench*. The sense 'to acquire, gain' is common in Elizabethan E. Cf. 1 *Timothy* iii. 13, "they that have used the office of a deacon well purchase to themselves a good degree' (Revised Version 'gain').

quaint, *Lyc.* 139, 'dainty.' Derived through O.F. *coint* from Lat. *cognitus*, 'well-known'; cf. *acquaint* from Lat. *adcognitare*. The original sense (1) was 'knowing, wise'; cf. Hampole's *Psalter*, *Ps.* cxix. 98, "Abouen myn enmys quaynt thou me made," i.e. "wiser than mine enemies." But (2) through a false notion that it came from Lat. *comptus*, 'trimmed, adorned,' *quaint* lost its old sense 'knowing' and got the sense 'trim, dainty, neat'—which it has always in Shakespeare; cf. "my quaint Ariel," *The Tempest*, I. 2. 317. Perhaps (3) *quaint*= 'odd, eccentric' arose from the notion '*too* trim, over-fine.'

quire, *Com.* 112. An older form of *choir*, Lat. *chorus*; cf. O.F. *quer* and F. *chœur*. "In Quires and places where they sing," Prayer-Book.

rapt, *Com.* 794, 'transported.' It should be written *rapped*, being the past participle of an old verb *rap*, 'to seize hurriedly'; cf. *Cymbeline*, I. 6. 51, "what...thus raps you?" i.e. what transports you thus? The form *rapt* comes through confusion with Lat. *raptus*, the p. p. of Lat. *rapere*, 'to seize.'

rathe, *Lyc.* 142 'early.' A.S. *hræð*, 'quick, soon'; cf. *rather*='sooner,' *rathest*='soonest' (e.g. in Bacon's *Colours of Good and Evil*). For *rathe*, 'early,' cf. *The Shepheards Calender*, December, "Thus is my harvest hastened all to rathe," i.e. too early).

rhyme, *Lyc.* 11; so spelt through confusion with *rhythm*, Gk. ῥυθμός; properly *rime*, from A.S. *rím*, 'a number.'

ruth, *Lyc.* 163, 'pity.' Cf. *Troilus and Cressida*, V. 3. 48, "Spur them to ruthful work, rein them from ruth," where *ruthful*='piteous'; contrast *ruthless*. Akin to A.S. *hreówan*, 'to *rue*,' Germ. *reue*, 'repentance.'

sad, *Com.* 189, 355, 'grave, serious,' without any notion of sorrow. Cf. *Henry V.* IV. I. 318, "the sad and solemn priests." Originally 'sated,' A.S. *sæd* being akin to Lat. *satis*, 'enough.'

scrannel, *Lyc.* 124. Skeat says: "*Scrannel*, thin, weakly, wretched (Scandinavian). Provincial English *scranny*, thin, lean; *scrannel*, a lean person (Lincolnshire)." He gives a Swedish word *skran*, 'weak,' and says that *shrink*, A.S. *scrincan*, is cognate; cf. its preterite *shrank*, A.S. *scranc*.

shrewd, *Com.* 846, 'malicious, mischievous'; from its common Elizabethan sense 'bad,' literally 'cursed' (*shrewd* being the p. p. of *schrewen*, 'to curse'). Cf. "a shrewd turn"='a bad turn,' *All's Well That Ends Well*, III. 5. 71. From *shrew*=A.S. *screáwa*, "a shrew-mouse, fabled to have a very venomous bite" (Skeat).

shroud; properly 'a garment' (A.S. *scrúd*)—cf. *Lyc.* 22; hence any 'shelter, covering,' *Com.* 147. Outside Old St Paul's Cathedral in London there was a covered place called "the Shrouds," where sermons were preached in wet weather, instead of at St Paul's Cross, which was in the open.

sooth, *Com.* 823, 'true.' A.S. *sōð*, 'true'; cf. *soothsayer*, *forsooth.*

sound, *Com.* 115, 'a strait, strip of water'; A.S. *sund*, literally 'a strait of the sea that could be *swum* across.'

sovran, *Com.* 41; spelt thus always in *Par. Lost*; cf. Ital. *sovrano.* The common form *sovereign*=O.F. *soverain.* Lat. *superanus*, 'chief,' from *super*, 'above.'

stole, *Com.* 195. Elizabethans often use the form of the past tense as a past participle—cf. **took** (*Com.* 558); and conversely with certain verbs, e.g. *begin*, *sing*, *spring*, the form of the past participle as a past tense. Thus Shakespeare and Milton nearly always use *sung* instead of *sang;* cf. *Par. Lost*, III. 18, "I *sung* of Chaos and eternal Night."

swart, *Lyc.* 138; more often *swarthy*, but cf. Keats, *Endymion*, "Swart planet in the universe of deeds." A.S. *sweart*, 'very dark'; cf. Germ. *schwartz.*

swink; A.S. *swincan*, 'to work hard, labour.' Hence the sense 'wearied with work' in *Com.* 293. A common verb in old writers; cf. *The Faerie Queene*, II. 7. 8:

"Honour, estate, and all this worldes good,
For which men swinck and sweat incessantly."

Shelley has it in his humorous *Letter to Maria Gisborne:*

"that dew which the gnomes drink,
When at their subterranean toil they swink."

take; used by Elizabethans of the influence of supernatural powers, e.g. fairies (*Hamlet*, I. 1. 163); cf. Cotgrave (1611), "*fée*, taken, bewitched." Hence 'to charm, fascinate'—as in *Com.* 558; cf. Tennyson's *Dying Swan*, III.:

"The wild swan's death-hymn took the soul
Of that waste place."

Cf. the colloquial use now of 'taking'='charming.'

toy, *Com.* 502, 'a trifle.' Cf. *Macbeth*, II. 3. 99, "All is but toys." Cognate with Germ. *zeug*, 'stuff, trash,' as in *spielzeug*, 'playthings.'

trains, *Com.* 151, 'snares.' Cf. *Samson Agonistes*, 533, "venereal snares"=snares of love (Venus). F. *traîner*, from Lat. *trahere*, 'to draw,' in Late Lat. 'to betray'—from the metaphor of drawing birds into snares.

trick, *Lyc.* 170, 'to dress anew.' From Dutch *trek*, 'a trick, a neat contrivance': whence the idea 'neat appearance.'

turkis, *Com.* 894, 'the turquoise,' literally 'Turkish stone.' Cf. Tennyson, *The Merman*, III., "Turkis and agate and almondine."

uncouth, *Lyc.* 186; A.S. *uncūð*, 'unknown'—from *un*, 'not,' + *cūð*, the p.p. of *cunnan*, 'to know.' In M. it almost always means 'unfamiliar,' with the implied notion 'unpleasant.'

unharboured, *Com.* 423, 'yielding no *harbourage*, i.e. shelter.' A *harbinger* was originally an officer who went in advance of an army or prince to make provision for the night's shelter. From Icelandic *herbergi*, 'an army shelter'; cf. the cognate Germ. words *heer* + *bergen*. F. *auberge*, 'an inn,' is also from this Icelandic word.

usher, *Com.* 279. The noun (F. *huissier*, Lat. *ostiarius*) meant properly 'a doorkeeper,' later 'someone who went in front of any great person in a procession': hence the idea 'to precede, introduce.'

virtue, *Com.* 165, 'efficacy, power'; a frequent Elizabethan use. Cf. *Luke* viii. 46, "Virtue is gone out of me." So **virtuous** = 'full of efficacy' (*Com.* 621). Lat. *virtus*, 'worth, manly excellence' (Lat. *vir*, man).

wanton. *Lyc.* 137. The radical sense is 'ill-restrained'; *wan* being a negative prefix expressing *want*, deficiency, and the latter part of the word being connected with A.S. *téon*, 'to draw.' For the prefix cf. the old words *wanhope*, 'despair,' *wantrust*, 'distrust.'

wassailer, *Com.* 179, 'a reveller.' *Wassail* is the old northern English *wæs hál*, 'be whole' = the imperative of *wesan*, 'to be' + *hál*, the same as *whole* and *hale*. Originally a salutation in drinking, like the Germ. *prosit!* ('may it benefit you'), used in drinking a man's health, *wassail* came to mean 'a drinking, carousing, revel.' Lady Macbeth promises to overcome the chamberlains "with wine and wassail" (I. 7. 64). The '*wassail*-bowl' was a great feature of the old Christmas feasting.

weed, *Com.* 16, 84, 390, 'garments, dress'; A.S. *wǽd*, 'a garment.' Commonly in the plural; cf. *Coriolanus*, II. 3. 161, "With a proud heart he wore his humble weeds." Now only in the phrase 'widow's weeds,' except in poetry; cf. Tennyson, "In words like weeds I'll wrap me o'er" (*In Memoriam*, V.).

welkin, *Com.* 1015, 'sky'; properly a plural word = 'clouds,' from A.S. *wolcnu*, the plural of *wolcen*, 'a cloud'; cf. Germ. *wolke*, 'a cloud.'

well, *Lyc.* 15, 'spring'; as often in Spenser; cf. *The Shepheards Calender*, April:

"And eke you Virgins [the Muses], that on Parnasse dwell,
Whence floweth Helicon, the learned well."

wizard, *Lyc.* 55. The first part is from the root seen in *wise*, *wit*, Germ. *wissen*. The suffix *-ard*, of Teutonic origin—cf. names like *Eberhard*—here has its original intensive force = '*hard*, strong in, i.e. very.' Usually depreciative, as in *coward*, *drunkard*, *braggart* (*d* softened to *t*).

APPENDIX.

I.

THE ENGLISH MASQUE[1].

In the last years of the sixteenth century England owed much to Italian culture. For the age of Spenser Italy was what France a hundred years afterwards became for the age of Dryden, the great authority and model in everything pertaining to literature and art. It was from Italy that the Masque came. Hall tells us in the passage from his *Chronicle* quoted later on that the entertainment which struck people as so novel in 1512 was introduced "after the manner of Italie." Marlowe puts these lines into the mouth of Piers Gaveston, the favourite of Edward II.:

"I must have wanton poets, pleasant wits,
Musicians, that with touching of a string
May draw the pliant king which way I please:
Music and poetry is his delight;
Therefore I'll have Italian masks by night,
Sweet speeches, comedies, and pleasing shows."—

Edward II. I. I.

In his *Chronicle History of the Stage*, pp. 22, 26, Mr Fleay notes that Italians "made pastime" for the Queen in 1574; that the Records of the Revels mention an Italian interpreter; and that the speeches of a Masque played before Elizabeth in 1579 were translated from English into Italian, at the Lord Chamberlain's direction.

[1] This sketch is mainly abridged from the longer account of the Masque prefixed to the edition of *Comus* in the "Pitt Press" edition, where the various sources from which information is taken are mentioned. Anyone who desires to consult a fuller (and most interesting) account of the Masque should turn to Symonds' book, *Shakspere's Predecessors.*

There can be no question therefore as to the Italian origin of the Masque.

The earliest description of an English Masque occurs in Hall's *Chronicle* under the date 1512. He says:

"On the daie of the Epiphanie at night the King with xi other were disguised after the manner of Italie, called a maske, a thing not sene afore in England: thei were appareled in garments long and brode, wrought all with golde, with visers and cappes of gold; and after the banket doen these Maskers came in with the sixe gentlemen disguised in silke, beryng staffe-torches, and desired the ladies to daunce: some were content, and some that knew the fashion of it refused, because it was not a thing commonly seen. And after thei daunced and communed together, as the fashion of the maskes is, thei toke their leave and departed; and so did the Queene and all the ladies."

The entertainment thus described was what we should call a 'masquerade': an entertainment, that is, in which 'masks' or vizards were worn and dances were the chief element. Often the dances were supposed to illustrate some story, as it were in 'dumb show,' and gradually allegorical characters, e.g. Love, were brought in to explain the story to the audience, and songs were introduced. Hence from being merely a series of dances performed by masked characters, the Masque came to be a kind of play which was accompanied by a good deal of music and therefore resembled an opera. Scenery was then required, and wealthy patrons of the Masque vied with each other in the splendour of their representations. Here the Masque was influenced by the Pageant. The latter was of even older origin. Mention is made as early as 1236 of the City-pageants celebrated in London by members of the trade guilds. Of these spectacular processions, representing symbolically the various trades, which passed through the London streets at great festivities, the Lord Mayor's Show is a survival. Sometimes, e.g. in Shirley's great Masque *The Triumph of Peace*, a procession formed the introduction to a Masque; and the general influence of the Pageant was to foster a taste for spectacular display. This taste was not gratified in the public theatres simply because the theatrical managers could not afford the expense. But it was gratified in the Masque-performances given by the Court, great nobles, and the four legal societies

(Inner Temple, Middle Temple, Gray's Inn and Lincoln's Inn), whose Christmas-tide festivities or 'Revels[1]' were of a costly description.

Gradually therefore the Masque developed from its simple origin as a masquerade into a complex form of entertainment scarcely distinguishable from an opera.

The Masque reached its zenith in the reign of James I. Ben Jonson was the great master of the art, and his Masques may be taken as specimens of the finest type. They present these features:

The characters are deities of classical mythology, nymphs and personified qualities such as 'Love,' 'Harmony,' 'Delight,' 'Laughter' (for throughout its history the Masque preserved a marked strain of allegory). The number of characters seldom exceeds six, and there are generally two bands to whom the title 'Masquers' is specially assigned and who serve as choruses, now separately and in contrast, now in union. Thus in the *Masque of Hymen* there are eight maidens personifying the powers exercised by Juno in her capacity of patroness of women in wedlock, and eight knights personifying the 'Humours' and 'Affections' of man. In the *Masque of Queens* there are twelve witches embodying evil qualities, such as 'Ignorance,' 'Suspicion,' and against them are set twelve queens representing the highest fame. The scenes are laid in ideal regions—Olympus, Arcadia, the Fortunate Isles, the Palace of Oceanus, and similar realms of fancy. The length of the pieces, of course, varies, but the average Masque is about equal to the first Act of *The Tempest*. They are written in various metres of rhymed verse, which is sometimes spoken, sometimes declaimed in recitative, and contain solos for the chief characters and part-songs and choruses.

Dances, executed by the 'Masquers,' are a very important element: stately 'measures,' 'corantos,' 'galliards,' and the like, of Italian or French origin, and all new to England. Most elaborate scenery is employed, giving the representations a highly spectacular character, and the dresses of the performers are of the costliest description and symbolical. It is interesting, in passing, to remember the contrast between the bare simplicity

1 *Twelfth Night* was acted at the Candlemas feast (Jan. 6) of the Middle Temple in 1602.

which characterised the representation of Shakespeare's pieces at the Globe Theatre[1] and the rich display of the Masque.

Generally there is a comic part called the Anti-masque. This serves as a contrast to the idealism of the Masque itself. It is a foil, an opposite: hence its name. Sometimes the Anti-masque consists of a scene or two of humorous dialogue and action, which have a satirical relation to the main subject and almost parody it; the characters being drawn from contemporary Elizabethan life. Sometimes the Anti-masque is merely a grotesque interlude. One moment personifications of Delight, and Harmony, and Love move across the scene, chanting some rhythmic choral strain to a slow recitative: the next all is confusion: the Anti-masquers rush forward, grotesque in dress and movement, execute fantastic dances and movements, and retire.

Milton does not attempt to work out an Anti-masque in *Comus;* very wisely, as he had little humour in his nature. But it may be conjectured that had Ben Jonson been the author of *Comus* at least two episodes in the poem would have been treated as burlesque interludes. These would have occurred at line 93, where Comus first appears, and at line 957: the Anti-masquers being in the one case the "rout of monsters," and in the other the "Country Dancers," with their clumsy "ducks and nods."

We have nothing in our own day that corresponds precisely with the Masque of the reign of James I. It was like an opera, because so much music was introduced; like a ballet, because there was so much dancing; like a pageant, because the scenery, setting and costumes were devised on so splendid a scale. It was certainly the forerunner of the opera, and composers like Lawes and Lock, to whom we owe our earliest operas, had in their youth written the incidental music of the latest Masques.

The Masque was a private form of entertainment, much patronised by the Court of James I. The Laureate Ben Jonson would write the *libretto*; the Court-composer Alfonso Ferrabosco often furnished the music, which would be rendered by the Court-orchestra and the choirs of the Chapels Royal; and the Court-architect, Inigo Jones, designed the scenery. Great nobles too, as we have said, and the legal societies gave Masque-performances. The Masque was peculiarly suited to be a form

[1] Cf. the first Prologue to *Henry V.*

of private theatricals because little skill in acting was required. The Queen and her maids of honour and courtiers could render the songs and execute the dances and rhythmic movements with all due effect, and satisfy the slender demands on their skill as players; though professional actors were sometimes employed for the Anti-masque, and professional musicians (usually the singers at the Chapels Royal) when the solo parts presented great difficulty.

Great ceremonies and occasions were signalised by Masque-performances, such as the Twelfth Night festivities at Whitehall, royal visits to noblemen's houses and weddings. Of course, the subject and allegory of a Masque were suited to the occasion for which it was composed. Thus in a Wedding-Masque the characters are Juno, Venus, Hymen, the Graces, etc., powers whose blessing is invoked on the wedded pair. And there is often, as in *Comus*, an element of personal compliment and local allusion.

The Masque declined somewhat on the death of James in 1625. Charles I. indeed was equally devoted to amusements. He was a good actor. As a boy he had played in several of Jonson's pieces, and *Love's Triumph through Callipolis* (1630) was performed "by his Majesty, with the Lords and Gentlemen Assisting." But the novelty was gone. An art or taste which depends on the whims of wealth and fashion has no element of permanence: what is in vogue to-day is voted obsolete to-morrow. Moreover the Masque had become too costly. We are told that Daniel's Masque *Hymen's Triumph* cost about £3000; Jonson's *Masque of Blackness* also about £3000, and his *Hue and Cry of Cupid* nearly £4000; while the expense of producing Shirley's *Triumph of Peace* reached the fabulous amount of £21,000 (which we must multiply by 4 to get its modern equivalent).

Entertainments which swallowed up a sum equivalent to the revenue of a small country could not be matters of frequent occurrence, especially when the royal purse was none too full. Moreover, as literature, the Masque had suffered inevitably by the mania for elaborate scenery, dresses and the like features of representation. Ben Jonson indeed insisted that the words were the real life and *anima* of the Masque: that the poetry should have the place of honour, and the other arts—music, sculpture, painting—serve as her handmaids. But this was not the popular view. Even his contemporary and fellow writer of Masques, Daniel in the preface to the *Masque of Tethys* declared that the poet's share in a Masque was "the least...and of least note: the only life consists in show, the art and invention of the architect gives the greatest graces, and is of the most importance."

The Masque in fact has come to be regarded as merely a peg whereon to hang costly extravagance. "Painting and carpentry are the soul of Masque" was Ben Jonson's final and bitterly ironical summing up of the whole matter. Just so nowadays a piece may attract by the splendour of its stage-spectacle rather than by any merit in the drama itself.

Curiously enough, when the period of its decadence was far advanced the Masque had a sudden and passing revival of life. This happened just before the composition of *Comus*. "In 1633 the Puritan hatred to the theatre had blazed out in Prynne's *Histriomastix*, and as a natural consequence, the loyal and cavalier portion of society threw itself into dramatic amusements of every kind. It was an unreal revival of the Mask, stimulated by political passion, in the wane of genuine taste for the fantastic and semi-barbarous pageant, in which the former age had delighted"—(Mark Pattison). This revival was marked by the production of the famous Masque already mentioned, Shirley's *Triumph of Peace*, and of Carew's *Cœlum Britannicum*. The former was acted on Feb. 3, 1634, by the four legal societies, who desired, says a writer of that period, to express thereby "their love and duty to their majesties...and to manifest the difference of their opinion from Mr Prynne's new learning." Carew's Masque was given by the Court a fortnight later. Probably Milton was then busy with the composition of *Comus*, acted some months after. Each of these Masques has some association with *Comus*, as Lawes wrote the music for each, while two of the performers in the *Cœlum Britannicum* were Viscount Brackley and Mr Thomas Egerton, the "Brothers" of Milton's Masque. The occasional representations of Masques after the Restoration, and even in this century, have merely an antiquarian interest. As a form of dramatic art the Masque lost its identity in the opera.

Ben Jonson's primacy in masque-writing stands unchallenged, but the art counted other distinguished exponents—e.g. Beaumont and Fletcher; Dekker and Middleton, who wrote city-pageants; Daniel, Chapman and Marston, patronised mainly by the Court and nobles; and Shirley and Carew, the representatives of its waning glories.

Nor was Shakespeare uninfluenced by the Masque. *A Midsummer-Night's Dream* is rather a Masque-comedy than comedy proper. The classical characters and locality, the supernatural beings, the picturesque scenery required, the fanciful story, the rhymed and various types of verse, the large element of music and dance, the comic "interlude" of Bottom and his friends, who not only serve as contrasts to the classical characters of Theseus and his courtiers and to the fairies, but also parody in their "tragical mirth" the love-element of the serious scenes: all these are features in which Shakespeare's play reveals its kinship with the Masque. The pageant of Hymen in *As You Like It*, v. 4, is an episode which might have been detached from an ordinary Masque; and so is the Vision in *Cymbeline*, v. 4. The Masquerade in *Henry VIII.* I. 4, reminds us of the simple type of Masque described by Hall. The Masque in the fourth Act of *The Tempest*, though brief, contains the characteristic features. The theme is an allegory of marriage-bliss. The characters are taken from mythology. The Nymphs and Reapers represent the bands of 'Masquers.' Their dresses[1] are emblematical. There are songs, a "graceful dance," music. The verse is rhymed and varied. And the interlude akin to a Masque in the third Act, scene 3, illustrates the use of scenery and stage-machinery.

II.

PASTORAL POETRY.

We must go back to the Greek poet Theocritus[2] for the beginnings of pastoral poetry such as *Lycidas*. Theocritus was born at Syracuse (a Greek colony) in Sicily, early in the third century B.C. It should be remembered that the Greek colonies in Sicily were as much 'Greek' then in civilization and culture

[1] Thus the "Nymphs" of the brooks are bidden to come with their "sedged crowns," IV. 129, sedge being symbolical of water-deities (cf. *Lyc.* 104), and the "Reapers" are "properly habited" (Stage-direction).

[2] "The first head and welspring" of pastoral verse, as Spenser's friend said; see "Globe" *Spenser*, p. 444.

as the capitals of Greater Britain—Toronto, say, and Sydney—are 'British' now. The works therefore of Theocritus represent Greek literature exactly as if he had been born in Greece itself. Theocritus spent part of his life at Alexandria, the great centre of culture and refinement at that time. His extant works, written in the Doric[1] dialect of Greek, consist of some thirty *Idyls* and a few *Epigrams*. His fame rests on his *Idyls*. They are called *Idyls*[2], 'little pictures,' from their highly-wrought, picturesque manner. About a third of them are pastoral or rural. They depict different aspects of rural life, more particularly shepherd-life, in Sicily and Southern Italy, and are partly cast in the form of a dialogue followed by a singing-match between two shepherds. The character of the *Idyls* will be best understood by those who are unacquainted with them if we give summaries of two or three from Mr Andrew Lang's translation.

Idyl v. "This Idyl begins with a debate between two hirelings, who, at last, compete with each other in a match of pastoral song. No other idyl of Theocritus is so frankly true to the rough side of rustic manners. The scene is in Southern Italy."

IX. "Daphnis and Menalcas, at the bidding of the poet, sing the joys of the neatherd's and of the shepherd's life. Both receive the thanks of the poet, and rustic prizes—a staff, and a horn, made of a spiral shell."

X. "The sturdy reaper, Milon, as he levels the swathes of corn, derides his languid and love-worn companion, Battus. The latter defends his gipsy love....Milon replies with the song of Lityerses—a string, apparently, of popular rural couplets, such as Theocritus may have heard chanted in the fields."

What distinguishes the *Idyls* of Theocritus from all later pastoral poetry is their reality, their fidelity to fact. The rural life of his poems is a genuine thing, idealised somewhat and represented with consummate art, but still genuine at bottom; not the fiction and mere literary convention which other bucolic verse gives us. Professor Jebb says: "His [Theocritus's] rural

[1] Syracuse was a Dorian colony.

[2] Cf. Tennyson's use of the title.

idyls are no sham pastorals, but true to the sights and sounds of his native Sicily. The Sicilian sunshine is there, the shade of oak-trees or pine, the 'couch, softer than sleep,' made by ferns or flowers; the 'music of water falling from the high face of the rock,' the arbutus shrubs, with their bright red berries, above the sea-cliffs, whence the shepherds watch the tunny-fishers on the sea below, while the sailors' song floats up to them; and if the form given to the strains of shepherd and goatherd is such as finished poetry demands, this is a very different thing from the affectation of the mock pastoral, as it existed, for instance, at the court of Louis XIV. The modern love-songs of Greek shepherds warrant the supposition that their ancient prototypes commanded some elegance of expression; and whatever may be the degree in which Theocritus has idealised his Sicilian peasants, at any rate we hear the voice and breathe the air of nature."

The first of these *Idyls* has a peculiar interest for the student of *Lycidas*. It is not merely a pastoral, but a pastoral elegy.

Mr Lang summarises it thus:

"The shepherd Thyrsis meets a goatherd, in a shady place beside a spring, and at his invitation sings the *Song of Daphnis*. This ideal hero [viz. Daphnis] of Greek pastoral song had won for his bride the fairest of the Nymphs. Confident in the strength of his passion, he boasted that Love could never subdue him to a new affection. Love avenged himself by making Daphnis desire a strange maiden, but to this temptation he never yielded, and so died a constant lover. The song tells how the cattle and the wild things of the wood bewailed him, how Hermes gave him counsel in vain, and how with his last breath he retorted the taunts of the implacable Aphrodite.

The scene is in Sicily."

This *Song* is the model on which *Lycidas* and all other pastoral elegies are framed, consciously or unconsciously.

Two other poets associated with Sicily lived about the same time as Theocritus and wrote, in Doric, *Idyls* of which a few are extant, viz. Bion and Moschus. Each wrote a poem of lament that may be compared with Theocritus's *Song of Daphnis*: Bion the *Lament for Adonis*, and Moschus the *Lament for Bion*. The latter is a very close parallel to *Lycidas*. Moschus was the pupil of Bion, and in his *Lament* he mourns for his friend and master under the same pastoral allegory which Milton uses in

Lycidas, i.e. as one shepherd mourning for another. Now this introduction of allegory into the pastoral marks the second stage in its history—the decline from its original reality and truth. For Theocritus's *Song of Daphnis* is, in kind if not exactly in form, a lament such as one shepherd might really have uttered over another; whereas in the *Lament for Bion* pastoralism is merely the imaginative garb in which one poet clothes his grief at the loss of another. Henceforth the drift of pastoral verse, whether descriptive or elegiac, is towards artificiality. This characteristic is very pronounced in Vergil. His pastoral poems, the *Eclogues*[1], are close, almost servile, imitations of Theocritus. His aim is not to paint in his own way the rural life of his own Mantuan land, but to repaint the pictures of Theocritus, with all their characteristic Sicilian features, whether appropriate to Italian scenes or not. Thus pastoralism ceases to be a faithful representation of shepherd-life, and becomes rather a literary exercise, and the *Eclogues* are admirable primarily for the same qualities as *Lycidas*—that is, qualities of art, not reality.

At the Renaissance the renewed interest in the classics brought the pastoral into vogue, especially in Italy. The revival of learning, says Professor Hales, "put fresh models before men, greatly modified old literary forms, originated new. The classical influence impressed upon Europe was by no means an unmixed good; in some respects it retarded the natural development of the modern mind by overpowering it with its prestige and stupefying it with a sense of inferiority; while it raised the ideal of perfection, it tended to give rise to mere imitations and affectations. Amongst these new forms was the Pastoral. When Virgil, Theocritus, 'Daphnis and Chloe,' and other writers[2] and works of the ancient pastoral literature once

[1] Latin *Eclogæ*, select poems; from Gk. ἐκλογή, a selection, especially a selection of poems. Note that the term for pastoral verse which prevailed among the earlier English poets was *Eclogue*, not *Idyl*—mainly, I suppose, because Vergil was a stronger influence than Theocritus. Every educated man knew Latin, but Greek (and that the Doric dialect) would be a mystery to most. Moreover, the common old spelling *Æglogue* shows that the word was supposed to be connected with Greek αἴξ, a goat, and therefore very appropriate to a class of poem in which goatherds often appear. Cf. "The General Argument" to *The Shepheards Calender*, lines 9 et seq. in the "Globe" edition; and see Conington's *Vergil*, I. pp. 17, 18.

[2] Latin pastoral writers later than Vergil are of little importance.

more gained the ascendency, then a modern pastoral poetry began to be. This poetry flourished greatly in Italy in the sixteenth century. It had been cultivated by Sannazaro, Guarini, Tasso[1]. Arcadia had been adopted by the poets for their country. In England numerous *Eclogues*[2] made their appearance. Amongst the earliest of these were Spenser's [i.e. the twelve *Eclogues*, one for each month of the year, of *The Shepheards Calender*]. It would perhaps be unjust to treat this modern pastoral literature as altogether an affectation. However unreal, the pastoral world had its charms—a pleasant feeling imparted of emancipation, a deep quietude, a sweet tranquillity."

Nevertheless, 'unreal' and 'artificial' are, in varying degrees, just descriptions of practically all pastoral verse since Theocritus. For whereas Theocritus depicted shepherd-life from the life—as he saw it lived by the shepherds of his native land—other pastoral writers, from Vergil onwards, have depicted it from poetic tradition. Vergil, as we saw, copied Theocritus, Italian writers copied Vergil, the English copied the Italians *plus* the classical poets. Thus from successive imitations of imitations arose a poetic tradition as to what shepherd-life should be, and pastoralism became neither more nor less than a literary *form*. The essential unreality of the modern pastoral is shown by the very fact that it generally "adopted" for its scene an *ideal* "Arcadia" where all was innocence and bliss. The invention of this Arcadia of pastoral verse, in which the characteristics of the Golden Age were supposed to be revived, was due to Sannazaro. The scene of Milton's own poem *Arcades* is laid in Arcadia, as the name shows ('the Arcadians'). One thing, it

[1] Each produced works which had a great influence in diffusing a taste for the pastoral, viz. Sannazaro the *Arcadia*, 1504, describing scenes and pursuits of pastoral life, and (in Latin) *Piscatory Eclogues*, 1520, imitated closely from Vergil; Tasso the dramatic pastoral *Aminta*, 1573; and Guarini, the *Pastor Fido*, 1585. These are the three writers to be mentioned in connection with the Italian pastoral.

[2] One of the earliest English writers of pastorals was Barnabe Googe, whose volume of miscellaneous poems, *Eglogs, Epytaphes, and Sonettes* (see Arber's *Reprint*), appeared in 1563. It contains eight pastoral poems, mostly in dialogue form: the speakers, shepherds and shepherdesses; the themes discussed, love, the evils of towns, the country-life, etc.; the verse full of old-fashioned alliteration.

should be added, in *Lycidas* which heightens the effect of unreality is the introduction of Christianity in the person of St Peter after the pagan deities Neptune and Æolus. But parallels might be quoted from earlier pastoral poems.

Lycidas was the last notable pastoral of the movement to which *The Shepheards Calender* had given a great impetus. The period between Spenser's poem and Milton's produced many specimens of the various types of pastoral—descriptive, dramatic, elegiac. The best known of these works were Spenser's own pastoral elegy *Astrophel* on the death of Sir Philip Sidney, and the Spenserian poems inspired by the same event; Browne's descriptive idyls entitled *Britannia's Pastorals* and the *Shepherd's Pipe*, Phineas Fletcher's *Piscatorie Eclogues*[1], and part of Giles Fletcher's verse; and in that sphere of dramatic pastoral where Tasso's *Aminta* was the approved model, John Fletcher's *Faithful Shepherdess*, Ben Jonson's *Sad Shepherd*, and Milton's *Arcades*. All these works illustrate aspects of *Lycidas*, and the *Faithful Shepherdess* bears a peculiar relation to it. Of pastoral verse written after *Lycidas* it is not necessary to speak.

III.

"SABRINA FAIR": *Comus*, 824—842.

The story of Sabrina, the "nymph" of the Severn, had been previously told by several poets: by Drayton in the *Polyolbion*, Sixth Song, by Warner in *Albion's England*, and Spenser in *The Faerie Queene*, II. 10. 14—19, and in the old play *Locrine* (absurdly attributed at one time to Shakespeare). The first presentment, however, of the legend occurs in the Latin History of the Britons by Geoffrey of Monmouth (made Bishop of St Asaph in 1152). This Milton reproduced in his own prose History of England. He relates how Brutus the great-grandson of Æneas, landed in Albion, built Troja Nova

[1] The title is copied from Sannazaro's Latin *Eclogues*, as that of John Fletcher's pastoral drama from Guarini's *Pastor Fido*. Such imitations, even in the matter of a title, are characteristic of the relation of the English pastoral school to the Italian.

(afterwards called Trinovantum=London), and at his death divided his territory between Locrine, Albanact, and Camber, his three sons. Locrine later on defeated Humber, king of the Huns, who had invaded Britain, and, says Milton, "among the spoils of his camp and navy were found certain young maids, and Estrildis above the rest, passing fair, the daughter of a king in Germany; whom Locrine, though before contracted to the daughter of Corineus [a Trojan warrior who accompanying Brutus to Britain had received Cornwall], resolves to marry. But being forced and threatened by Corineus, whose authority and power he feared, Guendolen the daughter he yields [consents] to marry, but in secret he loves the other [Estrildis]: and......had by her a daughter equally fair, whose name was Sabra. But when once his fear was off by the death of Corineus, divorcing Guendolen, he makes Estrildis now his queen. Guendolen, all in rage, departs into Cornwall, where Madan, the son she had by Locrine, was hitherto brought up by Corineus his grandfather. And gathering an army of her father's friends and subjects, gives battle to her husband by the river Sture [i.e. Stour]; wherein Locrine, shot with an arrow, ends his life. But not so ends the fury of Guendolen: for Estrildis, and her daughter Sabra, she throws into a river: and, to leave a monument of revenge, proclaims that the stream be thenceforth called after the damsel's name; which, by length of time, is changed now to Sabrina, or Severn"—*P. W.* v. 173, 174.

Cf. Spenser (II. 10. 19) describing how Guendolen, having taken "the faire Sabrina" (cf. *Comus*, 859) and her mother prisoners, slew the latter,

"But the sad Virgin, innocent of all,
Adoune the rolling river she did poure,
Which of her name now Severne men do call:
Such was the end that to disloyall love did fall."

So also at the close of the play *Locrine* (v. 5), where Sabren drowns herself, and Guendolen says:

"because this river was the place
Where little Sabren resolutely died,
Sabren for ever shall this stream be call'd."

Milton had hinted at the legend previously; cf. the *Vacation Exercise*, 96, "Or Severn swift, guilty of maiden's death."

CRITICAL OPINIONS ON COMUS AND LYCIDAS.

COMUS.

[JOHNSON: *LIFE OF MILTON*.]

"THE greatest of his juvenile performances is the 'Masque of Comus,' in which may very plainly be discovered the dawn or twilight of *Paradise Lost*. Milton appears to have formed very early that system of diction, and mode of verse, which his maturer judgment approved, and from which he never endeavoured nor desired to deviate.

Nor does *Comus* afford only a specimen of his language; it exhibits likewise his power of description and his vigour of sentiment, employed in the praise and defence of virtue. A work more truly poetical is rarely found; allusions, images, and descriptive epithets, embellish almost every period with lavish decoration. As a series of lines, therefore, it may be considered as worthy of all the admiration with which the votaries have received it.

As a drama it is deficient. The action is not probable. A masque, in those parts where supernatural intervention is admitted, must indeed be given up to all the freaks of imagination, but so far as the action is merely human, it ought to be reasonable, which can hardly be said of the conduct of the two brothers; who, when their sister sinks with fatigue in a pathless wilderness, wander both away together in search of berries too far to find their way back, and leave a helpless lady to all the sadness and danger of solitude. This, however, is a defect overbalanced by its convenience.

What deserves more reprehension is, that the prologue spoken in the wild wood by the attendant Spirit is addressed to the audience; a mode of communication so contrary to the nature of dramatic representation, that no precedents can support it.

The discourse of the Spirit is too long; an objection that may be made to almost all the following speeches; they have not the sprightliness of a dialogue animated by reciprocal contention, but seem rather declamations deliberately composed, and formally repeated, on a moral question. The auditor therefore listens as to a lecture, without passion, without anxiety.

The song of Comus has airiness and jollity; but, what may recommend Milton's morals as well as his poetry, the invitations to pleasure are so general, that they excite no distinct images of corrupt enjoyment, and take no dangerous hold on the fancy.

The following soliloquies of Comus and the Lady are elegant but tedious. The song must owe much to the voice, if it ever can delight. At last the Brothers enter with too much tranquillity; and, when they have feared lest their Sister should be in danger, and hoped that she is not in danger, the elder makes a speech in praise of chastity, and the younger finds how fine it is to be a philosopher.

Then descends the Spirit in form of a shepherd; and the Brother, instead of being in haste to ask his help, praises his singing, and inquires his business in that place. It is remarkable, that at this interview the Brother is taken with a short fit of rhyming. The Spirit relates that the Lady is in the power of Comus; the Brother moralises again; and the Spirit makes a long narration, of no use because it is false, and therefore unsuitable to a good being.

In all these parts the language is poetical, and the sentiments are generous; but there is something wanting to allure attention.

The dispute between the Lady and Comus is the most animated and affecting scene of the drama, and wants nothing but a brisker reciprocation of objections and replies to invite attention, and detain it.

The songs are vigorous and full of imagery; but they are harsh in their diction, and not very musical in their numbers.

Throughout the whole the figures are too bold, and the

language too luxuriant for dialogue. It is a drama in the epic style, inelegantly splendid, and tediously instructive."

[MACAULAY: *ESSAY ON MILTON.*]

"Milton attended in the *Comus* to the distinction which he afterwards neglected in the *Samson* [*Agonistes*]. He made his Masque what it ought to be, essentially lyrical, and dramatic only in semblance. He has not attempted a fruitless struggle against a defect inherent in the nature of that species of composition; and he has therefore succeeded, wherever success was not impossible. The speeches must be read as majestic soliloquies; and he who so reads them will be enraptured with their eloquence, their sublimity, and their music. The interruptions of the dialogue, however, impose a constraint upon the writer, and break the illusion of the reader. The finest passages are those which are lyric in form as well as in spirit. 'I should much commend,' says the excellent Sir Henry Wotton in a letter to Milton, 'the tragical part if the lyrical did not ravish me with a certain dorique delicacy in your songs and odes, whereunto, I must plainly confess to you, I have seen yet nothing parallel in our language.' The criticism was just. It is when Milton escapes from the shackles of the dialogue, when he is discharged from the labour of uniting two incongruous styles, when he is at liberty to indulge his choral raptures without reserve, that he rises even above himself. Then, like his own good genius bursting from the earthly form and weeds of Thyrsis, he stands forth in celestial freedom and beauty."

[HALLAM: *LITERATURE OF EUROPE.*]

"*Comus* was sufficient to convince anyone of taste and feeling that a great poet had arisen in England, and one partly formed in a different school from his contemporaries. Many of them had produced highly beautiful and imaginative passages; but none had evinced so classical a judgment, none had aspired to so regular a perfection. Johnson had learned much from the ancients; but there was a grace in their best models which he did not quite attain. Neither his *Sad Shepherd* nor the *Faithful Shepherdess* of Fletcher has the elegance or dignity of

Comus. A noble virgin and her young brothers, by whom this masque was originally represented, required an elevation, a purity, a sort of severity of sentiment, which no one in that age could have given but Milton. He avoided, and nothing loath, the more festive notes which dramatic poetry was wont to mingle with its serious strain. But for this he compensated by the brightest hues of fancy and the sweetest melody of song. In *Comus* we find nothing prosaïc or feeble, no false taste in the incidents, and not much in the language, nothing ever which we should desire to pass on a second perusal. The want of what we may call personality, none of the characters having names, except Comus himself, who is a very indefinite being, and the absence of all positive attributes of time and place, entrance the ideality of the fiction by a certain indistinctness not unpleasing to the imagination."

[BAGEHOT: *LITERARY STUDIES*.]

"The power of *Comus* is in its style. A grave and firm music pervades it: it is soft, without a thought of weakness; harmonious, and yet strong; impressive, as few such poems are, yet covered with a bloom of beauty and a complexity of charm that few poems have either. We have, perhaps, light literature in itself better, that we read oftener and more easily, that lingers more in our memories; but we have not any, we question if there ever will be any, which gives so true a conception of the capacity and the dignity of the mind by which it was produced. The breath of solemnity which hovers round the music attaches us to the writer. Every line, here as elsewhere, in Milton excites the idea of indefinite power."

[R. GARNETT: *LIFE OF MILTON*.]

"*Comus*, the richest fruit of Milton's early genius, is the epitome of the man at the age at which he wrote it. It bespeaks the scholar and idealist, whose sacred enthusiasm is in some danger of contracting a taint of pedantry for want of acquaintance with men and affairs. The Elder Brother's dialogues with his junior reveal the same solemn insensibility to the humorous which characterises the kindred genius of Wordsworth, and would have provoked the kindly smile of Shakespeare. It is singular to find the inevitable flaw of *Paradise Lost* prefigured here, and the wicked enchanter made the real hero of the piece. These defects are interesting, because they represent the nature of Milton as it was then, noble and disinterested to the height of imagination, but self-assertive, unmellowed, angular. They disappear entirely when he expatiates in the regions of exalted fancy, as in the introductory discourse of the Spirit, and the invocation to Sabrina. They recur when he moralizes; and his morality is too interwoven with the texture of his piece to be other than obtrusive. What glorious morality it is no one need be told; nor is there any poem in the language where beauties of thought, diction, and description spring up more thickly than in *Comus*... It is, indeed, true that many of these jewels are fetched from the mines of other poets: great as Milton's obligations to Nature were, his obligations to books were greater. But he has made all his own by the alchemy of his genius, and borrows little but to improve."

[DOWDEN: *TRANSCRIPTS AND STUDIES.*]

"*Comus* is the work of a youthful spirit, enamoured of its ideals of beauty and of virtue, zealous to exhibit the identity of moral loveliness with moral severity. The real incident[1] from which the mask is said to have originated disengages itself, in the imagination of Milton, from the world of actual occurrences, and becomes an occasion for the dramatic play of his own poetical abstractions. The young English gentlemen cast off their identity and individuality, and appear in the elementary shapes of 'First Brother' and 'Second Brother.' The Lady Alice rises into an ideal impersonation of virgin strength and virtue. The scene is earth; a wild wood; but earth, as in all the poems of Milton, with the heavens arching over it—a dim spot, in which men 'strive to keep up a frail and feverish being' set below the 'starry threshold of Love's Court.'... From its first scene to the last the drama is a representation of the trials, difficulties, and dangers to which moral purity is exposed in this

[1] Referring to the popular but very doubtful tradition as to the genesis of *Comus*; see the *Introduction*.

world, and of the victory of the better principle in the soul, gained by strenuous human endeavour aided by the grace of God. In this spiritual warfare the powers of good and evil are arrayed against one another; upon this side the Lady, her brothers (types of human helpfulness weak in itself, and liable to go astray), and the supernatural powers auxiliar to virtue in heaven and in earth—the Attendant Spirit and the nymph Sabrina.

The enchanter Comus is son of Bacchus and Circe, and inheritor of twofold vice. If Milton had pictured the life of innocent mirth in *L'Allegro*, here was a picture to set beside the other, a vision of the genius of sensual indulgence. Yet Comus is inwardly, not outwardly foul; no grim monster like that which the mediæval imagination conjured up to terrify the spirit and disgust the senses. The attempt of sin upon the soul as conceived by Milton is not the open and violent obsession of a brute power, but involves a cheat, an imposture. The soul is put upon its trial through the seduction of the senses and the lower parts of our nature. Flattering lies entice the ears of Eve[1]; Christ is tried[2] by false visions of power and glory, and beneficent rule; Samson is defrauded of his strength by deceitful blandishment[3]. And in like manner Comus must needs possess a beauty of his own, such beauty as ensnares the eye untrained in the severe school of moral perfection....He is sensitive to rich forms and sweet sounds, graceful in oratory, possessed, like Satan, of high intellect, but intellect in the service of the senses; he surrounds himself with a world of art which lulls the soul into forgetfulness of its higher instincts and of duty; his palace is stately, and 'set out with all manner of deliciousness.'

Over against this potent enchanter stands the virginal figure of the Lady, who is stronger than he... Something of weakness belongs to the Lady, because she is a woman, accustomed to the protection of others, tenderly nurtured; but when the hour of trial comes she shows herself strong in powers of judgment and of reasoning, strong in her spiritual nature, in her tenacity of moral truth, in her indignation against sin. Although alone, and encompassed by evil and danger, she is fearless, and so

1 *Paradise Lost*, IX. 532—732. 2 *Paradise Regained*, III. IV.
3 *Samson Agonistes*, 392—411.

clear-sighted that the juggling practice of her antagonist is wholly ineffectual against her. There is much in the Lady which resembles the youthful Milton himself, and we may well believe that the great debate concerning temperance was not altogether dramatic (where, indeed, is Milton truly dramatic?), but was in part a record of passages in the poet's own spiritual history. Milton admired the Lady as he admired the ideal which he projected before him of himself."

LYCIDAS.

[JOHNSON: *LIFE OF MILTON.*]

"Those who admire the beauties of this great poet sometimes force their own judgment into false approbation of his little pieces, and prevail upon themselves to think that admirable which is only singular. All that short compositions can commonly attain is neatness and elegance. Milton never learned the art of doing little things with grace; he overlooked the milder excellence of suavity and softness; he was a 'lion' that had no skill in 'dandling the kid.'

One of the poems on which much praise has been bestowed is *Lycidas*; of which the diction is harsh, the rhymes uncertain, and the numbers unpleasing. What beauty there is we must therefore seek in the sentiments and images. It is not to be considered as the effusion of real passion; for passion runs not after remote allusions and obscure opinions. Passion plucks no berries from the myrtle and ivy, nor calls upon Arethuse and Mincius, nor tells of rough 'satyrs' and 'fauns with cloven heel.' Where there is leisure for fiction, there is little grief.

In this poem there is no nature, for there is no truth; there is no art, for there is nothing new. Its form is that of a pastoral; easy, vulgar, and therefore disgusting; whatever images it can supply are long ago exhausted; and its inherent improbability always forces dissatisfaction on the mind. When Cowley tells of Hervey, that they studied together, it is easy to suppose how much he must miss the companion of his labours, and the partner of his discoveries; but what image of tenderness can be excited by these lines?—

'We drove afield, and both together heard
What time the grey fly winds her sultry horn,
Battening our flocks with the fresh dews of night.'

We know that they never drove afield, and that they had no flocks to batten; and though it be allowed that the representation may be allegorical, the true meaning is so uncertain and remote, that it is never sought, because it cannot be known when it is found.

Among the flocks, and copses, and flowers, appear the heathen deities; Jove and Phoebus, Neptune and Aeolus, with a long train of mythological imagery, such as a college easily supplies. Nothing can less display knowledge, or less exercise invention, than to tell how a shepherd has lost his companion, and must now feed his flocks alone, without any judge of his skill in piping; and how one god asks another god what is become of Lycidas, and how neither god can tell. He who thus grieves will excite no sympathy; he who thus praises will confer no honour.

This poem has yet a grosser fault. With these trifling fictions are mingled the most awful and sacred truths, such as ought never to be polluted with such irreverend combinations. The shepherd likewise is now a feeder of sheep, and afterwards an ecclesiastical pastor, a superintendent of a Christian flock. Such equivocations are always unskilful; but here they are indecent, and at least approach to impiety, of which, however, I believe the writer not to have been conscious.

Such is the power of reputation justly acquired, that its blaze drives away the eye from nice examination. Surely no man could have fancied that he read *Lycidas* with pleasure, had he not known its author."

[HALLAM: *LITERATURE OF EUROPE*.]

"It has been said, I think very fairly, that *Lycidas* is a good test of a real feeling for what is peculiarly called poetry. Many, or perhaps we might say, most readers, do not taste its excellence; nor does it follow that they may not greatly admire Pope and Dryden, or even Virgil and Homer. It is, however, somewhat remarkable that Johnson, who has committed his critical reputation by the most contemptuous depreciation of this poem, had in an earlier part of his life selected the tenth eclogue of Virgil for peculiar praise; the tenth eclogue, which, beautiful as it is, belongs to the same class of pastoral and personal allegory, and requires the same sacrifice of reasoning criticism as the *Lycidas* itself. In the age of Milton the poetical world had been accustomed by the Italian and Spanish writers to a more abundant use of allegory than has been pleasing to their posterity; but *Lycidas* is not so much in the nature of an allegory as of a masque; the characters pass before our eyes in imagination, as on the stage; they are chiefly mythological, but not creations of the poet. Our sympathy with the fate of Lycidas may not be much stronger than for the desertion of Gallus[1] by his mistress; but many poems will yield an exquisite pleasure to the imagination that produce no emotion in the heart; or none at least except through associations independent of the subject.

The introduction of St Peter after the fabulous deities of the sea has appeared an incongruity deserving of censure to some admirers of this poem. It would be very reluctantly that we could abandon to this criticism the most splendid passage it presents. But the censure rests, as I think, on too narrow a principle. In narrative or dramatic poetry, where something like illusion or momentary belief is to be produced, the mind requires an objective possibility, a capacity of real existence, not only in all the separate portions of the imagined story, but in their coherency and relation to a common whole. Whatever is obviously incongruous, whatever shocks our previous knowledge of possibility, destroys to a certain extent that acquiescence in the fiction which it is the true business of the fiction to produce. But the case is not the same in such poems as *Lycidas*. They pretend to no credibility, they aim at no illusion; they are read with the willing abandonment of the imagination to a waking dream, and require only that general possibility, that combination of images, which common experience does not reject as incompatible, without which the fancy of the poet would be only like that of the lunatic. And it had been so usual to blend sacred with mythological personages in allegory, that no one probably in Milton's age would have been struck by the objection."

[1] The shepherd in the tenth *Eclogue*.

[MARK PATTISON: *LIFE OF MILTON.*]

"In *Lycidas* (1637) we have reached the high-water mark of English Poesy and of Milton's own production. A period of a century and a half was to elapse before poetry in England seemed, in Wordsworth's *Ode on Immortality* (1807), to be rising again towards the level of inspiration to which it had once attained in *Lycidas*. And in the development of the Miltonic genius this wonderful dirge marks the culminating point. As the twin idylls[1] of 1632 show a great advance upon the *Ode on the Nativity* (1629), the growth of the poetic mind during the five years which follow 1632 is registered in *Lycidas*. Like the *L'Allegro* and *Il Penseroso*, *Lycidas* is laid out on the lines of the accepted pastoral fiction; like them it offers exquisite touches of idealised rural life. But *Lycidas* opens up a deeper vein of feeling, a patriot passion so vehement and dangerous, that, like that which stirred the Hebrew prophet, it is compelled to veil itself from power, or from sympathy, in utterance made purposely enigmatical. The passage which begins 'Last came and last did go,' raises in us a thrill of awe-struck expectation which I can only compare with that excited by the Cassandra of Æschylus's *Agamemnon*. For the reader to feel this, he must have present in memory the circumstances of England in 1637. He must place himself as far as possible in the situation of a cotemporary. The study of Milton's poetry compels the study of his time; and Professor Masson's six volumes[2] are not too much to make us to understand that there were real causes for the intense passion which glows underneath the poet's words—a passion which unexplained would be thought to be intrusive.

The historical exposition must be gathered from the English history of the period, which may be read in Professor Masson's excellent summary. All I desire to point out here is, that in *Lycidas*, Milton's original picturesque vein is for the first time crossed with one of quite another sort, stern, determined, obscurely indicative of suppressed passion, and the resolution to do or die. The fanaticism of the covenanter and the sad

[1] *L'Allegro* and *Il Penseroso*. They may be called *idyls*, being short but elaborately wrought descriptive poems. Gk. εἰδύλλιον = a short, descriptive poem.

[2] His great *Life* of Milton.

grace of Petrarch seem to meet in Milton's monody. Yet these opposites, instead of neutralising each other, are blended into one harmonious whole by the presiding, but invisible, genius of the poet. The conflict between the old cavalier world—the years of gaiety and festivity of a splendid and pleasure-loving court, and the new puritan world into which love and passion were not to enter—this conflict which was commencing in the social life of England, is also begun in Milton's own breast, and is reflected in *Lycidas*.

'For we were nurs'd upon the self-same hill.'

Here is the sweet mournfulness of the Spenserian time, upon whose joys Death is the only intruder. Pass onward a little, and you are in the presence of the tremendous

'Two-handed engine at the door,'

the terror of which is enhanced by its obscurity. We are very sure that the avenger is there, though we know not who he is. In these thirty lines we have the preluding mutterings of the storm which was to sweep away mask and revel and song, to inhibit the drama, and suppress poetry. In the earlier poems Milton's muse has sung in the tones of the age that is passing away; the poet is, except in his austere chastity, a cavalier. Though even in *L'Allegro* Dr Johnson truly detects 'some melancholy in his mirth.' In *Lycidas*, for a moment, the tones of both ages, the past and the coming, are combined, and then Milton leaves behind him for ever the golden age, and one half of his poetic genius."[1]

POLITICAL AND SOCIAL ASPECTS OF MILTON'S EARLY POEMS.

[STOPFORD BROOKE: "*CLASSICAL WRITERS*," *MILTON*.]

"Puritanism, when Milton began to write, was not universally apart from literature and the fine arts. In its staid and pure

[1] I think that most students would regard this as somewhat an over-statement of the case. Mr Mark Pattison grudged Milton's intervention in politics and theological controversy, and perhaps rather over-estimated its evil effect on the poet and under-estimated the good.

religion Milton's work had its foundation, but the temple he had begun to build upon it was quarried from the ancient and modern arts and letters of Greece and Italy and England. And filling the temple rose the peculiar incense of the Renaissance. The breath of that spirit is felt in the classicalism of the *Ode to the Nativity*, in the love proclaimed for Shakespeare, in the graceful fancy of the *Epitaph to Lady Winchester*, and in the gaiety of the *Ode to a May Morning*. But a new element, other than any the Renaissance could produce, is here; the element that filled the Psalms of David, the deep, personal, passionate religion of the Puritan, possessing, and possessed by, God. Over against the Renaissance music is set the high and devout strain of the first sonnet and of the *Odes to Time* and *A Solemn Musick*. Even while at Cambridge, the double being in Milton makes itself felt, the struggle between the two spirits of the time is reflected in his work. These contrasted spirits in him became defined as the political and social war deepened around his life. The second sonnet still is gay, fresh with the morn of love, Petrarca might have written it; the *Allegro* does not disdain the love of nature, the rustic sports, the pomp of courts, the playhouse and the land of faery, nor does the *Penseroso* refuse to haunt the dim cathedral. But yet, in these two poems more than in the Cambridge poems, the deepening of the struggle is felt. Milton seems to presage in them that the time would come when the gaiety of England would cease to be shared in by serious men; when the mirth of the Cavalier would shut out the pleasures derived from lofty Melancholy, because they shut out the devil; as the Puritan pensiveness would be driven to shut out the pleasures of Mirth, because they shut out God. While he gives full weight in the *Allegro* to 'unreproved pleasures free,' he makes it plain in the *Penseroso* that he prefers the sage and holy pleasures of thoughtful sadness. These best befitted the solemn aspect of the time.

A few years later and the presage had come true. Milton is driven away from even the *Allegro* point of view. In *Comus* the wild licence of the Court society is set over against the grave and temperate virtue of a Puritan life. The unchastity, the glozing lies, the glistering apparel that hid moral deformity, the sloth and drunkenness, the light fantastic round of the enchanter's character and court, are (it seems likely) Milton's allegory of the Court society of his time. The stately philosophy of the Brothers which had its root in subduing passion and its top in the love of God; the virginal chastity of the Lady, and at the end the releasing power of Sabrina's purity, exalt and fill up more sternly the idea of the *Penseroso* and symbolise that noble Puritanism which loved learning and beauty only when they were pure, but holiness far more than either. It may be, as Mr Browne supports, that there is a second allegory within the first, of Laud and his party as the Sorcerer commending the cup of Rome by wile and threat to the lips of the Church and enforcing it by fine and imprisonment; paralysing in stony fetters the Lady of the Church. It may be that Milton called in this poem on the few who, having resisted like the Brothers, but failed to set the Church free, ought now to employ a new force, the force of Purity; but this aspect of the struggle is at least not so clear in *Comus* as in *Lycidas*.

In *Lycidas* Milton has thrown away the last shreds of Church and State and is Presbyterian. The strife now at hand starts into prominence, and not to the bettering of the poem as a piece of art. It is brought in—and the fault is one which frequently startles us in Milton—without any regard to the unity of feeling in the poem. The passage on the hireling Church looks like an after-thought, and Milton draws attention to it in the argument. 'The author...by occasion foretells the ruin of our corrupted clergy then in their height.' But he does not leave Laud and his policy nor the old Church tenderly. When he felt strongly, he wrote fiercely. The passage is a splendid and a fierce cry of wrath, and the rough trumpet note, warlike and unsparing, which it sounds against the unfaithful herdsmen who are sped and the 'grim wolf with privy paw,' was to ring louder and louder through the prose works, and finally to clash in the ears of those very Presbyterians whom he now supported.

There is then a steady progress of thought and of change in the poems. The Milton of *Lycidas* is not the Milton of *Comus*. The Milton of *Comus* is not the Milton of the *Penseroso*, less still of the *Allegro*. The Milton of the *Penseroso* is not the Milton of the *Ode to the Nativity*. Nothing of the Renaissance is left now but its learning and its art."

I. INDEX OF WORDS AND PHRASES.

This List applies to the **Notes** *only; words of which longer explanations are given will be found in the* **Glossary.** *The references are to the pages.*

Abbreviations: n. = noun. vb = verb.

II. GENERAL INDEX TO NOTES.

For EU product safety concerns, contact us at Calle de José Abascal, 56–1°,
28003 Madrid, Spain or eugpsr@cambridge.org.

www.ingramcontent.com/pod-product-compliance
Ingram Content Group UK Ltd.
Pitfield, Milton Keynes, MK11 3LW, UK
UKHW020320140625
459647UK00018B/1936

* 9 7 8 1 1 0 7 6 2 0 0 1 8 *